Locating the Mediterranean

Connections and Separations across Space and Time

Edited by
Carl Rommel and
Joseph John Viscomi

Published by Helsinki University Press
www.hup.fi

© Authors 2022

First published in 2022

Cover design: Ville Karppanen
Cover photo: Lena Malm

ISBN (Paperback): 978-952-369-076-9
ISBN (PDF): 978-952-369-077-6
ISBN (EPUB): 978-952-369-078-3

https://doi.org/10.33134/HUP-18

The full text of this book has been peer reviewed to ensure high academic standards. For full review policies, see http://www.hup.fi/

VERTAISARVIOITU
KOLLEGIALT GRANSKAD
PEER-REVIEWED
www.tsv.fi/tunnus

Suggested citation:
Rommel, Carl, and Joseph John Viscomi, eds. 2022. *Locating the Mediterranean: Connections and Separations across Space and Time*. Helsinki: Helsinki University Press. DOI: https://doi.org/10.33134/HUP-18.

To read the free, open access version of this book online, visit https://doi.org/10.33134/HUP-18 or scan this QR code with your mobile device:

Contents

Figures

Tables

Acknowledgements

Locating the Mediterranean has been a long time coming and it has been shaped by many people and events along the way. The book's central conceptual intervention – the understanding of location as inherently relative and a result of connections and separations to locations elsewhere – was originally formulated by Sarah Green and refined within the ERC-advanced grant funded research project 'Crosslocations: Rethinking Relative Location in the Mediterranean' (grant no. 694482) that she led at the University of Helsinki between 2016 and 2022. Six members of the Crosslocations core team have contributed chapters to the book (Green, Soto Bermant, Douzina-Bakalaki, Lähteenaho, and the editors); one more chapter is written by an affiliated Crosslocations researcher (Bullen). Other scholars in the same research project (Patricia Scalco, Viljami Kankaanpää-Kukkonen, and Marion Lecoquierre), as well as the project's advisory board, played key roles in developing and sharpening the concepts and ideas that we mobilise in this volume. Input from the whole team was invaluable to make this book happen.

While Crosslocations has been the volume's intellectual home, the volume was first conceived by the editors as a panel for the European Association for Social Anthropologists (EASA) biannual conference in Stockholm in August 2018. The panel, as well as the subsequent dinner at an Eritrean restaurant in central Stockholm, were both fun and intellectually stimulating; there was an excitement in the air that one experiences among likeminded people with a shared new-found cause. When we left Sweden, we felt that we were at the beginning of a larger intellectual project.

Compiling an edited volume is always collective effort that requires coordination and patience, and even more so in the ever-changing circumstances of 2020 and 2021. Over the last two years, we have all faced pandemic-induced delays, and the editorial process has been an unevenly paced ride. We are especially grateful to the contributors for their resilience in staying committed to the project during these exceptional circumstances. It was not easy, but we did it together. This volume connected us at our most disconnected moment. For the same reasons, we wish to thank the editorial team at Helsinki University Press for their encouragement and understanding as we managed countless delays. Leena Rautjärvi's excitement for the project helped us push through the final months. Rupert Stasch and two anonymous reviewers provided astute comments and perceptive suggestions that added depth as well as coherence. Many of the images in the volume (including the cover) come from Lena Malm. We are thankful that she gave us permission to use her vivid photographic work, which weaves through this constellation. The same can be said of Philippe Rekacewicz, who designed the map for the book.

Last but not least, Carl would like to thank his family in Sweden for love and support, in the past and in the future. A special thanks go to Karin – always there, somewhere, somehow – for flair and fun, and for rendering the world more lustrous. Joseph would like to thank his many students over the last years who have listened and responded as he rehearsed parts of the introduction's arguments. Much of the nuance is owed to their insights. He would also like to thank Maria and Teo, who are always supportive (and patient) as these Mediterranean ramblings shape and permeate their own locations.

Contributors

Carl Rommel is a researcher at the Department of Cultural Anthropology and Ethnology at Uppsala University. His ongoing research – 'Egypt as a Project: Dreamwork and Masculinity in a Projectified Society' – is funded by Riksbankens Jubileumsfond. Rommel's anthropological research in Egypt focuses on masculinity, emotions, future-making, sports, revolution and 'projects'. In 2015, Rommel earned his PhD from SOAS, University of London. Between 2017 and 2021, he was a postdoctoral researcher in the ERC project 'Crosslocations' at the University of Helsinki. Rommel has published articles in *Men & Masculinity*, *Critical African Studies*, *Middle East – Topics & Arguments*, and *Soccer & Society*. His first monograph, *Egypt's Football Revolution: Emotion, Masculinity and Uneasy Politics*, was published with the University of Texas Press in July 2021.
https://orcid.org/0000-0003-0301-6131

Joseph John Viscomi is a lecturer in European History in the Department of History, Classics and Archaeology at Birkbeck, University of London. He trained in anthropology and history at the University of Michigan, Ann Arbor, and is specialised in temporality, migration, and political processes in the Mediterranean region. He is currently completing a book that examines migration, political membership, and historical time in the Mediterranean by studying the departure of Italians from Egypt in the twentieth-century. This research has been published in *The Journal of Modern History*, *History and Anthropology*, and *Modern Italy*. He has begun new research on depopulation in Southern Italy since 1783.
https://orcid.org/0000-0002-1147-8689

Claire Bullen is a postdoctoral researcher at the Institute for Sociology at the University of Tübingen in Germany, as well as an affiliated researcher at IDEMEC, the Institute for Mediterranean, European and Comparative Ethnography, at Aix-Marseille University in France. Her research interests include transforming urban socio-spatial relations, ethnographic urban comparisons, and the anthropology of the Mediterranean. She has carried out fieldwork in Algeria, France, and the UK. Her latest publications include a thematic section in the *International Journal of Heritage Studies* on heritage associations operating around the Mediterranean basin.
https://orcid.org/0000-0001-5722-0205

Matei Candea is professor of social anthropology at the University of Cambridge. He is the author of *Corsican Fragments* (2010, Indiana University Press) and *Comparison in Anthropology* (2018, Cambridge University Press). Please see www.candea.org.
https://orcid.org/0000-0001-7260-4194

Phaedra Douzina-Bakalaki is a social anthropologist specialised in the ethnographic study of Greece, Southern Europe, and the Mediterranean. Her research interests lie in patterns of social reproduction and processes of sociopolitical transformation. Among others, she has explored provisioning practices amid the Greek economic crisis, ongoing reconfigurations of church–state relations in contemporary Greece, and emergent landscapes of religious tourism. Her ongoing research 'From Extractivist Pasts to Post-Carbon Futures: An Ethnographic study of lignite phase-out in Southern Greece' is funded by the Finnish Cultural Foundation. She earned her doctoral degree in social anthropology from the University of Manchester in 2017. Shortly afterwards she joined the University of Helsinki as a postdoctoral researcher for 'Crosslocations: Rethinking Relative Location in the Mediterranean'. She is the co-editor of Anthropology Matters, the ASA's early-career open-access journal.
https://orcid.org/0000-0001-5575-5636

Laust Lund Elbek holds a PhD in social anthropology from Aarhus University (2020). He has a particular ethnographic interest in the politics of location and a regional focus on Italy and Scandinavia. His doctoral work on Lampedusa has appeared in journals such as *Ethnos* and *History and Anthropology*. He is currently a postdoctoral research

fellow at the Danish Centre for Welfare Studies at the University of Southern Denmark.
https://orcid.org/0000-0002-6719-9478

Sarah Green is professor of social and cultural anthropology at the University of Helsinki. She has spent her academic career studying issues of space, place, location, and borders. She moved on to study the reopening of the Greek–Albanian border following the end of the Cold War, and to look at the introduction of internet and digital technologies to Manchester. She is the principal investigator in the ERC project 'Crosslocations'. Her own research in that project involves looking at the transportation of livestock across borders, the tracking of wild animals across borders, and efforts to stop the spread of zoonotic disease. Her chapter in this book is part of that research.
https://orcid.org/0000-0002-7026-383X

Samuli Lähteenaho is a PhD candidate in social and cultural anthropology at the University of Helsinki. His wider research interests cover ethnographic theorisations of space, place, and location, alongside questions of ecology and social movements. His doctoral research focuses on the politics and poetics of the coastline in Lebanon, based on ethnographic fieldwork with civil society and volunteer groups engaged with the country's littoral. He holds a master's degree in anthropology from the University of Helsinki. His current research is a part of the European Research Council project 'Crosslocations: Rethinking Relative Location in the Mediterranean'.
https://orcid.org/0000-0003-1757-2331

Carmelo Russo is assistant professor in cultural anthropology and Marie Curie Global researcher with a project on religious superdiversity at SARAS Department, Sapienza University, Rome (Italy). In 2020, he obtained the Italian Scientific Qualification as associate professor in anthropology, two years after defending his doctoral thesis. He has conducted fieldwork in Italy and Tunisia focusing on migration process and religious dynamics. He is the author of numerous journal articles and volume chapters. His monograph *Nostra Signora del limite* (*Our Lady of the Boundaries*), concerning Marian worship in Tunisia, was published in September 2020.
https://orcid.org/0000-0003-1140-1566

Laia Soto Bermant is a social anthropologist specialised in the anthropology of borders, identity, and location, with a regional interest in Europe and the Mediterranean. She earned her MA (2007) and PhD (2012) in social and cultural anthropology from the University of Oxford. After graduating, she held postdoctoral research fellowships at the School of Transborder Studies at Arizona State University, and at the University of Helsinki, where she participated in the ERC project 'Crosslocations: Rethinking Relative Location in the Mediterranean' and the Academy of Finland project 'Trade, Transit and Travel'. Presently, she is the editor-in-chief of the EASA's flagship journal *Social Anthropology/Anthropologie Sociale*. Her current research, funded by the KONE Foundation, explores the global spread of conspiracy theories about Covid-19.
https://orcid.org/0000-0002-1676-1432

Janine Su is a PhD candidate in the Department of Anthropology at University College London, with research and professional interests centering around issues of youth, masculinities, and mobilities. Her doctoral study was first conceived during her tenure as research scholar at the British Institute at Ankara, and the faculty and postgraduate students at the Middle East Technical University Department of Sociology have generously supported her work on an ongoing basis.
https://orcid.org/0000-0002-0282-7576

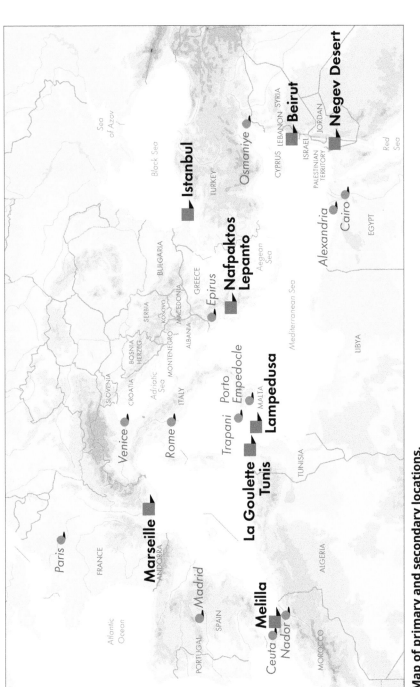

Map of primary and secondary locations.
Designed by Philippe Rekacewicz.

CHAPTER 1

Introduction: Locating the Mediterranean

Carl Rommel
Uppsala University

Joseph John Viscomi
Birkbeck, University of London

Abstract

In recent years, the Mediterranean region has reasserted itself in the world: popular uprisings have unsettled long-standing political regimes, economic crises have generated precarity, and nationalist movements have reified some borders while condemning others. The circulation and stagnation of people, ideas, and objects provoked by these events draw attention to regional connections and separations that, in turn, challenge strict geopolitical renderings of Europe, the Middle East, and North Africa. In considering this resurgence of interest in the Mediterranean, this introduction asks: what role does 'location' play in our conception of region and region-formations? What kinds of locations are generated in the contemporary Mediterranean? How do historical, legal, political, and social connections and separations shape the experience of being located somewhere in particular? Furthermore, the introduction explores how, by placing in dialogue

How to cite this book chapter:
Rommel, Carl, and Joseph John Viscomi. 2022. 'Introduction: Locating the Mediterranean'. In *Locating the Mediterranean: Connections and Separations across Space and Time*, edited by Carl Rommel and Joseph John Viscomi, 1–29. Helsinki: Helsinki University Press. DOI: https://doi.org/10.33134/HUP-18-1.

diverse approaches and traditions, this collective volume works on two levels at once. First, each contribution posits its own Mediterranean 'constellation'. Second, the collective volume presents a wider understanding of what historically inclined anthropologists might conceive of as a Mediterranean 'constellation'. In doing this, the introduction proposes a theoretical apparatus through which we can understand cultural and historical values of region and region-making in and beyond the Mediterranean.

Two (Mediterranean) Locations

In Alexandria, Egypt, tucked behind the Bibliotheca Alexandrina, across from the Greek school campus, and next to the old tram line, there is an Italian care home (Casa di Riposo, see Image 1.1). The home was built in 1928 to house over 200 elderly or disabled Italians and then expanded several years later when there was need for additional rooms. At the time, there were over 30,000 Italian residents in Alexandria (out of around 55,000 in all of Egypt). When inaugurated, the Italian architects, charity organisations, and diplomats dedicated the Casa di Riposo to Mussolini and named it after the then king, Vittorio Emanuele III. In 1946, after the collapse of the Fascist govern-

Image 1.1: Casa di Riposo Vittorio Emanuele III, Alexandria, Egypt.
Photo: Joseph John Viscomi.

ment and the declaration of the Italian Republic, Vittorio Emanuele III departed Italy for Egypt where he died one year later; his corpse remained buried behind the altar of St Catherine's Cathedral of Alexandria until it was repatriated in 2017. After the Second World War, an ageing community populated the care home as many of the younger Italian residents left Egypt. By the mid-1960s, over 40,000 Italians had departed, and the community continued to shrink as the walls around the old people's home grew. In 2013, inside the Casa's emptied halls, where around 20 elderly Italians lived (nearly one third have since passed away), a number of residents discussed past and present revolutionary futures. Outside, the sounds of demonstrators chanting '*yisqut yisqut hukm al-murshid*' (down, down with the rule of the [Muslim Brotherhood's] Supreme Guide) filled the street. Inside, with idyllic nostalgia, three residents debated the 'turn' (*svolta*) away from the 'cosmopolitan' Mediterranean worlds that, they claimed, had dissipated between 1948 and 1967. In this post-war 'turn' away from 'cosmopolitanism', Egyptian and Italian governments had strengthened political, economic, and military ties. After the 1952 coup d'état, the two governments negotiated relations in terms of a history of cultural and political exchange. Even following the 2016 death of Giulio Regeni, the Italian PhD student abducted and tortured by Egyptian security agents while conducting doctoral research in Egypt, these relations have been evoked and reinforced while material indexes of this past, such as the Italian care home, are emptied and resignified within Alexandria's urban landscape.

Some 200 kilometres south, in the heart of the capital, Cairo, boys and men play recreational football on a small artificial-grass pitch inside the courtyard of an old school building. Less than a kilometre from Cairo's iconic Tahrir Square and adjacent to Muhammad Mahmoud Street – famous for clashes between protesters and security forces in 2011 and 2012 – the shiny green football field was constructed by a thrifty entrepreneur, Mustafa, in 2017 (see Image 1.2).[1] The surrounding buildings are much older. The school was originally founded by French educators in 1909 but brought under state control after the 1956 Suez Crisis; the present building – combining European and Islamic architectural features to showcase the merging of two worlds – was built in the 1930s. Until the late 1960s, all teaching was carried out by French teachers, many of whom resided in dormitories in the school's upper floors. These days, the European pedagogues are

Image 1.2: Mustafa's football pitch, Cairo, Egypt.
Photo: Lena Malm.

long gone, although the school – run as a cooperative by the pupils' parents – is still known as a 'French school' (part of the teaching takes place in French). Over the last decades, the school complex has been expanded multiple times. In the 1980s, the world-famous Egyptian architect Hassan Fathy designed a nursery that featured Nubian-styled domes and materials ensuring natural year-around ventilation. A while later, a small kiosk was built that allows students to buy snacks and soft drinks during breaks. The football pitch constitutes the latest addition. Mustafa worked hard to finance it through informal credit circles (*gama'iyyat*) involving friends and family all over Egypt and as far away as Northern Europe. The grass comes from a factory in Osmaniye, south-eastern Turkey. It was constructed by a family-run company who holds the exclusive licence to import this high-quality but relatively cheap grass to Egypt. Mustafa rents the pitch from the school on a five-year-long contract. From 4pm until long after midnight, seven days a week, he in turn rents it out to coaches running football academies or groups of friends playing the game for fun. On any given night, one might see boys and men playing in match shirts representing clubs from every corner of the Mediterranean: Egypt's al-Ahly and al-Zamalek; the Tunisian champions Taragi; Galatasaray and Beşiktaş from Istanbul; Real Madrid, Atletico Madrid, Barcelona, Marseille, Rome, Milan, and more.

***

The care home in Alexandria and the football pitch in central Cairo are both well demarcated spaces located squarely within Egypt's political borders. At the same time, the qualities of their *located-ness* stem from a multitude of relations that well exceed the confines of the post-1952 Egyptian nation state. Bringing together elderly Italians, Italian, French, Islamic, and Nubian architectures, imperial nostalgia, French curricula, Turkish artificial grass, and match shirts of football clubs in Spain, Tunisia, Italy, and Turkey, the two sites are not delimited by national political boundaries; they extend back in time to moments when borders had different meanings and outwards in space to seemingly detached locations. In other words, the two locations only become meaningful within a complex meshwork of historical, material, and discursive links. They are constituted by multiple connections and separations, through time and across space.

Building on a long history of intellectual engagement in the Mediterranean region, *Locating the Mediterranean* brings together ethnographic examinations of projects and processes that make locations and render them meaningful. The book's overarching aims are to highlight the centrality of located-ness in people's lives and to reinvigorate anthropological debates about the interplay between location and region-making. Our intervention is first and foremost empirical and ethnographic. From different theoretical and topographical angles, the volume's eight contributions illustrate how historical, legal, religious, economic, political, and social connections and separations shape the experience of being located 'somewhere in particular' in the geographical space commonly known as the Mediterranean region. This anthropological attention to the local allows us to see the region – and region-making, more general – anew. The volume's chapters demonstrate how qualitatively distinct threads conjoin (or dissolve) to give locations value, usefulness, and political charge.

Locating Location in Anthropology

When 'the local' arose as a key concern for anthropologists in the 1980s and 1990s, it did so in opposition to other units of analysis that ostensibly did not do the job. In an era combining a devastating crisis of representation (Clifford and Marcus 1986) with expanding interests in globalisation (Hannerz 1989), transnationalism (Hannerz 1996), cultural flows (Appadurai 1996), and multisitedness (Marcus 1995), the disciplinary habit to premise comparative analyses on fieldwork in and on presumably coherent 'culture areas', 'societies', or 'nations' inhering in discrete geographical spaces appeared more and more suspect (Clifford 1988; Gupta and Fergusson 1997a, 1997b; Wimmer and Glick Schiller 2002, 2003). Efforts to overcome the discipline's looming crisis proceeded along multiple paths. Whereas some anthropologists turned ethnographic attention to projects and processes of scale-making that render global, regional, and local cultures comprehensible in the first place (Gupta and Ferguson 1997b; Mazzarella 2004; Tsing 2000; Wilk 1995), others advocated a re-envisioning of 'the local' as an analytical category. One early blueprint was Anthony Cohen's work on rural Britain (1982, 1986, 1987), in which an 'anthropology of locality' ultimately aimed at deconstructing the purportedly hegemonic and homogenising industrial nation-state by highlighting symbolic construction and reproduction of idiosyncratic 'local' communities (see also Knight 1994).[2] Arjun Appadurai's proposal to reconceive anthropology in line with a new globalised, mediatised, postcolonial, and postnational world order is another case in point (1990, 1996). Appadurai understood locality as an always fragile 'phenomenological quality' or 'structure of feeling' produced in 'disjunctures' between deterritorialised 'scapes' through dialectical work between the materiality of local spaces and meaning-making local subjects.[3] His approach inspired numerous studies of the interplay between, on the one hand, belonging, memory, and agency and, on the other, the making of 'local' spaces in the midst of global flows (e.g. Ghannam 2002; Korff 2003; Lovell 1998).

Until today, anthropological examinations of locality have taken primary interest in local subjects leading local lives in local communities. Through a shift of conceptual emphasis from *locality* to *location*, the present volume departs from previous preoccupations with identity and belonging and inverts central optics of ethnography.

In *Locating the Mediterranean*, we begin by examining questions of *where* spaces are *located*. Each ethnographic chapter aims to arrive at a characterisation of how particular locations are articulated and realised through intersecting processes of (dis)entanglement and by socio-historical actors. Only thereafter do we consider how the particularities of this located-ness shape lives, experiences, and identities. This adjustment of analytical stress should be read neither as a retreat to a primordial and untouched local field site nor as a reliance on a fixed spatiality. Relationality is inherent to the locations that we consider, some connecting to distant elsewheres and others mired in the complexity of microspatial particularity. More precisely, the volume attends to the constitution of what anthropologist Sarah Green calls 'relative locations' (Green 2005, 13–14; 2013a; 2013b; 2019) – i.e. the way in which a location's quality of being 'somewhere in particular' results from connections and separations to other locations (see also Gupta and Ferguson 1997a).[4] When making sense of such processes of relative positioning, it is generative to delineate how different *spatial logics* intersect (or do not) to make a location what it is. The individual chapters illustrate how legal codes, bureaucratic organisations, urban planning, migration, trade networks, infrastructure, narrations of historical events, and political borders divide up, connect, and separate space, how distinct logics overlap, and how locations – always relative, multiple, and contingent – are carved out at their interstices. Sometimes the spatial logics are shown to be additive and cumulative, at other times they are dissonant and tension-inducing (see Green 2005, 128–48).

Locating the Mediterranean understands locations as constituted by a multiplicity of connections and separations. This approach to the local necessitates empirical examinations of processes, logics, and events that ostensibly unfold *elsewhere*, across the Mediterranean region and at times far beyond it. For example, Douzina-Bakalaki (Chapter 4) draws attention to the expansion outwards from a spectacular Greek bridge said to link 'nowhere much to nowhere at all' towards an imaginary Europe based on longue durée historical narratives that situate Greece at the nexus between East and West. Soto Bermant (Chapter 3) and Elbek (Chapter 2) both demonstrate how grand projects of 'European' geopolitics are accentuated and collapse into the remote border locations of Melilla and Lampedusa, respectively. In both cases, remoteness is a measure of distance from and centrality within broader geographical imaginaries. The spatial logics that Lähteenaho (Chapter 7) examines draw on French imperial and national legal codes but take shape and form materially in the location of Beirut's last remaining public beach. This is one of several chapters in which urban landscapes demonstrate the important and complex palimpsest processes converging on and defining locations. In other cases, the ethnography draws upon past movements to understand ethnographic locations. Bullen (Chapter 5) and Su (Chapter 8) begin on specific streets and neighbourhoods to understand how mobility cultivates relational meaning for social actors living within specific material conditions in Marseille and Istanbul. Mobility, then, is more than individual movement through space; it spans and forms life-worlds as well as regions. Russo (Chapter 6) and Green (Chapter 9), finally, illustrate how institutional transformations in colonial and postcolonial settings have resignified the values of religious icons in Tunisia and animal lives across the sea. These cases show how institutions generate meaning in locations but also elaborate wider regional configurations.

All of these inquiries are rooted in the position afforded by specific locations. By starting from the question of *where* and with an interrogation of what it means to be *here* and not *there*, they spotlight connections, separations, and spatial logics of inclusion and exclusion refracted from a particular *somewhere*. As we shall return to below, this ethnographic insistence on standing still in a world that twists and turns gives us a unique vantage point from which to locate the Mediterranean anew. By zooming in on the constitution of specific Mediterranean locations, we are inevitably also zooming out in order to re-envision region-making in and beyond the sea. Before returning to these locations and the regions that they spawn, however, we shall consider the approaches and traditions that have developed in and around the anthropology in/of the Mediterranean.

Which Mediterranean?

Fernand Braudel's *La Méditerranée et le Monde Méditerranéen à l'Epoque de Philippe II* (1949) challenged scholars to see how distinct historical processes shaped landscapes in and around the sea. His approach highlighted ecological, social, and political processes that together constituted the Mediterranean worlds of the 16th century. To do this, Braudel directed his analysis away from the events that punctuated historical narratives. His layered approach instead sought to articulate the totality of the region through three distinct, yet interconnected temporalities: event history, social or economic histories, and the longue durée of geohistorical time. This temporal division of labour has been interpreted unsurprisingly as hierarchically determined, especially given the analytical space he devotes to the longue durée. Importantly, Braudel's multidimensional approach also undermined the political borders that have conventionally framed historical analyses (Trevor Roper 1972, 467).

Braudel initially wrote of the 16th-century Mediterranean from the confines of prison in Mainz during the Second World War, where his own experience of historical time was shaped as much by his experience of the war as it was by more protracted processes ('slower temporalities') such as the 'colonial sea' of the French empire in North Africa (Borutta and Gekas 2012; Braudel 2009, 181). Howard Caygill argues that '[t]ime for the detainees was a burden, not only because of the dreary routines of the prison regime but also because of the sense of being detached from crucial historical events and helpless to intervene in them' (2004, 152). Braudel's specific *location* in space and time fostered his thinking through the complex manner by which political histories impose themselves upon the so-called slower temporalities. One might suggest that his was an attempt to locate the present within (or to dislocate it from) a more complex historical trajectory of the violence of the Second World War (Braudel 2009, 182). The threefold temporality at the heart of Braudel's intellectual project, therefore, located his experience – as well as those that constituted the 16th-century worlds about which he wrote – through a set of (temporal) relations.[5] In a similar multidimensional fashion, the present volume aims to articulate location by paying attention to the complex overlapping, incorporation, and obfuscation of distinct social and historical processes.

After the publication of Braudel's *La Méditerranée* (1949), the Mediterranean (and especially its Southern European shores) emerged as a site of increasing anthropological importance. Ethnographers in the region employed categorical containers that situated, in some way, the ethnographic present upon a backdrop of timeless sharedness often buttressed by allusions to Braudel's longue durée. These containers – honour and shame (Campbell 1964; Gilmore 1987; Peristiany 1966; Schneider 1971), amoral familism (Banfield 1958), patron–client networks (Boissevain 1966; Brown 1977; Gellner and Waterbury 1977;

Gilmore 1982) – depicted societies connected through deep-rooted structures that in turn determined conditions of possibility for a kind of society – peasantry – located in a grey zone between 'civilised' Europe and the 'primitive' South. In line with Braudel's dissatisfaction with a nation-centred (and political event-oriented) historiography, anthropologists such as Julian Pitt-Rivers posited the Mediterranean as a regional framework that could challenge privileged national cultures (1963, 1977). Indeed, it was Pitt-Rivers's Mediterranean, which cut across political boundaries of nation states and framed the region as a 'zone', that John Davis, in *People of the Mediterranean* (1977), suggested offers 'distinctive opportunities to be *comparative and historical*' (10, our emphasis).

The comparative project at the heart of that nascent ethnographic interest (Boissevain 1979) rested on troubling premises. For Davis, history was a matrix upon which comparison within the contemporary Mediterranean was made possible. It was a unifying backdrop, yet the ethnographic observations facilitated by these historical connections were atomistic and disjointed. He claimed that peoples 'of' the Mediterranean 'have been trading and talking, conquering and converting, marrying and migrating for six or seven thousand years', and then he posed the question 'is it unreasonable to assume that some anthropological meaning can be given to the term "Mediterranean"?' (1977, 13). Davis's Mediterranean was constituted by means of these interactions, historical and social in their substance. Comparison as a mechanism for realising this complexity thus functioned teleologically on the basis of that substructure. Davis's historical Mediterranean is flat and atemporal, and, in consequence, his anthropological one is atomistic and fragmented.[6] He reduced the multidimensionality of Braudel's Mediterranean and installed in its place a trajectory wherein the past presupposes the present, perpetuating the myth of a cultural area at once written out of time and yet determined by it.[7]

Furthermore, just as Braudel was deeply embedded within the colonial sea when he conceived of his project, and later Nazi-occupied France and the Algerian War in its writing and initial reception (Borutta and Gekas 2012; Dobie 2014), these post-Second World War ethnographic iterations of the Mediterranean interplayed with a world that had become strategically central to burgeoning American imperialism and NATO's Cold War geopolitics. The comparative study of peoples 'of' the Mediterranean located the region uncomfortably between democracy and the need for democratisation (Schneider 2012; Silverman 2001). While its historical determination predisposed its contemporary importance as a region, the way in which the sea was studied systematically obscured dynamism and connectivity across space and time.

Whether we speak of Pitt-Rivers's 'metaphysical', transcendent Mediterranean (1963, 1977) or Davis's 'atomistic' one (1977), as Dionigi Albera has observed (2006, 113), both models were founded upon comparative frameworks that divide the ethnographic present and the historical past in arbitrary ways. Both scholars also employed the language of 'cultural area' despite their outspoken opposition to the idea (Albera and Blok 2001, 18). In this sense, they left little room for the layered and multiple experiences of immigrant arrivals, embodied geopolitics, marketplaces, bridges and transportation networks, urban landscapes, and human and non-human border-crossings. In short, the foundational texts of Mediterranean anthropology paid scant attention to the actual connections and separations that constitute Mediterranean *locations*, thus taking for granted the 'Mediterranean' as a regional framework by functioning on the premise that the Mediterranean itself is already *there*.

Not long after Davis's *People of the Mediterranean* was published, Edward Said's *Orientalism* (1978) inverted the frames through which scholars wrote about Others. This found its Mediterranean expression in Michael Herzfeld's classic critique of the 'horns' of the Mediterraneanist dilemma, which all but silenced discussion of regional sharedness (see Herzfeld 1980, 1984). The epistemological shift to perceive of taken-for-granted analytical categories as constructed (Pina-Cabral 1989) made it possible to think of the Mediterranean as a contested category in itself – a move that continues to inform postcolonial and cultural studies of/in the region (see, for example, Dobie 2014; elharity and Talbayev 2018; Proglio et al 2020; Smythe 2018; Yashin 2014). As a result, the Mediterranean became a historically contingent category rather than one generated in comparison.[8] Later, and turning the ethnographic concept in on itself, 'Mediterraneanism' came to be interpreted as part of a politicised cultural repertoire by means of which sociocultural hierarchies could be reconfigured (Herzfeld 2005).

During the 1990s, attention turned towards the more complex relations between past and present *in* and *around* the Mediterranean, without much pretence to regional generalisation or comparison (on different sides of this moment, see Behar 1991; Leontidou 1990; Sutton 2000). With scholars aware of Herzfeld's critique of regional comparisons, and at the height of the age of ethnographic relativism (accounted for above), interplay across and between sites specifically located in a Mediterranean configuration remained below the surface, at least until the late 1990s and early 2000s when attempts were made in Aix-en-Provence to revive the regional debate and justify the viability of a Mediterranean anthropology (Albera 2006; Albera, Blok, and Bromberger 2001; Bromberger 2006, 2007; Sacchi and Viazzo 2013). Reflecting on earlier controversies, Sydel Silverman noted a colleague's reflection on 'the possibility that the very concept of a "Mediterranean anthropology" is no longer useful'. In response, she argued that indeed migration, nationalisms, the reconfiguration of state and society, and globalisation are all 'processes ... *still worked out in localities*' (2001, 53, emphasis ours). To what extent does Silverman's insight pave the way for an anthropology that embraces abstracted regional frameworks *and* specific locations? That is the point to which this volume turns.

Mediterranean Locations, Mediterranean Constellations

Locating the Mediterranean is guided by an attempt to rethink regional constellations by taking locations, always relative and constituted by particular connections, separations, and spatial logics, as our starting points. Constellations enter the analysis in two ways and on two different scales. First, they do so in the individual chapters, which offer insights into particular locations, the connections and separations that bring them into being, and their often independently emergent constellations. Second, they do so through the collective and accumulative project of *Locating the Mediterranean*'s eight following chapters, which constitutes a Mediterranean constellation in its own right. We contend that our approach unveils powerful hierarchies that give particular form to a particular region. The locations with which we began – the Italian care home in Alexandria and the football pitch in Cairo – together conjure a range of connections and separations that give each location, and the region, meaning and value. Therefore, we take into account Silverman's 2001 observation that processes of all scales by necessity are worked out in localities, but we do so by engaging with more recent reassessments of the analytical value of regional frameworks (e.g. Ben-Yehoyada 2017; Ben-Yehoyada, Cabot, and Silverstein 2020). In framing this volume, we ask: how do we move from micro interactions and dynamics worked out in specific locations, and characterised by particular cultural and historical worlds, into broader processes that are not always visibly (or materially) connected? How can we elaborate such an approach without sacrificing one perspective for the other (that is, without insisting on innate comparability or incommensurable difference)? And, importantly, how do these multi-directional processes locate places, and regions, within particular sets of relations through space and time?

Our approach is inspired in part by Nicholas Purcell and Peregrine Horden's path-breaking *The Corrupting Sea* (2000), with its strong focus on connectivity within and between the Mediterranean's many microregions. In developing a more complex study of the mechanisms of connection from micro-level processes to regional phenomena, from the ancient to the contemporary periods, Purcell and Horden have inspired a new wave of Mediterranean studies and a thorough rehashing of older conversations and debates (on the sea and its global histories, Abulafia 2011; on region-making, Ben-Yehoyada 2014; on postcolonial Mediterranean literary studies, Chambers 2008; on Mediterranean ports, Driessen 2005; on the Mediterranean city, Leontidou 2004, 2015, 2019; on critical theory and literary studies, elhariry and Talbayev 2018; on rethinking the broad field of Mediterranean studies, Harris 2005; Horden and Kinoshita 2014; on legal regimes in the 19th century, Marglin 2014; Sant Cassia and Schäfer 2005; on the Mediterranean viewed from its southern shores, Tucker 2019). These new works conjure a sea that circumvents homogeneity through its microregional complexity, one that is interconnected by transport and infrastructure, sociocultural perceptions, shared dependencies, and asymmetrical political forms of exchange. *The Corrupting Sea*'s Mediterranean is not a region on the basis of its being the same everywhere, nor of shared historical processes manifesting in a generalisable present. Instead, its intellectual underpinnings aim to attend to the 'polybian problem' of 'making sense of more than one place at a time' (Purcell 2006). In doing so, processes of connection become ever more important in understanding region.

The resurgence in scholarly interest in the Mediterranean as a field of connections has also been spurred by a recent evocation of relations that connect space and time across the sea. The Mediterranean has emerged as a site of negotiation for the century's most pressing concerns: the Barcelona Process in 1995 paved the way for Sarkozy's 2007 Union pour la Méditerranée; the 2011 revolutions and uprisings in the Middle East and North Africa stimulated popular revolts against global capitalism and austerity measures from Spain's *indignados* to Athens's Syntagma Square to Occupy Wall Street; the creation of 'Fortress Europe' and the Operation Mare Nostrum (OMN) sought to block migrant and refugee arrivals and externalise EU boundaries since the early 2000s; and the surge of right-wing nationalism following the 2008 economic recession and the migrant 'crisis' has recast the sea's northern shores within a discourse of civilisational conflict (Albahari 2015; Andersson 2014; Ben-Yehoyada 2015; Cabot 2014; Elliot 2021; Heller and Pezzani 2017; Knight 2015, 2021; Soto Bermant 2017). Scholarship in the region has also raised questions about how decolonisation after the Second World War has connected and separated places and peoples across borders through the lens of these abovementioned events and processes (Ballinger 2020; Malia Hom 2020; Lorcin and Shepard 2016; Viscomi 2019, 2020).[9]

A subsection of this outpouring of scholarly engagement explicitly addresses the constitution of the Mediterranean as a region. Naor Ben-Yehoyada's *The Mediterranean Incarnate* (2017), for example, examines sociopolitical geographies in the Mediterranean by arguing that scale-making processes of region formation are at play both in grand political projects, such as Sarkozy's Union, and in micro-level cultural, material and historical encounters, such as those between Sicilian and Tunisian fishermen.[10] We find Ben-Yehoyada's intervention a much-welcomed challenge to previous decades' epistemological hesitancy. Indeed, if it is true that 'the Mediterranean is back', as Ben-Yehoyada, Cabot, and Silverstein argue, then a revitalised field of Mediterranean studies must take seriously how processes of 'connection, movement, and relatedness' engender 'socio-cultural and ecological realities' that span, constitute and even exceed the region (2020, 1, 6).

The processes explored by scholars in this new 'wave' of Mediterranean studies are rich in connections. Yet, in an incisive critique of Purcell and Horden's approach to connectivity, Gadi Algazi asks: '[i]s connectivity the sum total of enabling natural conditions and techniques, of economic structures, cultural perceptions, and configurations of power that predispose agents to engage in exchange, or the end result of all of these forces?' (2006, 242; a similar critique has been levied by

Fentress and Fentress 2001). In other words, the stress on connectivity does not tell us much about constitutive processes. Does an emphasis on connectivity suggest a new form of 'total history' (a way of putting everything together into a whole image) or is it generative (emerging from existing, but not necessarily connected processes)? Is connectivity an analytic predisposition or is it an empirical result? These questions are left unanswered. A similar critique might be made about *The Mediterranean Incarnate*. Ben-Yehoyada's Mediterranean is a region that connects, forms, and extends but which rarely dissolves, deforms, or breaks apart. For him and other scholars who follow travel, trade, transport links, shared vocabularies and infrastructure, the spotlight will always be on tying, knitting, and knotting rather than on dead ends, loose threads, and unfinished connections. In this framing, the ways in which the Mediterranean is contemporaneously an epitome of connectivity and mobility *and* one of the most deadly and heavily policed border risk sliding out of view.

Does an overemphasis on connectivity create gaps and biases in our knowledge of the material conditions of social life in the region? We argue that it does. In this volume, therefore, we are less concerned with connectivity per se and more focused on how *locations* are calibrated by *constellations* of money, materiality, movement, and stories that cross or do not cross the Mediterranean in space and through time. By constellation, and in accordance with Ben-Yehoyada, Cabot, and Silverstein (2020, 7), we refer to a specific, yet inevitably transforming arrangement of meanings and values that render a location legible or internally coherent. While partly a result of contingent spatial and temporal relations, a constellation is also constituted by separation. Locations are also constituted by deliberate processes of region *un*-making, by excluding other locations from a given constellation, or by being distinguished and situated within power-laden hierarchies. While attentive to the processes that Ben-Yehoyada calls 'region formation', our approach thus also highlights practices that intentionally work to *dissolve* region, to foster separation, and to generate remoteness.[11]

Stepping into the Mediterranean

By examining constellations that incorporate connections and separations across space and time, the individual chapters and *Locating the Mediterranean* as a whole demonstrate how Mediterranean locations affect and shape daily lives, practices, opportunities, and social and political conditions. Drawing on research in Lampedusa, Melilla, Nafpaktos/Lepanto, Marseille, Tunis, Beirut, Istanbul, and Mediterranean-wide networks of animal mobility, each chapter creates diverse kinds of distinctions between places and times and demonstrates how locations are actualised.

The first two chapters work through remote or isolated locations to understand such spatiotemporal constellations. In Chapter 2, Elbek shows how Lampedusans depict their island's isolation in historical time and in the ethnographic present. In doing this, they understand their own isolation as pulled in multiple directions contemporaneously. Soto Bermant explores Spain's and the European Union's remote borders in Melilla in Chapter 3, illustrating the enclave's role as distanced gatekeeper for Europe's centres of geopolitical power. The constellation that renders Melilla meaningful as a location is most clearly one where drastic separations and performative connections work in tandem.

The following two chapters use infrastructure – bridges and roads – to unravel temporal processes wrapped up in locations. In Chapter 4, Douzina-Bakalaki examines how commemorative practices around the Battle of Lepanto situate Nafpaktos's changing locations vis-à-vis Europe and the Mediterranean. The constellation under scrutiny in the chapter combines history and geopolitics to locate Nafpaktos as a contemporary incarnation of Lepanto. Bullen (Chapter 5) looks at the social networks that intersect on one street in Marseille to understand the location of lives and practices in relation to French and Algerian shores. Her interlocutors are contemporaneously located along a busy urban road and in a Mediterranean region criss-crossed by history, travel, and postcolonial debates.

Chapters 6 and 7 concentrate more explicitly on constellations informed by colonial and postcolonial locations. Russo (Chapter 6) explores the rituals around the celebration of the Virgin Mary of Trapani in Tunisia to understand how its use has manifested La Goulette's religious diversity at different historical conjunctures. Through the cult that surrounds Notre Dame de Trapani, La Goulette is at the crossroad of spatial and temporal trajectories that define the city as a distinctly cosmopolitanism location. Lähteenaho (Chapter 7), then, shows how public spaces in Beirut are located through colonial and postcolonial legal and bureaucratic regimes. Here, the location of the city's coastline is shown to be both relative and contested, an always-shifting sum of political struggles in the present and spatial logics of bygone eras that haunt the present.

The last two chapters turn to questions of mobility, each from radically different perspectives. In Chapter 8, Su looks at how location, in relation to notions of belonging, creates possibilities for migrants in Istanbul to subvert social and political borders. It spotlights how the notion of *gurbet* (exile) is both an experience and a location, which fundamentally shapes ideas about masculinity. Green explores in Chapter 9 the classificatory logics of locating animals in the Mediterranean region, in terms of both science and their actual travels, whose movements frequently evade political bordering regimes. Here, we see how the Mediterranean takes shape at the intersection of a multiplicity of spatial logics that only partly contain the region's unruly fauna.

By taking the unique vantage point in concrete locations, each chapter approaches Mediterranean constellations from a specific position, somewhere in particular. This ethnographic insistence on watching the world's complexity from an 'arbitrary' location (Candea 2007, 2010; see also Douzina-Bakalaki, Chapter 4) provides an analytical fix-point from which to 'cut the network' (Strathern 1996) and partially unravel the 'knotted' temporal and spatial threads (Viscomi 2020) that compose the constellation under consideration.[12] In keeping this dual perspective – on the one hand, specific locations; on the other hand, the Mediterranean as a regional constellation (especially visible in Green's contribution, Chapter 9) – we are able to explore located understandings of the Mediterranean, while still maintaining and, indeed, insisting that locations fluctuate and overlap in their meanings and values. We also demonstrate how multiple locations materialise and coexist in the same space, emphasising the centrality of certain locations while marginalising others. Bullen (Chapter 5) and Russo (Chapter 7), for instance, demonstrate how particular neighbourhoods and streets, in their material landscapes, evoke local and regional values that endow them with specific yet multiple meanings.

The shift from micro-level specificity to broader regional constellations is imbued with historical and cultural tensions that, although always beginning somewhere, often finish nowhere in particular. In embracing such an approach, *Locating the Mediterranean* aims to avoid several dichotomous interpretations that have long dominated conversations about the Mediterranean. One such binary delineates proponents of the *reality* of the Mediterranean (as grounds for comparison) from those insisting on its constructed-ness (as a cultural tool to be employed, strategically or otherwise; see Herzfeld 1984, 2005). As the empirical material incorporated in this volume demonstrates, the Mediterranean *has* an undeniable material presence in infrastructure (Elbek, Chapter 2), cadastral archives (Lähteenaho, Chapter 7), border regimes (Soto Bermant, Chapter 3), and the regulatory frameworks of the World Organisation for Animal Health (Green, Chapter 9). Our aim, however, is to work towards its articulation *between* conceptual fields *and* material realities. To do so, we do not presuppose (or impose) the Mediterranean as a concept across the chapters. The Mediterranean might well be an 'imagined' or polysemic space (*al-bahr al-abyad al-mutawassat* [the white middle sea], *al-bahr al-malih* [the salt sea], *bahr al-rum* [the Roman sea], or localised nomenclature such as *bahr tanja* [the sea of Tangier], to draw from the recent work on the Mediterranean through Arab eyes; Matar 2019), yet there is, concurrently, one that is a material reality (for example, the political economic conditions described by Tabak 2008 and 2010). Moreover, we see the sea – in its conceptualisation *and* its empirical realities – as a product of locations cultivated to a significant degree by (European) imperial projects and projections (Borutta and Gekas 2012; Fogu 2018, 2020; Lorcin and Shepard 2016; Silverstein 2002). Like Proglio et al (2020), Proglio (2018) and Grimaldi (2019) show in their articulation of the Black Mediterranean, regional configurations demarcate lived and remembered paths across space and through time that interconnect migrants' experiences and yet distinguish them from other experiences within a political contested Mediterranean (see also di Maio 2012).

Asymmetries of power between the northern and southern shores constitute another persistent and troubling binary. No doubt, Mediterranean studies has habitually adopted a distinctly northern perspective and European gaze. As literary scholar Roberto Dainotto notes, 'Any Italian might write about the Mediterranean … without bothering with citing Abdelkebir Khatibi, Albert Memmi, or Taieb Belghazi. For a Turkish or Algerian author, it is instead impossible (or suicidal) not to confront the "Mediterranean" canonised in European literature' (2003, 7). Recent efforts to remedy this asymmetry have typically highlighted how the Mediterranean has been understood, created, and mapped by people populating its southern (and eastern) – that is, Arab, Muslim, and African – shores (Ardizzoni and Ferme 2015; Kahlaoui 2018; Tucker 2019; Wick 2014). While we recognise that this is a praiseworthy and vital move, we also identify a risk of becoming trapped in the loathed binary division that one wants to challenge. Singling out the north–south divide as *the* fundamental principle that has to be broken down by necessity emphasises certain differences (i.e. religious and linguistic) while flattening other, 'internal' nuances[13]: how similar are Mediterranean experiences in 'northern' countries such as Greece and Spain? In Lebanon and Morocco? In cities such as Naples and Palermo? Or, as we began, in Alexandria and Cairo? Due to its insistence on examining relative locations, the chapters in *Locating the Mediterranean* aim to sidestep this impasse. Our minute analyses of the connections and separations that locate actors and processes somewhere in particular demonstrate that north-vs-south is but one of many logics determining where Mediterranean locations are located.[14] Sometimes (e.g. Soto Bermant, Chapter 3; Douzina-Bakalaki, Chapter 4; Su, Chapter 8) what is West and what is Rest *is* key for the experiences of located-ness under scrutiny; in other instances (e.g. Elbek, Chapter 2; Bullen, Chapter 5; Russo, Chapter 6; Lähteenaho, Chapter 7; Green, Chapter 9) other logics – infrastructural, religious, legal, scientific – play more decisive roles. Rather than assuming that the division between a European/Christian North and an African/Muslim South constitutes the region's hegemonic divide, then, the volume allows localised encounters to determine what is pertinent and what is not.

'Mediterranean modernity' constitutes another long-standing field of contestation. To what extent is it possible to imagine and live modern Mediterranean lives, given the region's associations with a golden, pre-modern age and the fact that it was conceptualised as an antidote to north-western Europe as the epitome of modernity? Is the notion of Mediterranean modernity a contradiction in terms, leaving contemporary Mediterranean subjects forever nostalgic for a lost past? How could a modern version of the sea be discursively and materially re-erected (Ben-Yehoyada 2014, 2017; Chambers 2008; elhariry and Talbayev 2018; Goldwyn and Silverman 2016; Tucker 2019; Yashin 2014)? Once again, we do not question the relevance of these questions but ask what they potentially obfuscate when taken as the premise for ethnographic research (see Russo's engagement with nostalgia,

Chapter 6). As much as the region has been historically constructed as modern Europe's internal other, we note that this is a positioned and partial perspective. For many people, the Mediterranean instead represents an accessible vision of modernity (Elliot 2021; Schielke 2015) or a path to it (Douzina-Bakalaki, Chapter 4). In the wake of the 2008 economic crisis, cross-Mediterranean identities and solidarities might be more likely to conjure a shared sense of precarity and marginalisation than would nostalgia for a pre-modern past (Elbek, Chapter 2). Our focus on locations gestures to a different set of questions and a different kind of region. Examining connections and separations, our Mediterranean transpires in material and discursive constellations that might or might not encompass the question of modernity and the nostalgia elicited by it. This circumventing manoeuvre does not imply that we propose a wholly synchronic Mediterranean detached from historical time.[15] By contrast, one of the volume's primary interests is to expose how spaces and times get folded or knotted into one another (for example, Douzina-Bakalaki's and Russo's contributions, Chapters 4 and 6). And, yet, whether or not modernity, or the lack thereof, is implicated in these Mediterranean constellations must be an empirical question. It should not be one posed at the outset.

We hope that *Locating the Mediterranean* opens the path for an anthropology both *in* and *of* the Mediterranean (see Horden and Purcell 2000), and that it does so without relying on comparison as the primary methodological approach. We recognise that comparison always creeps into a collected volume; yet, taking that insight with 'a pinch of salt', as anthropologist Matei Candea has suggested, the volume seeks to foreground empirical connections or processes that *lead to* comparison rather than begin with conceptual prefigurations (for more on this, see Candea 2018, and the Epilogue in this volume). As outlined above, anthropologists committed to the region's viability have, since Herzfeld's scathing critique, been at pains to justify why the comparative project is worthwhile. Arguably, doubts about the regional framework's very possibility have, over the last decades, troubled Mediterraneanist anthropologists more than any other regionally assembled community of scholars. While there has been no dearth of groundbreaking anthropological work in various parts of the Mediterranean region, scholars have been hesitant both to label themselves 'Mediterraneanists' and to address broader questions about region formation. For reasons that would require another book to disentangle, it has been much less problematic for anthropologists working in Egypt or Tunisia to place themselves with bodies of scholarship labelled as 'Middle Eastern' or 'North African'. Could ethnographic research premised on locations and the connections and separations that sustain them provide a way out of this impasse? We are convinced that it could, but only if the question of *what* the Mediterranean *is* is substituted by that of *where* the sea *is located*. The volume ultimately proposes that 'Mediterranean' – and, arguably, any other regional label – can function as a generative framework for analysis if it is studied as malleable, transforming and performative *constellations* fostered in specific *locations*. As each contribution to this volume illustrates, the study of locations – relative, connected, separated, overlapping – makes visible constellations that constitute actually existing Mediterraneans. In this sense, *Locating the Mediterranean* is accumulative. The ethnographic chapters that we now turn to do not provide Mediterranean 'examples' but rather offer windows into expansive Mediterranean worlds.

Notes

1 Mustafa is a pseudonym.
2 This is the same moment in which 'nation' and 'nationalism' underwent intellectual scrutiny, best epitomised in Benedict Anderson, *Imagined Communities* (1983) and Eric Hobsbawm and Terence Ranger (eds.), *The Invention of Tradition* (1983).
3 This stems in part from a long-standing critique within cultural studies, such as Raymond Williams's reading of the concentration on urban locations as delimiting historical and cultural understandings of modernity in *The Country and the City* (1975).
4 Although our project involves a certain degree of what theorist Henri Lefebvre calls 'spatialization' – or 'the production of space' – we seek to go beyond that analytical framework to understand how various spaces might be used to constitute specific locations in relation to others. For us, then, location is a more central and palpable concept, in contrast to an abstracted understanding of socio-spatial production. See Lefebvre's *The Production of Space* (1991) for a full elaboration of his ideas.
5 Caygill importantly points to Braudel's critique of Bergson by noting that Braudel 'compares the history of events to a film trailer', in which, however 'gripping they may be, these trailers never tell us the whole film, all of the story (*histoire*)' (2004, 157n22).
6 Purcell and Horden make a similar observation (2000, 467). They also importantly note that anthropologists in this period almost entirely neglected to give serious consideration to one key historically informed ethnographic work: Evans-Pritchards's *The Sanusi of Cyrenaica* (1949).

7 See also Purcell and Horden's discussion on *Cristo si è fermato a Eboli* (2000, 463).

8 There are, of course, importance resonances with later works that challenged the assumed concreteness of geographical specificity; see e.g., Lewis and Wigen's *The Myth of Continents* (1997). Perhaps nowhere better is this encapsulated than in Jane Schneider's edited volume *Italy's 'Southern Question': Orientalism in One Country* (1998).

9 Similar insights on regional connectivity have formed the basis of a thorough reassessment of the cultural, political, and religious categories that shaped early modern and long-19th-century contexts of slavery, piracy, nationalism, and the circulation of political ideas; see Greene 2002; Hershenzon 2018; Isabella and Zanou 2015; White 2017; Zanou 2018.

10 For further anthropological discussions on the production of scales and scalability, see e.g., Mazzarella 2004; Tsing 2000, 2012; Wilk 1995.

11 By emphasising this duality between connection and separation, we are not interested in describing the existence of or relation between points of a network, as is the dominant analytical approach in actor network theory; see Latour 2005. Rather, we aim to consider how these two processes (connection and separation) can give shape to constellations that emanate from and at the same time constitute particular locations.

12 As Matei Candea has argued (2007), this is an approach that both builds on and deviates from multisided methodologies that 'follow' the movement of things, concepts, or people across geographical space.

13 For an example of how this debate figures in Italian thinking, see Cassano (1996).

14 Importantly, we do acknowledge that this volume is missing a sufficient discussion of Adriatic and Balkan worlds. On this, see the interesting collective project 'Decolonize Hellas/Decolonize the Balkans' (decolonizehellas.org/en) and Ballinger (1999).

15 We are not arguing for a Mediterranean coevality à la Fabian (2014 [1983]) but rather a multiplicity of time. See Bevernage (2016).

References

Abulafia, David. 2011. *The Great Sea: A Human History of the Mediterranean*. London: Penguin.

Albahari, Maurizio. 2015. *Crimes of Peace: Mediterranean Migrations at the World's Deadliest Border*. Philadelphia, PA: University of Pennsylvania Press.

Albera, Dionigi. 2006. 'Anthropology of the Mediterranean: Between Crisis and Renewal'. *History and Anthropology* 17 (2): 109–33. https://doi.org/10.1080/02757200600633272

Albera, Dionigi, and Anton Blok. 2001. 'The Mediterranean as an Ethnological Field of Study: A Retrospective'. In *L'antropologie de la Méditerranée / Anthropology of the Mediterranean*, edited by Dionigi Albera, Anton Blok, and Christian Bromberger, 15–37. Paris: Maisonneuve et Larose.

Albera, Dionigi, Anton Blok, and Christian Bromberger, eds. 2001. *L'antropologie de la Méditerranée / Anthropology of the Mediterranean*. Paris: Maisonneuve et Larose.

Algazi, Gadi. 2006. 'Diversity Rules: Peregrine Horden and Nicholas Purcell's The Corrupting Sea'. *Mediterranean Historical Review* 20 (2): 227–45. https://doi.org/10.1080/09518960500495172

Anderson, Benedict. 2006. *Imagined Communities: Reflections on the Origin and Spread of Nationalism*. London: Verso.

Andersson, Ruben. 2014. *Illegality, Inc.: Clandestine Migration and the Business of Bordering Europe*. Berkeley, CA: University of California Press.

Appadurai, Arjun. 1990. 'Disjuncture and Difference in the Global Cultural Economy'. *Public Culture* 2 (2): 1–24.

Appadurai, Arjun. 1996. *Modernity at Large: Cultural Dimensions of Globalization*. Minneapolis, MN: University of Minnesota Press.

Ardizzoni, Michela, and Valerio Ferme, eds. 2015. *Mediterranean Encounters in the City: Frameworks of Mediation Between East and West, North and South*. Lanham, MD: Lexington Books.

Ballinger, Pamela. 1999. 'Definitional Dilemmas: Southeastern Europe as "Culture Area"?' *Balkanologie: Revue d'études pluridisciplinaires* 3 (2). https://doi.org/10.4000/balkanologie.745

Ballinger, Pamela. 2020. *The World Refugees Made: Decolonization and the Foundation of Postwar Italy*. Ithaca, NY: Cornell University Press.

Banfield, Edward C. 1958. *The Moral Basis of a Backward Society*. New York, NY: Free Press.

Behar, Ruth. 1991. *The Presence of the Past in a Spanish Village: Santa Maria del Monte*. Princeton, NJ: Princeton University Press.

Ben-Yehoyada, Naor. 2014. 'Mediterranean Modernity?' In *A Companion to Mediterranean History*, edited by Peregrine Horden and Sharon Kinoshita, 107–21. London: John Wiley & Sons.

Ben-Yehoyada, Naor. 2015. '"Follow Me, and I Will Make You Fishers of Men": The Moral and Political Scales of Migration in the Central Mediterranean'. *Journal of the Royal Anthropological Institute* 22 (1): 183–202.

Ben-Yehoyada, Naor. 2017. *The Mediterranean Incarnate: Region Formation between Sicily and Tunisia since World War II*. Chicago, IL: University of Chicago Press.

Ben-Yehoyada, Naor, Heath Cabot, and Paul A. Silverstein. 2020. 'Introduction: Remapping Mediterranean Anthropology'. *History and Anthropology* 31 (1): 1–21. https://doi.org/10.1080/02757206.2019.1684274

Bevernage, Berber. 2016. 'Tales of Pastness and Contemporaneity: On the Politics of Time in History and Anthropology'. *Rethinking History* 20 (3): 352–74. https://doi.org/10.1080/13642529.2016.1192257

Boissevain, Jeremy. 1966. 'Patronage in Sicily'. *Man* 1 (1): 18–33.

Boissevain, Jeremy. 1979. 'Towards a Social Anthropology of the Mediterranean'. *Current Anthropology* 20 (1): 81–93.

Borutta, Manuel, and Sakis Gekas. 2012. 'A Colonial Sea: The Mediterranean, 1798–1956'. *European Review of History: Revue europeenne d'histoire* 19 (1): 1–13. https://doi.org/10.1080/13507486.2012.643609

Braudel, Fernand. 1949. *La Méditerranée et le Monde Méditerranéen a l'époque de Philippe II* (vol. 1). Paris: Armand Colin.

Braudel, Fernand. 2009. 'History and the Social Sciences: The Longue Durée'. Translated by Immanuel Wallerstein. *Review* 32 (2, Commemorating the Longue Durée): 171–203.

Bromberger, Christian. 2006. 'Towards an Anthropology of the Mediterranean'. *History and Anthropology* 17 (2): 91–107. https://doi.org/10.1080/02757200600624339

Bromberger, Christian. 2007. 'Bridge, Wall, Mirror: Coexistence and Confrontations in the Mediterranean World'. *History and Anthropology* 18 (3): 291–307. https://doi.org/10.1080/02757200701389030

Brown, Kenneth. 1977. *Changing Forms of Patronage in a Moroccan City*. London: Duckworth.

Cabot, Heath. 2014. *On the Doorstep of Europe: Asylum and Citizenship in Greece*. Philadelphia, PA: University of Pennsylvania Press.

Campbell, John K. 1964. *Honour, Family and Patronage: A Study of Institutions and Moral Values in a Greek Mountain Community*. New York, NY: Clarendon Press.

Candea, Matei. 2007. 'Arbitrary Locations: In Defence of the Bounded Field-Site'. *Journal of the Royal Anthropological Institute* 13 (1): 167–84.

Candea, Matei. 2010. *Corsican Fragments: Difference, Knowledge, and Fieldwork*. Bloomington, IN: Indiana University Press.

Candea, Matei. 2018. *Comparison in Anthropology: The Impossible Method*. Cambridge: Cambridge University Press.

Cassano, Franco. 1996. *Il pensiero meridiano*. Bari: Laterza.

Caygill, Howard. 2004. 'Braudel's Prison Notebooks'. *History Workshop Journal* 57 (1): 151–60. https://doi.org/10.1093/hwj/57.1.151

Chambers, Iain. 2008. *Mediterranean Crossings: The Politics of an Interrupted Modernity*. Durham, NC: Duke University Press.

Clifford, James. 1988. *The Predicament of Culture: Twentieth-Century Ethnography, Literature, and Art*. Cambridge, MA: Harvard University Press.

Clifford, James, and George E. Marcus, eds. 1986. *Writing Culture: The Poetics and Politics of Ethnography*. Berkeley, CA: University of California Press.

Cohen, Anthony P., ed. 1982. *Belonging: Identity and Social Organisation in British Rural Cultures*. Manchester: Manchester University Press.

Cohen, Anthony P. 1986. 'Of Symbols and Boundaries, or, Does Ertie's Greatcoat Hold the Key?' In *Symbolising Boundaries: Identity and Diversity in British Cultures*, edited by Anthony P. Cohen, 1–19. Manchester: Manchester University Press.

Cohen, Anthony P. 1987. *Whalsay: Symbol, Segment and Boundary in a Shetland Island Community*. Manchester: Manchester University Press.

Dainotto, Roberto. 2003. 'Asimmetrie mediterranee: Etica e mare nostrum'. *NAE* 3: 3–18.

Davis, John. 1977. *People of the Mediterranean: An Essay in Comparative Social Anthropology*. London: Routledge & K. Paul.

Di Maio, Alessandra. 2012. 'Il mediterraneo nero: Rotte dei migranti nel millennio globale'. In *La Città Cosmopolita*, edited by Giulia de Spuches, 143–63. Palermo: Palumbo Editore.

Dobie, Madeleine. 2014. 'For and against the Mediterranean: Francophone Perspectives'. *Comparative Studies of South Asia, Africa and the Middle East* 34 (2): 389–404. https://doi.org/10.1215/1089201X-2773923

Driessen, Henk. 2005. 'Mediterranean Port Cities: Cosmopolitanism Reconsidered'. *History and Anthropology* 16 (1): 129–41. https://doi.org/10.1080/0275720042000316669

elhariry, yasser, and Edwige Tamalet Talbayev, eds. 2018. *Critically Mediterranean: Temporalities, Aesthetics, and Deployments of a Sea in Crisis*. Basingstoke: Palgrave Macmillan.

Elliot, Alice. 2021. *The Outside: Migration as Life in Morocco*. Bloomington, IN: Indiana University Press.

Evans-Pritchard, E.E. 1949. *The Sanusi of Cyrenaica*. London: Clarendon Press.

Fabian, Johannes. 2014 [1983]. *Time and the Other: How Anthropology Makes Its Object*. New York, NY: Columbia University Press.

Fentress, Elizabeth, and James Fentress. 2001. 'The Hole in the Doughnut'. *Past & Present* 173 (1): 203–19. https://doi.org/10.1093/past/173.1.203

Fogu, Claudio. 2018. 'We Have Made the Mediterranean; Now We Must Make Mediterraneans'. In *Critically Mediterranean: Temporalities, Aesthetics, and Deployments of a Sea in Crisis*, edited by yasser elhariry and Edwige Tamalet Talbayev, 181–97. Cham: Springer.

Fogu, Claudio. 2020. *The Fishing Net and the Spider Web: Mediterranean Imaginaries and the Making of Italians*. Basingstoke: Palgrave Macmillan.

Gellner, Ernest, and John Waterbury, eds. 1977. *Patrons and Clients in Mediterranean Societies*. London: Gerald Duckworth & Company.

Ghannam, Farha. 2002. *Remaking the Modern: Space, Relocation, and the Politics of Identity in a Global Cairo*. Berkeley, CA: University of California Press.

Gilmore, David D. 1982. 'Anthropology of the Mediterranean Area'. *Annual Review of Anthropology* 11 (1): 175–205.

Gilmore, David D., ed. 1987. *Honor and Shame and the Unity of the Mediterranean*. Washington, DC: American Anthropological Association.

Goldwyn, Adam J., and Reneé M. Silverman. 2016. 'Introduction: Fernand Braudel and the invention of a modernist's Mediterranean'. In *Mediterranean Modernism: Intercultural Exchange and Aesthetic Development*, edited by Adam J. Goldwyn and Reneé M. Silverman, 1–26. Basingstoke: Palgrave Macmillan.

Green, Sarah F. 2005. *Notes from the Balkans: Locating Marginality and Ambiguity on the Greek-Albanian Border*. Princeton, NJ: Princeton University Press.

Green, Sarah. 2013a. 'Borders and the Relocation of Europe'. *Annual Review of Anthropology* 42: 345–61. https://doi.org/10.1146/annurev-anthro-092412-155457

Green, Sarah. 2013b. 'Money Frontiers: The Relative Location of Euros, Turkish Lira and Gold Sovereigns in the Aegean'. In *Objects and Materials: A Routledge Companion*, edited by Penny Harvey, Eleanor Conlin Casella, Gillian Evans, Hannah Knox, Christine McLean, Elizabeth B. Silva, Nicholas Thoburn, and Kath Woodward, 302–11. London: Routledge.

Green, Sarah. 2019. 'Entangled Borders'. *Archivio antropologico mediterraneo* 21 (2). https://doi.org/10.4000/aam.1749

Greene, Molly. 2002. 'Beyond the Northern Invasion: The Mediterranean in the Seventeenth Century'. *Past and Present* 174: 42–71.

Grimaldi, Giuseppe. 2019. 'The Black Mediterranean: Liminality and the Reconfiguration of Afroeuropeanness'. *Open Cultural Studies* 3: 414–27. https://doi.org/10.1515/culture-2019-003

Gupta, Akhil, and James Ferguson, eds. 1997a. *Anthropological Locations: Boundaries and Grounds of a Field Science*. Berkeley, CA: University of California Press.

Gupta, Akhil, and James Ferguson, eds. 1997b. *Culture, Power, Place: Explorations in Critical Anthropology*. Durham, NC: Duke University Press.

Hannerz, Ulf. 1989. 'Notes on the Global Ecumene'. *Public Culture* 1 (2): 66–75. https://doi.org/10.1215/08992363-1-2-66

Hannerz, Ulf. 1996. *Transnational Connections: Culture, People, Places*. London: Routledge.

Harris, William V., ed. 2005. *Rethinking the Mediterranean*. Oxford: Oxford University Press.

Heller, Charles, and Lorenzo Pezzani. 2017. 'Liquid Traces: Investigating the Deaths of Migrants at the EU's Maritime Frontier'. In *The Borders of 'Europe': Autonomy of Migration, Tactics of Bordering*, edited by Nicholas de Genova, 95–119. Durham, NC: Duke University Press.

Hershenzon, Daniel. 2018. *The Captive Sea: Slavery, Communication, and Commerce in Early Modern Spain and the Mediterranean*. Philadelphia, PA: University of Pennsylvania Press.

Herzfeld, Michael. 1980. 'Honour and Shame: Problems in the Comparative Analysis of Moral Systems'. *Man* 15 (2): 339–51. https://doi.org/10.2307/2801675

Herzfeld, Michael. 1984. 'The Horns of the Mediterraneanist Dilemma'. *American Ethnologist* 11 (3): 439–54.

Herzfeld, Michael. 2005. 'Practical Mediterraneanism: Excuses for Everything, from Epistemology to Eating'. In *Rethinking the Mediterranean*, edited by William V. Harris, 45–63. Oxford: Oxford University Press.

Hobsbawm, Eric, and Terence Ranger, eds. 1983. *The Invention of Tradition*. Cambridge: Cambridge University Press.

Horden, Peregrine, and Nicholas Purcell. 2000. *The Corrupting Sea: A Study of Mediterranean History*. Hoboken, NJ: Wiley-Blackwell.

Horden, Peregrine, and Sharon Kinoshita, eds. 2014. *A Companion to Mediterranean History*. Chichester: John Wiley & Sons.

Isabella, Maurizio, and Konstantina Zanou, eds. 2015. *Mediterranean Diasporas: Politics and Ideas in the Long 19th Century*. London: Bloomsbury Press.

Kahlaoui, Tarek. 2018. *Creating the Mediterranean: Maps and the Islamic Imagination*. Amsterdam: Brill.

Knight, John. 1994. 'Questioning Local Boundaries: A Critique of the "Anthropology of Locality"'. *Ethnos* 59 (3–4): 213–31. https://doi.org/10.1080/00141844.1994.9981500

Knight, Daniel. 2015. *History, Time and Economic Crisis in Central Greece*. Basingstoke: Palgrave Macmillan.

Knight, Daniel. 2021. *Vertiginous Life: An Anthropology of Time and the Unforeseen*. New York, NY: Berghahn.

Korff, Rüdiger. 2003. 'Local Enclosures of Globalization'. *Dialectical Anthropology* 27 (1): 1–18. https://doi.org/10.1023/A:1025466127833

Latour, Bruno. 2005. *Reassembling the Social: An Introduction to Actor-Network-Theory*. Oxford: Oxford University Press.

Lefebvre, Henri. 1991. *The Production of Space*. Oxford: Blackwell.

Leontidou, Lila. 1990. *The Mediterranean City in Transition*. Cambridge: Cambridge University Press.

Leontidou, Lila. 2004. 'The Boundaries of Europe: Deconstructing Three Regional Narratives'. *Identities: Global Studies in Culture and Power* 11 (4): 593–617. https://doi.org/10.1080/10702890490883876

Leontidou, Lila. 2015. '"Smart Cites" of the Debt Crisis: Grassroots Creativity in Mediterranean Europe'. *Greek Review of Social Research* 144A: 69–101. https://doi.org/10.12681/grsr.8626

Leontidou, Lila. 2019. 'Mediterranean City'. In *The Wiley Blackwell Encyclopaedia of Urban and Regional Studies*, edited by Anthony M. Orum, 1-8. Hoboken, NJ: John Wiley & Sons Ltd.

Lewis, Martin W., and Kären E. Wigan. 1997. *The Myth of Continents: A Critique of Metageography*. Berkeley, CA: University of California Press.

Lorcin, Patricia M., and Todd Shepard, eds. 2016. *French Mediterraneans: Transnational and Imperial Histories*. Lincoln, NE: University of Nebraska Press.

Lovell, Nadia, ed. 1998. *Locality and Belonging*. London: Routledge.

Malia Hom, Stephanie. 2020. *Empire's Mobius Strip: Historical Echoes in Italy's Crisis of Migration and Detention*. Ithaca, NY: Cornell University Press.

Marcus, George E. 1995. 'Ethnography in/of the World System: The Emergence of Multi-sited Ethnography'. *Annual Review of Anthropology* 24 (1): 95–117.

Marglin, Jessica. 2014. 'Mediterranean Modernity through Jewish Eyes: The Transimperial Life of Abraham Ankawa'. *Jewish Social Studies* 20 (2): 34–68. https://doi.org/10.2979/jewisocistud.20.2.34

Massey, Doreen. 2005. *For Space*. London: Sage.

Matar, Nabil. 2019. 'The "Mediterranean" through Arab Eyes in the Early Modern Period: From Rumi to "White-In-Between Sea"'. In *The Making of the Modern Mediterranean: Views from the South*, edited by Judith E. Tucker, 16–35. Berkeley, CA: University of California Press.

Mazzarella, William. 2004. 'Culture, Globalization, Mediation'. *Annual Review of Anthropology* 33: 345–67.

Peristiany, John G. 1966. 'Honour and Shame in a Cypriot Highland Village'. In *Honour and Shame: The Values of Mediterranean Society*, edited by John G. Peristiany, 171–90. Chicago, IL: University of Chicago Press.

Pina-Cabral, João de. 1989. 'The Mediterranean as a Category of Regional Comparison: A Critical View'. *Current Anthropology* 30 (3): 399–406.

Pitt-Rivers, Julian Alfred, ed. 1963. *Mediterranean Countrymen: Essays in the Social Anthropology of the Mediterranean*. Paris: Mouton.

Pitt-Rivers, Julian Alfred. 1977. *The Fate of Shechem: or, the Politics of Sex: Essays in the Anthropology of the Mediterranean*. Cambridge: Cambridge University Press.

Proglio, Gabriele. 2018. 'Is the Mediterranean a White Italian-European Sea? The Multiplication of Borders in the Production of Historical Subjectivity'. *Interventions* 20 (3): 406–27. https://doi.org/10.1080/1369801X.2017.1421025

Proglio, Gabriele, Camilla Hawthorne, Ida Danewid, P. Khalil Saucier, Giuseppe Grimaldi, Angelica Pesarini, Timothy Raeymaekers, Giulia Grechi, and Vivian Gerrand, eds. 2020. *The Black Mediterranean: Bodies, Borders and Citizenship*. Basingstoke: Palgrave Macmillan.

Purcell, Nicholas. 2006. 'The Boundless Sea of Unlikeness? On Defining the Mediterranean'. *Mediterranean Historical Review* 18 (2): 9–29. https://doi.org/10.1080/0951896032000230462

Sacchi, Paola, and Pier Paolo Viazzo. 2013. 'Honour, History, and the History of Mediterranean Anthropology'. *Journal of Mediterranean Studies* 22 (2): 275–91.

Said, Edward. 1994 [1978]. *Orientalism*. New York, NY: Vintage.

Sant Cassia, Paul, and Isabel Schäfer. 2005. '"Mediterranean Conundrums": Pluridisciplinary Perspectives for Research in the Social Sciences'. *History and Anthropology* 16 (1): 1–23. https://doi.org/10.1080/02757200500103400

Schielke, Samuli. 2015. *Egypt in the Future Tense: Hope, Frustration, and Ambivalence before and after 2011*. Bloomington, IN: Indiana University Press.

Schneider, Jane. 1971. 'Of Vigilance and Virgins: Honor, Shame and Access to Resources in Mediterranean Societies'. *Ethnology* 10 (1): 1–24. https://doi.org/10.2307/3772796

Schneider, Jane, ed. 1998. *Italy's 'Southern Question': Orientalism in One Country*. London: Routledge.

Schneider, Jane. 2012. 'Anthropology and the Cold War Mediterranean'. *Urban Anthropology and Studies of Cultural Systems and World Economic Development* 41 (1, Italy): 107–29.

Silverman, Sydel. 2001. 'Defining the Anthropological Mediterranean: Before Aix 1966'. In *L'anthropologie de la Méditerranée / Anthropology of the Mediterranean*, edited by Dionigi Albera, Anton Blok, and Christian Bromberger, 43–57. Paris: Maisonneuve et Larose.

Silverstein, Paul A. 2002. 'France's *Mare Nostrum*: Colonial and Postcolonial Constructions of the French Mediterranean'. *Journal of North African Studies* 7 (4): 1–22. https://doi.org/10.1080/13629380208718480

Smythe, S. A. 2018. 'The Black Mediterranean and the Politics of the Imagination'. *Middle East Report* 286.

Soto Bermant, Laia. 2017. 'The Mediterranean Question: Europe and Its Predicaments in the Southern Peripheries'. In *The Borders of 'Europe': Autonomy of Migration, Tactics of Bordering*, edited by Nicholas de Genova, 120–40. Durham, NC: Duke University Press.

Strathern, Marilyn. 1996. 'Cutting the Network'. *Journal of the Royal Anthropological Institute* 2 (3): 517–35. https://doi.org/10.2307/3034901

Sutton, David. 2000. *Memories Cast in Stone: The Relevance of the Past in Everyday Life*. London: Routledge.

Tabak, Faruk. 2008. 'Imperial Rivalry and Port-Cities: A View from Above'. *Mediterranean Historical Review* 24 (2): 79–94. https://doi.org/10.1080/09518960903487933

Tabak, Faruk. 2010. *The Waning of the Mediterranean, 1550–1870: A Geohistorical Approach*. Baltimore, MD: Johns Hopkins University Press.

Trevor Roper, Hugh R. 1972. 'Fernand Braudel, the Annales, and the Mediterranean'. *The Journal of Modern History* 44 (4): 468–79.

Tsing, Anna. 2000. 'The Global Situation'. *Cultural Anthropology* 15 (3): 327–60.

Tsing, Anna. 2012. 'On Non-Scalability: The Living World Is Not Amenable to Precision-Nested Scales'. *Common Knowledge* 18 (3): 505–24. https://doi.org/10.1215/0961754X-1630424

Tucker, Judith E., ed. 2019. *The Making of the Modern Mediterranean: Views from the South*. Berkeley, CA: University of California Press.

Viscomi, Joseph John. 2019. 'Mediterranean Futures: Historical Time and the Departure of Italians from Egypt, 1919–1937'. *The Journal of Modern History* 91 (2): 341–79. https://doi.org/10.1086/703189

Viscomi, Joseph John. 2020. 'Pontremoli's Cry: Personhood, Scale, and History in the Eastern Mediterranean'. *History and Anthropology* 31 (1): 43–65. https://doi.org/10.1080/02757206.2019.1687463

White, Joshua M. 2017. *Piracy and Law in the Ottoman Mediterranean*. Palo Alto, CA: Stanford University Press.

Wick, Alexis. 2014. 'Sailing the Modern Episteme: Al-Tahtāwī on the Mediterranean'. *Comparative Studies of South Asia, Africa and the Middle East* 34 (2): 405–17. https://doi.org/10.1215/1089201X-2773935

Wilk, Richard. 1995. 'Learning to be Local in Belize: Global Systems of Common Difference'. In *Worlds Apart: Modernity through the Prism of the Local*, edited by Daniel Miller, 110–33. London: Routledge.

Williams, Raymond. 1975. *The Country and the City*. Oxford: Oxford University Press.

Wimmer, Andreas, and Nina Glick Schiller. 2002. 'Methodological Nationalism and Beyond: Nation-State Building, Migration and the Social Sciences'. *Global Networks: A Journal of Transnational Affairs* 2 (4): 301–34. https://doi.org/10.1111/1471-0374.00043

Wimmer, Andreas, and Nina Glick Schiller. 2003. 'Methodological Nationalism, the Social Sciences, and the Study of Migration: An Essay in Historical Epistemology'. *International Migration Review* 37 (3): 576–610.

Yashin, Veli N. 2014. 'Beginning with the Mediterranean: An Introduction'. *Comparative Studies of South Asia, Africa and the Middle East* 34 (2): 364–67. https://doi.org/10.1215/1089201X-2773899

Zanou, Konstantina. 2018. *Transnational Patriotism in the Mediterranean, 1800–1850: Stammering the Nation*. Oxford: Oxford University Press.

CHAPTER 2

Spotlights in the Middle of Nowhere
Everyday Marginality and
'the Border' on Lampedusa

Laust Lund Elbek
University of Southern Denmark

Abstract

A main entry point for boat migrants, the Italian island of Lampedusa is a strategically important and highly symbolic location on Europe's Mediterranean border, and, owing to heavy militarisation and political and media attention, the island has acquired a central place in national as well as European political imaginaries. Yet, for the island's population of 6,000, things look rather different. Rather than a fixation point for political attention, Lampedusa is experienced by its inhabitants as a deeply marginal place with weak ties to the mainland and, by extension, the border, which is described by locals as 'not our business'. Drawing inspiration from Doreen Massey, the chapter argues that Lampedusa's simultaneous centrality and marginality should not be understood as a kind of paradox to be 'solved' but as the outcome of different, yet overlapping, political histories that go well beyond the island itself. Lampedusa thus testifies to 'location' as a potentially multiple concept that never stands on its own but is inherently constituted in relation

How to cite this book chapter:
Elbek, Laust Lund. 2022. 'Spotlights in the Middle of Nowhere Everyday Marginality and "the Border" on Lampedusa'. In *Locating the Mediterranean: Connections and Separations across Space and Time*, edited by Carl Rommel and Joseph John Viscomi, 31–52. Helsinki: Helsinki University Press. DOI: https://doi.org/10.33134/HUP-18-2.

to other locations across time and space. By approaching the Mediterranean as both a periphery and politically important border zone, the chapter draws together two ethnographically well-known 'Mediterraneans' that are typically studied in separate contexts.

Introduction

In the winter of 2011, a group of local fishermen gathered on the harbour of the Italian island of Lampedusa to demonstrate against the increasing unaffordability of boat fuel. The fishermen's primary working method is motorised trawling (*pesca a strascico*), and, owing to the island's isolated location in the middle of the Central Mediterranean, fuel is an expensive and often scarce resource. Each year, the higher cost of fuel will set a Lampedusan fisherman back thousands of euros more than his Sicilian competitors. 'We are being punished,' Paolo, one of the fishermen, told me when we met some six years later, describing the persisting inequality brought about by Lampedusa's geographical remoteness.

The demonstration itself was unremarkable. It took place quietly, and none of the participants seriously expected anyone beyond the island's perimeter to take much notice, as is usually the case regarding such local affairs. But, this time around, the fishermen's predicament did in fact make national headlines. Within a few weeks, media outlets from across the country began reporting on the demonstration with a well-developed sense of sensationalist creativity: allegedly, the demonstration had concerned boat migrants occupying the pier and thus obstructing the fishermen's work and disturbing the public order. A portrayal that, in Paolo's words, amounted to 'crazy stuff'.

If anything, such media representations underline how Lampedusa has become synonymous with irregular boat migration across the Mediterranean Sea in the past few decades. Situated halfway between Malta and Tunisia, the tiny island is Italy's southernmost piece of territory and a notorious first destination for boat migrants attempting to enter Europe via the deadly 'Central Mediterranean Route'. In addition to the boat migrants who land here, a patchwork of military corps, national and international NGOs, European agencies, and other border workers have become a more or less permanent presence. By adding a sense of location to the images of overcrowded migrant boats and notions of migrant crisis that haunt political and popular imaginaries,

Lampedusa has acquired a symbolic potency that greatly exceeds the island's 20 square kilometres.

Put differently, Lampedusa testifies to how the Schengen Agreement in no way resulted in the *removal* of Europe's borders; they were simply moved to other locations. At the 'local' level, however, the fishermen's demonstration simultaneously exemplified how Lampedusa remains – despite the enormity of outside attention – a deeply remote location where a profound lack of reliable infrastructure, health services, and recurring scarcity of basic commodities are pressing everyday concerns. Literally and metaphorically out of sight beyond the Mediterranean horizon, too far south to be represented on many maps of the national territory, the island and its 6,000 inhabitants who predominantly live off fishing and seasonal tourism seem very much cut off from any political centre of gravity. 'We are closer to Africa than Europe' is a commonly heard phrase on the island, and this is not merely a neutral cartographic observation but a statement that implicitly evokes a long history of marginalisation on Lampedusa in particular and southern Italy in general.

Drawing on approximately a year's fieldwork[1] on Lampedusa, this chapter takes a closer ethnographic look at these two very different 'Lampedusas', as it were: by foregrounding how Lampedusa has evolved into a political focal point as a border while remaining 'out of sight' from a local perspective, the chapter is essentially concerned with how the island constitutes a political centre and margin at the same time. A key point here is how the local experience of detachment is accompanied by a high degree of non-identification with Lampedusa's role as a border, as migration – and particularly migration management – is commonly experienced as external to the community. Operated almost entirely by people from elsewhere, 'the border' on Lampedusa seems to exist largely separate from, or perhaps rather in parallel with, the everyday lives of many islanders.

The theoretical hinge of the chapter, which I elaborate in the following section, is to conceptualise the marginal and the central not as contradictory configurations per se but rather as different 'relative locations' that, over time, have come to coexist within the same geographical space (see Green 2005; Viscomi and Rommel, Chapter 1 in this volume). Inspired especially by Doreen Massey's theorisation of space as the accumulation of heterogeneous historical trajectories (2005), the chapter makes the case that Lampedusa testifies to 'location' as inherently relational and potentially multiple, and hence that Lampedusa never stands on its own but is continuously constituted in relation to other locations across time and space. Thus, by drawing questions of migration and borders as well as the experience of inhabiting marginal locations into the same ethnographic space, the chapter weaves together two empirically well-established Mediterranean constellations that are, however, usually studied in separate realms (see also Ben-Yehoyada 2014).

Locating Multiplicity

The notion that 'centres' and 'margins' may overlap in spatial terms is not new. In *We, the People of Europe?*, for example, Étienne Balibar noted that, while borders are typically located 'at the edge of the territory', they simultaneously occupy 'the middle of political space' (2004, 109). Balibar's formulation alluded specifically to how growing political concerns over migration have rendered borders defining institutions in Western politics. A related perspective is found in Veena Das and Deborah Poole's now canonical volume, *Anthropology in the Margins of the State* (2004), in which 'margins' are conceptualised in an Agambenian fashion as spaces of exception that, owing to their lack of full legibility, are constitutive of mainstream politics through a logic of negative mirroring. The 'margins', from this angle, need not even be located at the geographical edges of a polity but may also be found in places such as refugee camps or urban 'ghettos' (e.g. Asad 2004). The overall point to be made here is that neither centres nor margins/edges/peripheries are constituted simply in geographical terms (see also Ardener 1987) – rather, they are the outcomes of particular relations between people, power, and place.

But if the central and the marginal may in some instances become 'one', as suggested above, this chapter takes a slightly different approach by treating the central and the marginal as distinct 'relative locations' that coexist within the same geographical space (see Green 2005). Indeed, if Lampedusa has moved to the 'centre' of national and European politics as a border, this has not rendered its inhabitants' experiences of self-location any less marginal. In developing this argument, I am particularly inspired by Doreen Massey's thinking about the 'liveliness' of space (2005). In her view, space should not be understood as fixed but as constituted through variable and multiple contemporaneous relations (2005, 9–12). This means that places are rarely defined by singular identities and should not be thought of as self-contained enclosures with clearly discernible insides and outsides. Rather, they come into being as the product of heterogeneous (power) relations across space and time. And, while Massey's view of space-as-relations resonates well with, for example, Balibar's and Das and Poole's ideas, she adds the crucial point that these cannot be the relations of a closed system where 'everything is (already) related to everything else' (2005, 10). This implies an understanding of 'relationality' as an open-ended and potentially multi-temporal process, and so Massey invites us to understand space as 'a *simultaneity* of stories-so-far', i.e. a sphere in which 'distinct trajectories *coexist*' (Massey 2005, 9, my emphasis).

It is Massey's notion of space as composed of contemporaneous 'trajectories' or 'stories' in the plural that I find particularly insightful here. Indeed, 'border' and 'remote island', respectively, would seem to correspond to distinct relations in both space and time: if Lampedusa is at the same time central and marginal, this seems the result of a 'layering' of various political histories that have taken the island as its object in rather different ways (see also Elbek 2020). However, as Matei Candea has pointed out, such contrasting formulations of place may constitute a challenge to a 'traditional' anthropological imagination (2010; see also Gupta and Ferguson 1992). This is the case, Candea argues, because the lack of a coherent identity makes places 'seem messy, disintegrated, or difficult to study not because they are, but because of the assumptions we have about what they *should* be like' (2010, 25; see also Otto and Bubandt 2010). In line with Candea, I am not suggesting that Lampedusa's simultaneous centrality and marginality constitute a paradox to be 'solved' by looking for coherence where there may, in fact, be none. Instead, with Massey in mind, I propose to understand such multiple place-identities as relationships that, at different points in time, have fashioned Lampedusa as a particular kind of place. To pursue this argument ethnographically, the following sections provide a series of reflections on Lampedusa's recent transformation into a border hub 'par excellence'. The final parts of the chapter will, in turn, deal in historical and ethnographic detail with Lampedusa's marginality and isolation.

Placing 'the Border'

Falcone e Borsellino Airport, Palermo. The small turboprop airplane that connects Sicily and Lampedusa leaves from an underground section of the airport. If the slightly run-down boarding area – equipped with benches and a small bar – comes across as entirely ordinary, many of the people present constitute a stark contrast to the inconspicuousness of the place. The briefest glance at the boarding queue confirms that Lampedusa has long ceased to be simply a distant outpost of the Republic: in addition to islanders returning home from Sicily, the passengers boarding for Lampedusa constitute a motley crew of people connected only by a professional interest in the island's function as a border. There are NGO workers, military representatives, ecclesiastics, reporters, and at least one anthropologist. Some of the more conspicuous travellers are a group of journalists with large cameras, microphones, and press card lanyards around their necks – not to mention a squad of uniformed and quite gruff-looking Carabinieri, who, without any kind of questioning, carry their firearms and batons aboard the plane.

Although technically not on Lampedusa, the boarding area is a perfect site for gauging the island's unusually high degree of 'borderness' (see Cuttitta 2012). Here, it is visible how a patchwork of actors concerned with border management has set up shop on Lampedusa in recent years: the people in the queue – from armed soldiers to aid workers – provide a window into how the politics of humanitarianism and securitisation intertwine, and occasionally collide,[2] at the EU's external borders (see e.g. Andersson 2017; Cuttitta 2018; Dines, Montagna, and Ruggiero 2014). To recall Étienne Balibar's formulation, such scenes leave no doubt that Lampedusa has indeed moved to the 'centre of political space' on both the national and European levels. More specifically, the boarding queue reflected how Lampedusa has become home to a host of military, paramilitary, and police corps and an equally long list of humanitarian NGOs, all with varying levels of involvement, authority, and responsibility. Their tasks include, for example, search-and-rescue operations, sea and air patrolling, identification, transfers, legal assistance for migrants, and the daily operation of Lampedusa's migrant reception centre (Cuttitta 2014). As geographer Paolo Cuttitta has accurately observed on the matter,

> Lampedusa has effectively attracted all that makes a 'place' a 'border':
> from migrants to smugglers, from law enforcement to humanitarian
> workers, from Italian military vessels to the patrols of the EU agency
> Frontex, from the police officers of emigration and transit countries to
> those of the United Nations, from inspectors of EU institutions to jour-
> nalists and researchers from across the world. (2012, 12, my translation)

In addition to being an operational hub for all the border related
activities described above, Lampedusa has – perhaps more than any
other place – become a symbol of the Mediterranean 'migration crisis'.
Not least due to extensive media coverage and political attention, the
island has become synonymous with undocumented migrant flows,
deadly shipwrecks, and maritime border controls (Friese 2014). In this
manner, Lampedusa arguably constitutes 'the very incarnation of the
concept of border' for politicians, migrants, and a wider public alike
(Cuttitta 2012, 11, my translation).

Two events arguably stand out regarding Lampedusa's rise to public
notoriety. Although the island had already attracted significant attention as a site of irregular border-crossings into Europe for some years,
Lampedusa became the object of a national and European discourse
on 'migrant emergency' when thousands of Tunisians fled to the island
in the wake of the so-called Arab Spring in 2011 (Elbek 2020). The second event occurred on 3 October 2013, when a cataclysmic shipwreck
took place just off the island. Three hundred and sixty-eight passengers, most of whom came from Eritrea, lost their lives in this tragedy.
Photographs of hundreds of coffins, each adorned with a single rose
and lined up in an airport hangar – among them several children-
sized ones, each with a smiling teddy bear on top – travelled across the
globe. Such occasions made it clear that Lampedusa has become the
stage for a veritable 'border spectacle' (De Genova 2002): a key node in
the 'visual economy of clandestine migration' (Andersson 2014).

Yet, such spectacular imagery is hardly unambiguous, and to invoke
an anthropological classic, the island certainly carries a good amount
of symbolic 'multivocality' (Firth 1973). As the simultaneous presence
of humanitarian and military actors indicates, Lampedusa seems to
lend itself well to appropriation by the entire political spectrum: Pope
Francis's very first official visit outside the Vatican was, of all places, to
Lampedusa, and all imaginable kinds of politicians, artists, and other
public figures have travelled to the island to claim their share of the

spotlight – including actress Angelina Jolie in the capacity of 'goodwill ambassador' for the UNHCR, as well as Marine Le Pen, leader of the French anti-immigration party Front National.[3] As Heidrun Friese has noted,

> Lampedusa stands for the imagination, and especially fear, of the black masses, invasions, loss of control and national cultural identity and, simultaneously, humanitarian participation, compassion, philanthropy, vulnerability and help for the victims, solidarity and such notions. … Lampedusa provides a place for the fear of strangers and images of victims and ties friend and foe together. (Friese 2014, 31, my translation)

Friese clearly hits the nail on the head in pointing to Lampedusa's capacity to *provide a place*. Covering large stretches of national as well as international waters and extending well beyond the perimeter of Europe into the offices of sub-Saharan authorities (Andersson 2014; Lucht 2013), the Euro-African border is hardly a fixed location; on the contrary, it is a highly mobile and deterritorialised phenomenon with a largely liquid material form (see also Chambers 2008). In such an institutionally complex, ever-changing, and spatially heterogeneous border constellation, Lampedusa provides exactly what appears to be missing: fixity and location. In the following section, I will provide an ethnographic snapshot of the multifaceted border machinery that I have just described.

A Migrant Landing

On a December afternoon in 2015, at the peak of the so-called 'refugee crisis', I had gone for a walk with a journalist working for a small-time migration-oriented NGO. Around L'isola dei Conigli, a picturesque natural reservation some five kilometres west of Lampedusa town, we bumped into Marco, a fingerprint specialist employed at the island's migrant reception centre. I had not met Marco before but my journalist companion knew him peripherally through work. We exchanged a few niceties and Marco told us that he had just been notified that a *sbarco* – a migrant landing – would take place in the small hours of the following morning.

This information was of particular interest to the NGO that the journalist worked for. In a setting otherwise dominated by uniforms and military equipment, one of their primary activities is to be physically present during landings to 'show the migrants a human face' and 'break the militarised monopoly on reception', as one of the managers, a Roman in his thirties, explained. At landings, the NGO hands out snacks, a cup of hot tea, and a friendly greeting for the exhausted newcomers. Under normal circumstances, civilians not employed within official border management procedures are not allowed to attend landings; however, the then-parish priest of Lampedusa had managed to negotiate an exception for this particular NGO. But it was rarely without complaints and insults from the Finanza or the Carabinieri that they would enter Molo Favaloro, the restricted military quay where landings are usually carried out. Later that day, I asked for permission to join the NGO at the next morning's *sbarco*, and so, before sunrise, three or four NGO workers and I loaded the boot of a Fiat Doblo with freshly brewed tea, juice, snacks, and isothermal blankets to observe and play an active, however minimal, role in the very sort of event that had placed Lampedusa on the political map of Europe.

When we arrived at Molo Favaloro around 6am, the quay was empty and quiet, so we decided to go to a nearby bar to wait and have some breakfast. The bar was already full of other early birds, mainly fishermen and police officers. Soon, however, Giorgio, a local Red Cross volunteer, joined us at our table and told us that he had heard from the Coast Guard that the *sbarco* would begin around 8 o'clock. Estimating the arrival time of migrants in this way was possible because landings are typically coordinated by Italian authorities: rather than migrants arriving of their own accord, their boats are typically intercepted on the high seas and the passengers are subsequently transferred to a migrant reception centre, for example on Lampedusa.[4]

When we returned to the quay an hour's time later, a diverse gathering of border workers – armed and unarmed – had arrived. The following list of actors present at Molo Favaloro should give a sense of the range of interests involved:

- Azienda Sanitaria Palermo (a regional health service provider)
- Carabinieri (the Italian military police)
- Guardia Costiera (the Coast Guard)
- Croce Siciliana (a privately run ambulance service)
- EASO (the European Asylum Support Office)
- Frontex (the European Border Management Agency)

- Guardia di Finanza (Italian military police dealing with, e.g., smuggling)
- IOM (the International Organization for Migration)
- Misericordia (a private Catholic community service organisation operating the migrant reception centre)
- Marina Militare (the navy)
- Polizia statale (the Italian police)
- The Red Cross (the local Lampedusan division, volunteering at the migrant reception centre)
- Save the Children
- Various church representatives.

After half an hour or so, the *sbarco* began. The first boat to approach Molo Favaloro was one of the Guardia Costiera's search-and-rescue vessels: the characteristic *Classe 300 Ammiraglio Francese* high-speed boat with an inflated orange fender all the way around the hull. The deck was jam-packed with mainly African men and a smaller number of women and children. The boat docked at the far end of the quay and, one by one, the migrants were helped ashore by the Misericordia, the Red Cross and the Guardia Costiera. The latter were sporting white full-body protection suits, while the Red Cross and Misericordia were wearing rubber gloves and face masks to protect them from potential infections that the migrants might have contracted en route to Europe.

Once on solid ground, visibly ill and pregnant migrants were taken directly to an ambulance that, in the meantime, had arrived at the other end of the quay. The rest were instructed to wait before being allowed to walk in single file to a bus that would take them to the migrant reception centre a ten-minute drive from Molo Favaloro. Most of the newcomers looked tired, but in good condition, all things considered. A small group of men were instructed to wait behind; I was told that they had scabies.

As these events unfolded, most migration management professionals did little more than observe the scene with an air of routine about them. A few made encouraging comments in broken English about the football jerseys that some of the migrant children were wearing, but most were simply standing there quietly, some smoking cigarettes or distracting themselves with their phones. The group of NGO workers that I had latched onto, however, were all smiles, handing out plastic cups of warm tea, isothermal blankets, and crackers to the migrants that were now walking towards the bus. The tea and snacks were accompanied by an enthusiastic 'welcome to Italy!' or a 'where are you from?'

Once the bus was full, it left the harbour and headed towards the reception centre. The remaining refugees were told to line up and wait for the bus to return. While they were waiting, the NGO workers served more snacks and water. A total of about 400 refugees landed on Molo Favaloro that morning, representing a wide range of nationalities. Based on the answers to 'where are you from?', Syrians, Moroccans, Somalis, Sudanese, and Iraqis landed on Lampedusa in what seemed to be a well-rehearsed, almost choreographed, fashion on the authorities' part.

One aspect of this glimpse of 'the border' deserves to be explicitly highlighted: save for a couple of Red Cross volunteers, like Giorgio, everyone present on Molo Favaloro – from Carabinieri to humanitarian workers – came from elsewhere (mainland Italy, elsewhere in Europe, North Africa), and they were solely present on the island for migration management purposes. It was only those 'in the loop' that knew that the *sbarco* was taking place at all; I myself only found out when I incidentally met Marco. Most islanders would have had little or no knowledge of what was going on at the quay. Indeed, the events of that morning underlined that, if Lampedusa has come to constitute a political 'centre', as it were, this development has remained largely cut off from local lives.

Not Our Border, Not Our Wars

Via Roma, Lampedusa town's main street, ends in a small plateau with a panoramic view of the port. This is a popular spot among locals to hang out and observe the quiet traffic of fishing boats and indulge in the colours of the Mediterranean sunsets. It is, however, also a perfect spot for watching something rather less meditative: migrant landings. Molo Favaloro is located just across the port basin from here.

But few Lampedusans seem to devote much attention to the politically potent events taking place literally next to their moored fishing boats. On occasion, a few elderly islanders may be seen half-observing a landing from the plateau at the end of the street for a few minutes before turning to other business. But, by and large, the landings are of no observable interest to the majority of the local population, as many locals appear to perceive the border as something fundamentally external to the community – as if the island has merely become a strategic node in a system to which it does not quite belong, or at least only marginally so. Fabrizio, a civil servant, put it this way: 'It is not our border and not our wars. If we see something at sea, we will notify the coast guard. But dealing with migration is not our business.'

In a completely mundane way, Fabrizio's statement is reflected in the practically non-existing interaction between Lampedusans and the armed forces whose presence serves as a constant reminder of the island's geopolitical importance.[5] Many islanders display a downright scornful attitude towards those wearing uniforms, accusing them of laziness and indifference (see also Elbek 2021): 'They are not exactly busy catching criminals, eh?' Fabrizio said one day we were walking on the main street, nodding towards a squad of Carabinieri who were finishing what appeared to be their second round of coffee and pastries at an outside café table. Valentina, a teacher who had moved to Lampedusa from Sicily to work some 30 years ago and had stayed on since, expressed a similarly dismissive sentiment when telling me about 'the primary tasks' of the migration management officials: 'having coffee in winter and going swimming in summer. Such a hard life!'

But local lives and migrant reception were not always this disjoined (see also Quagliariello 2021). When migrants began to arrive on Lampedusa in the wake of the Schengen Agreement in the early 1990s, the local population would care for and accommodate migrants on an ad hoc basis, providing food and temporary shelter (see also Elbek 2020; Friese 2012). In 1998, however, a state-subsidised reception centre was established, replacing such local hospitality initiatives. This marked the beginnings of a process of professionalisation of migrant reception on Lampedusa, and hence a fundamental reconfiguration of the relationship between Lampedusans and migrants, but also between Lampedusans and 'the border' more generally. As the migrant landing previously described illustrated, the jobs went almost entirely to non-local actors when migration management was professionalised. Unsurprisingly, this caused some local consternation over what was perceived as lost opportunities for work.

But, even though migration is no longer 'our business' and the local community has been effectively placed on the sideline of border management, 'our business' is literally feared to be at stake. Since the early 1990s, the local tourist industry has overtaken fishing as the island's primary economic sector, and locals frequently worry that this source of livelihood could suffer permanent damage from the media attention that the border attracts.[6] This has especially been the case since the so-called Arab Spring, when thousands of Tunisians were stranded on Lampedusa, and the images of distress and despair that circulated in worldwide media led to a dramatic, if temporary, decrease in the earnings of the tourist industry, and it is commonly feared that something similar could happen in the future (Elbek 2020).

Yet, the experience of being 'sidelined' is in no way new on Lampedusa – on the contrary, the notion that 'we' are profoundly disconnected from the country's political centre of gravity has deep historical roots that long precedes the island's becoming a border – a 'trajectory' of its own, as Massey would have it. Looking more closely at Lampedusa's geographical and political marginality, the following section provides some further ethnographic and historical subtext to Fabrizio's description of the border as 'not ours'.

Disconnections

The A4-sized sign at the closed petrol station on the pier was laconically precise: *gasolio e benzina esaurita*. We are out of diesel and petrol. The ferry that connects Lampedusa and Porto Empedocle in Sicily had been unable to land for several days in a row because of what the operator referred to as 'adverse weather conditions'. The ferry carries both passengers and cargo, but its primary importance is located below the passenger deck. Owing to Lampedusa's geographical remoteness and low degree of self-sufficiency, practically all commodities must be shipped to the island – including necessities such as fuel, clean drinking water, and flour.

The importance of the ferry should be measured against the economic landscape of the island. Although Lampedusa was originally populated to establish an agricultural colony in the 1840s, farming efforts were undermined by rapid erosion of the soil and uncontrolled deforestation related to charcoal production – a resource that had to be produced locally because of the island's geographical circumstances (Li Causi 1987). Today, no agriculture remains on the island except for some private vegetable gardens. And, unlike the neighbouring island of Linosa, there is no livestock on Lampedusa except for a few herds of sheep that sustain a very limited local production of ricotta and milk.

With fishing and tourism being the primary means of local subsistence, the ferry is really the community's lifeline.

In principle, the ferry should arrive and depart daily, providing a stable supply of goods and a reliable means of transportation for Lampedusa's inhabitants. Too often, however, reality falls short of the ideal, and the ferry is continuously cancelled, particularly in autumn and winter (the off-season both in fishing and tourism), when weather conditions at sea often render the passage from Sicily impossible. The ferry may be absent for days, occasionally weeks, on end, and even on clear days the ferry may be unable to land on Lampedusa if conditions are windy. This means that even the most basic commodities can be in scarce supply. Consequently, the ferry is always a topic of conversation among Lampedusans, many of whom frantically follow weather forecasts to assess the probability of the ferry's possible arrival ('It might come on Thursday or Friday; they say that the wind will be down to four knots'). Edwin Ardener's observation that 'remote areas are obsessed with communications: the one road, the one ferry' (1987, 46) springs to mind here.

On a windy February afternoon, I was having coffee with Valentina, the teacher, at her meeting point of choice: the portside bar where the NGO workers and I had waited for the migrant landing to take place. When we met, the ferry had been absent for the better part of a week, which was nothing out of the ordinary for this time of year. Valentina recalled one particularly rough winter that had, nevertheless, made the potential consequences of Lampedusa's isolation clear to her. After a series of the 'typical' seasonal cancellations, the ferry's engine had broken, and the repairs had taken several weeks to complete. The island had been completely disconnected from the rest of the country for so long that flour and other indispensable foodstuffs had to be rationed: 'I had never heard about anything like that before – apart from what my grandmother had told me about the war!'

Such infrastructural disconnections are a challenge in relation not only to importing goods to Lampedusa but also to getting them away. The unreliability of the ferry constitutes a recurrent economic threat to the island's fishermen, whose livelihoods mainly revolve around the export of squid and oily fish (slightly less so in summer, when tourists consume large amounts of locally caught fish and seafood). Most of the year, the primary markets for the Lampedusan fishermen are in Sicily (Catania and Palermo) – and, with a transfer time to southern Sicily of approximately ten hours, delivering freshly caught fish to the island's urban centres is already a battle against time. 'The fish is thrown away too often,' Paolo (the fisherman to whom I referred in the beginning) said, explaining how just a few days' delay will result in a spoiled catch and labour and money wasted for the fishermen.

But there are even graver implications to isolation than a limited selection of fresh produce, a spoiled catch every now and then, and the occasional shutdown due to fuel shortages. For many islanders, the lack of health services constitutes the single biggest everyday challenge to living on Lampedusa. Take Giuseppe, for example, a retired sailor probably in his late fifties. One morning, I bumped into him *per caso* in Via Roma after not having seen him for a few weeks. We shook hands, and I asked him how he was doing. 'You know about my illness?' he asked. I said that I did not, and he explained that he had been hospitalised in Sicily to receive surgical cancer treatment some years ago, and that the result was never really followed up on. I asked him how that was possible, and he simply replied that 'the system doesn't work'. For Giuseppe, the apparent dysfunction of 'the system' was inseparable from Lampedusa's remote geography: 'I pay the same taxes as those in Rome and Milan, but I don't get the same out of it.' He continued: 'You know, Lampedusa is far away from everything, so you just need to take care of yourself.' Giuseppe passed away a few months after our conversation.[7]

While there is a helicopter service available for immediate transfer to Sicily in case of acutely life-threatening incidents, the only medical clinic on Lampedusa is a minor *poliambulatorio* without possibilities for actual hospitalisation, let alone treatment of complicated illnesses. Such cases require that Lampedusans bear the significant expenses of moving temporarily to Sicily to seek long-term medical attention. In the case of childbirth, mothers-to-be must leave Lampedusa approximately a month before giving birth due to air-travel restrictions and the ferry's unreliability. Additionally, it is rare that medical professionals stay on Lampedusa for very long – instead, doctors from the mainland are stationed for shorter periods of time only to be replaced by others, unable to build rapport with locals and acquire knowledge of individual needs and situations. 'They [the health system] simply let them die,' according to a woman engaged in community work with the elderly.

An Island with a Capital 'I'

As the previous section illustrated, infrastructure can reveal difficult relations between people, materiality, and the realm of the political (see also Appel, Anand, and Gupta 2015; Larkin 2013). This seems to be the case not least due to the link between infrastructural connections and notions of territorial integrity and cohesion (Harvey and Knox 2015; Reeves 2017). Indeed, on Lampedusa, the relative lack of functioning infrastructure is a recurring source of frustration and insecurities, but, just as importantly, it serves as an ever-present confirmation of the island's marginality and the immobility of its people. In broader terms, I consider all of the 'infrastructural anecdotes' recounted in this chapter to be indicative of a more general experience of being somewhat cut off from the rest of the polity – i.e. physical and symbolic disconnections that produce a sense of apartness, of inhabiting a deeply marginal place. This experience revolves particularly around the necessity of self-sufficiency, what Giuseppe described as the need 'to take care of yourself'. To reverse James Scott's observation that infrastructural connections can be 'distance-demolishing technologies' (Scott 2009, xxi), malfunctioning ones may be 'distance-*producing*'.

Now, in the age of the internet and social media – a sort of infrastructure that does, in fact, work reasonably well when power cuts do not occur – marginality has a rather different face than, say, in the 1950s and 1960s, when Giuseppe was growing up and Lampedusa had neither electricity nor sewers. Back then, the almost complete absence of public investment combined with a lack of economic reward in the fishing industry resulted in 'third-world living conditions' (Taranto 2016, 41). Donkeys and mules were perfectly common means of transportation around the time that car manufacture and road construction in the country's northern provinces placed Italy at the forefront of Western Europe's post-war industrial boom (Ginsborg 1990, 212–14). One very rarely encounters this kind of destitution on Lampedusa today. Even though Gianfranco Rosi's film *Fuocoammare* (*Fire at Sea*) – winner of the Golden Bear at the 2016 Berlinale and one of a great many recent cultural productions that testify to Lampedusa's political importance as a border – may have given its audience the impression that the island's children only play with sticks, stones, and slingshots, modern technology and social media have become an integral part of life on Lampedusa as much as everywhere else. Virtual connections seem especially important when physical ones are hard to come by. 'We, too, have iPads, you know,' as a friend put it rather sourly after having watched the film. Yet, if Third World conditions have been relegated to the (quite recent) past, this is almost entirely due to the advent of the island's tourist industry, which attracts as many as 60,000 paying visitors each summer. In the past 25 years or so, mass tourism has brought a certain level of affluence to Lampedusa – including, not least, iPads.

But a sense of isolation and difference does remain deep-seated. Several of my interlocutors described the 'special sensation' of remoteness as one of Lampedusa's primary tourist attractions – in addition, of course, to seafood and splendid beaches. And, while tourism has arguably brought Lampedusa 'closer' to the mainland, it has also become a new arena for explicit articulations of difference vis-à-vis the national mainstream. The local tourist industry largely brands itself on the island's 'Oriental' nature: tourists are often reminded how Lampedusa is 'closer to Africa than Sicily', and local restaurants carry names such as Il Saraceno (the Saracen) and Le Mille e Una Notte (The Thousand and One Nights). Inside these establishments, the island's geological attachment to the African continent rather than the European one is sure to come up in many a conversation over plates of fish *couscous*, a local signature dish.[8] Only half-jokingly, if at all, did my interlocutors refer to tourists arriving from 'up there in Italy'.

Such 'self-Orientalisation' may well be understood as a plain and benign case of authenticity branding in the tourism business, but it is also superimposed on the semantics of the historical marginalisation of Italy's south. Since national unification in the mid-19th century, associations with Africa have functioned as a 'governing metaphor' in placing the country's southern provinces on the sideline of the national community (Pugliese 2009, 665). Within the new unified Kingdom of Italy, which was largely a Piedmontese (i.e. northern) project, the southern provinces became increasingly marginalised politically and economically. Throughout the 19th century, an image of the historically poorer south as culturally 'backward' and fundamentally inferior to its northern counterpart became deeply ingrained in the country's symbolic geography[9] (Dickie 1999; Moe 2002; Riall 1994). Suffice it to note here that the undifferentiated 'south' in many ways emerged as the negative pole of a north–south axis, a 'margin' against which the new nation, ostensibly committed to 'progress' and 'civilization', defined itself (Forgacs 2014). This tenacious north–south binarism, which is commonly referred to as 'the southern question' (*la questione meridionale*), has been construed as a form of intra-national 'neo-Orientalism' (Schneider 1998).

Against this backdrop, it is not an insignificant detail that Lampedusa is literally the south of the south. In Italy, 'south' is not just a marker of location or direction but also a signifier of marginalisation and cultural, political, and economic subordination. Lampedusa is, in addition to its cartographic 'southernness', materially disconnected from the already marginalised south. Valentina, the teacher, described Lampedusa's state of being doubly marginal in this way: 'Lampedusa … it is definitely an island with a capital "I".'

Conclusion

'The Mediterranean,' as Fernand Braudel noted many years ago, 'speaks with many voices' (1972, 13). This seems a fitting closing note for this chapter, insofar as the two 'Lampedusas' that I have described – the border hub and the remote island, respectively – point to how 'the Mediterranean' may be construed as a (conceptual and physical) space that is simultaneously out of sight and at the centre of attention. While Lampedusa's recent role as a symbolic and strategic border is tightly linked to the post-Schengen fashioning of the Mediterranean as the contentious threshold between the European Union and its exterior, the tenacious local experience of being on the fringes of the national and European communities evokes much older Mediterranean 'voices' that speak of political and economic peripherality (see also Ben-Yehoyada, Cabot, and Silverstein 2020; Viscomi and Rommel, Chapter 1 in this volume). By foregrounding such multiplicity, the chapter has gone against the grain of what could be called a 'palimpsestic' understanding of Lampedusa's becoming a border: even if the island has moved to the centre of political and media attention, this has not overwritten other and quite different senses of location.

Inspired especially by Massey's theorisation of space as a heterogeneous accumulation of 'stories-so-far', I have thus portrayed Lampedusa as a condensed setting for observing the interface between two quite different Mediterranean constellations that exist in parallel and tension with one another within the same limited geographical space. The border is understood by locals as 'not our business' – a description that refers to how migration is managed almost entirely by non-local actors, but also more broadly evokes an understanding of the border as related to political processes to which 'we' do not quite belong. This points to how, from a local perspective, the border is commonly made sense of through the prism of Lampedusa's marginality. To borrow another phrase from Doreen Massey, the border in this way appears to be experienced by locals as a sort of "'outside" that can be found within' (2007, 193): while physically close, it is experienced as an external force that has made its way 'in', as it were. Indeed, from the perspective of my Lampedusan interlocutors, locating oneself and locating the border appear to be two quite different things: the border has certainly acquired a physiognomy on Lampedusa, but the logics that dictate it appear to be historically and experientially located elsewhere.

Notes

1 Fieldwork was carried out during my doctoral studies at Aarhus University (2015–2020).
2 This was certainly evidenced when Italian then-minister of the interior, Matteo Salvini, ordered the closure of the country's ports for vessels carrying migrants, which resulted in the impounding of *The Aquarius* and *The Sea Watch 3*, search-and-rescue vessels belonging to Médecins Sans Frontières and the aid organisation Sea Watch, respectively (Morosi 2019; Ziniti 2018).
3 Now Rassemblement National.
4 This dynamic has changed somewhat in recent years as search-and-rescue efforts have been lessened. This has led to an increase in so-called *sbarchi fantasma* – 'ghost landings' – where migrants arrive on their own.
5 Minimal interaction is generally the rule, but there is a noteworthy exception: a minor portion of Lampedusans have come to benefit from a small-scale 'border economy', most importantly grocers, restaurateurs, and hotel owners. Like everybody else, border workers need to sleep and eat (see Elbek 2021).
6 This points to a significant comparative perspective: beyond Lampedusa, the 'migrant crisis' has repercussions across the entire Mediterranean space, and the Greek islands especially seem to be caught in a similar tension between economic reliance on a fragile 'hospitality industry' and negotiations of the 'limits of hospitality' (see also Friese 2010).
7 See Greco (2016) for further reflections on regional health inequalities in Italy.
8 Originating in North Africa, couscous is a common staple across the south of Italy. On the one hand, such culinary connections bear obvious testament to how the Mediterranean has always been a space of interaction and exchange. But, on the other hand, they also implicitly invoke the sea's symbolic role as a space of separation between 'the West and the Rest'. In fact, the dish was used actively in an anti-southern political campaign by the northern chauvinist party Lega Nord some years ago: 'Sì alla polenta, no al cous cous' was one of many

controversial slogans employed by the party. The overall message seemed to be that 'real' Italians do not eat 'African' food (cf. Woods 2009).

9 In his famous autobiographical novel *Cristo si è fermato a Eboli* (Christ stopped at Eboli), Carlo Levi made a noteworthy observation on the relationship between infrastructure and the marginality of the South: in Levi's narrative, Eboli represented the southernmost outpost of 'civilisation', in part because the roads and the train tracks did not go any further south (1970, ix).

References

Andersson, Ruben. 2014. *Illegality, Inc.: Clandestine Migration and the Business of Bordering Europe*. Berkeley, CA: University of California Press.

Andersson, Ruben. 2017. 'Rescued and Caught: The Humanitarian-Security Nexus at Europe's Frontiers'. In *The Borders of 'Europe': Autonomy of Migration, Tactics of Bordering*, edited by Nicholas De Genova, 64–94. Durham, NC: Duke University Press.

Appel, Hannah, Nikhil Anand, and Akhil Gupta. 2015. 'Introduction: The Infrastructure Toolbox'. *Cultural Anthropology Online* 24.

Ardener, Edwin. 1987. '"Remote Areas": Some Theoretical Considerations'. In *ASA Monographs 25: Anthropology At Home*, edited by Anthony Jackson, 38–54. London: Travistock Publications.

Asad, Talal. 2004. 'Where Are the Margins of the State?' In *Anthropology in the Margins of the State*, edited by Veena Das and Deborah Poole, 279–88. Santa Fe, NM: School for Advanced Research Press.

Balibar, Etienne. 2004. *We, the People of Europe? Reflections on Transnational Citizenship*. Princeton, NJ: Princeton University Press.

Ben-Yehoyada, Naor. 2014. 'Mediterranean Modernity?' In *A Companion to Mediterranean History*, edited by Peregrine Horden and Sharon Kinoshita, 107–21. Malden, MA: Wiley Blackwell.

Ben-Yehoyada, Naor, Heath Cabot, and Paul A. Silverstein. 2020. 'Introduction: Remapping Mediterranean Anthropology'. *History and Anthropology* 31 (1): 1–21. https://doi.org/10.1080/02757206.2019.1684274

Braudel, Fernand. 1972. *The Mediterranean and the Mediterranean World in the Age of Philip II*. Vol. 1. New York, NY: Harper & Row.

Candea, Matei. 2010. *Corsican Fragments: Difference, Knowledge, and Fieldwork*. Bloomington, IN: Indiana University Press.

Chambers, Iain. 2008. *Mediterranean Crossings: The Politics of an Interrupted Modernity*. Durham, NC: Duke University Press.

Cuttitta, Paolo. 2012. *Lo spettacolo del confine, Lampedusa tra produzione e messa in scena della frontiera*. Milan: Mimesis.

Cuttitta, Paolo. 2014. '"Borderizing" the Island: Setting and Narratives of the Lampedusa Border Play'. *ACME: An International E-Journal for Critical Geographies* 13 (2): 196–219.

Cuttitta, Paolo. 2018. 'Repoliticization through Search and Rescue? Humanitarian NGOs and Migration Management in the Central Mediterranean'. *Geopolitics*, 23 (3): 632–60. https://doi.org/10.1080/14650045.2017.1344834

Das, Veena, and Deborah Poole, eds. 2004. *Anthropology in the Margins of the State*. Santa Fe, NM: School for Advanced Research Press.

De Genova, Nicholas P. 2002. 'Migrant "Illegality" and Deportability in Everyday Life'. *Annual Review of Anthropology* 31 (1): 419–47.

Dickie, John. 1999. *Darkest Italy. The Nation and Stereotypes of the Mezzogiorno, 1860–1900*. London: Macmillan Press.

Elbek, Laust Lund. 2020. 'Rupture, Reproduction, and the State: The Arab Spring on Lampedusa as "Layered Event"'. *History and Anthropology* E-pub ahead of print: 1–18. https://doi.org/10.1080/02757206.2020.1793761

Elbek, Laust Lund. 2021. 'There's a Hole in the Fence: Civil Pragmatism in Ambiguous Encounters on Lampedusa, Italy'. *Ethnos: Journal of Anthropology* E-pub ahead of print: 1–19. https://doi.org/10.1080/00141844.2021.1887912

Firth, Raymond. 1973. *Symbols: Public and Private*. London: Allen & Unwin.

Forgacs, David. 2014. *Italy's Margins: Social Exclusion and Nation Formation Since 1861*. Cambridge: Cambridge University Press.

Friese, Heidrun. 2010. 'The Limits of Hospitality: Political Philosophy, Undocumented Migration and the Local Arena'. *European Journal of Social Theory* 13 (3): 323–41. https://doi.org/10.1177/1368431010371755

Friese, Heidrun. 2012. 'Border Economies. Lampedusa and the Nascent Migration Industry'. *Shima: The International Journal of Research into Island Cultures* 6 (2): 66–84.

Friese, Heidrun. 2014. *Grenzen der Gastfreundschaft: die Bootsflüchtlinge von Lampedusa und die europäische Frage*. Bielefeld: Transcript Verlag.

Ginsborg, Paul. 1990. *A History of Contemporary Italy: Society And Politics 1943–1988*. London: Penguin.

Greco, Cinzia. 2016. 'Blaming the Southern Victim: Cancer and the Italian "Southern Question" in Terra dei fuochi and Taranto'. *Anthropology Today* 32 (3): 16–9. https://doi.org/10.1111/1467-8322.12255

Green, Sarah F. 2005. *Notes from the Balkans: Locating Marginality and Ambiguity on the Greek-Albanian Border*. Princeton, NJ: Princeton University Press.

Gupta, Akhil, and James Ferguson. 1992. 'Beyond "Culture": Space, Identity, and the Politics of Difference'. *Cultural Anthropology* 7 (1): 6–23. https://doi.org/10.1525/can.1992.7.1.02a00020

Harvey, Penny, and Hannah Knox. 2015. *Roads: An Anthropology of Infrastructure and Expertise*. Ithaca, NY: Cornell University Press.

Larkin, Brian. 2013. 'The Politics and Poetics of Infrastructure'. *Annual Review of Anthropology* 42: 327–43. https://doi.org/10.1146/annurev-anthro-092412-155522

Levi, Carlo. 1970. *Cristo si è Fermato a Eboli*. Turin: Einaudi.

Li Causi, Luciano. 1987. 'Lampedusa: The Road to Marginality'. *Ekistics* 54 (323/324): 165–69.

Lucht, Hans. 2013. 'Pusher Stories: Ghanaian Connection Men and the Expansion of the EU's Border Regimes into Africa'. In *The Migration Industry and the Commercialization of International Migration*, edited by Thomas Gammeltoft-Hansen and Ninna Nyberg Sørensen, 173–89. London: Routledge.

Massey, Doreen. 2005. *For Space*. London: Sage Publications.

Massey, Doreen. 2007. *World City*. Cambridge: Polity Press.

Moe, Nelson. 2002. *View from Vesuvius: Italian Culture and the Southern Question*. Berkeley, CA: University of California Press.

Morosi, Silvia. 2019. 'Sea Watch sequestrata dalla GdF: i 47 migranti scendono. Salvini: "Chi li ha autorizzati? Li denuncio"'. *Corriere della Sera*, 20 May.

Otto, Ton, and Nils Bubandt. 2010. 'Anthropology and the Predicaments of Holism'. In *Experiments in Holism: Theory and Practice in Contemporary Anthropology*, edited by Ton Otto and Nils Bubandt, 1–16. Hoboken, NJ: John Wiley & Sons.

Pugliese, Joseph. 2009. 'Crisis Heterotopias and Border Zones of the Dead'. *Continuum* 23 (5): 663–79. https://doi.org/10.1080/10304310903183627

Quagliariello, Chiara. 2021. '*Caring* for Others, *Managing* Migrants: Local and Institutional Hospitality in Lampedusa (Italy)'. In *Migrant Hospitalities in the Mediterranean: Encounters with Alterity in Birth and Death*, edited by Vanessa Grotti and Marc Brightman, 15–38. London: Palgrave Macmillan.

Reeves, Madeleine. 2017. 'Infrastructural Hope: Anticipating "Independent Roads" and Territorial Integrity in Southern Kyrgyzstan'. *Ethnos* 82 (4): 711–37. https://doi.org/10.1080/00141844.2015.1119176

Riall, Lucy. 1994. *The Italian Risorgimento: State, Society, and National Unification*. London: Psychology Press.

Schneider, Jane, ed. 1998. *Italy's 'Southern Question': Orientalism in One Country*. Oxford: Berg.

Scott, James C. 2009. *The Art of Not Being Governed: An Anarchist History of Upland Southeast Asia*. New Haven, CT: Yale University Press.

Taranto, Antonino. 2016. *Breve Storia di Lampedusa*. Naples: Associazione Culturale Archivio Storico Lampedusa.

Woods, Dwayne. 2009. 'Pockets of Resistance to Globalization: The case of the Lega Nord'. *Patterns of Prejudice* 43 (2): 161–77. https://doi.org/10.1080/00313220902793906

Ziniti, Alessandra. 2018. 'Sequestrata Nave Aquarius di Msf: "Smaltivano scarti e vestiti infetti dei migranti come rifiuti normali". Dodici indagati'. *La Repubblica*, 20 November.

CHAPTER 3

Remote Areas in the Mediterranean
A View from Europe's Southern Borderland

Laia Soto Bermant

University of Helsinki

Abstract

This chapter examines how the variable geopolitical dynamics of the EU's border regime have affected the Mediterranean's southern shore. I focus on one of Europe's most controversial border areas: the city of Melilla, a territory of 12 km^2 located in north-eastern Morocco under Spanish sovereignty since 1497. When Spain joined the Schengen Area in 1991, both Melilla and Ceuta, the two Spanish territories in North Africa, became the gatekeepers of 'Fortress Europe'. This put Melilla at the centre of the EU's political agenda, but was locally experienced with a sense of increased detachment and isolation. In this chapter, I explore ethnographically this general experience of marginality and how it is connected to the constitution of Melilla as an offshore border zone. I build on Edwin Ardener's notion of 'remote areas' as a distinct and identifiable type of place to explain why the problem of identity is experienced with particular intensity in places like Melilla, and argue that this feeling of vulnerability evokes a larger constellation of relations, connections and disconnections across the Mediterranean region and beyond.

How to cite this book chapter:
Soto Bermant, Laia. 2022. 'Remote Areas in the Mediterranean: A View from Europe's Southern Borderland'. In *Locating the Mediterranean: Connections and Separations across Space and Time*, edited by Carl Rommel and Joseph John Viscomi, 53–76. Helsinki: Helsinki University Press. DOI: https://doi.org/10.33134/HUP-18-3.

Introduction

The question organising this volume concerns how the Mediterranean has been shaped historically by connections and disconnections spanning space and time. Locating the Mediterranean from this perspective involves considering the historical, legal, political, and social entanglements not only between specific locations, but also between conceptual (and geopolitical) domains such as 'East' and 'West' and 'North' and 'South'. To do this, we must examine the spatial logics, material infrastructure and discursive systems that shape the experience of living *somewhere* in the Mediterranean, and ask how this constellation of connections and disconnections determines the significance of particular places, how it puts them in relation to other locations, and how it situates them within a larger regime of value. The asymmetrical but also mutually constitutive nature of these encounters force us to reconsider how we use 'centre' and 'periphery' as categories, and to rethink our mental map of this part of the world (Hauswedell, Körner, and Tiedau 2019).[1]

My take on these questions is based on my research in north-eastern Morocco, and focuses on how the rebordering of the Mediterranean (Suárez Navas 2004) at the turn of the 20th century 'relocated' certain territories in the EU's periphery.[2] I draw my material from one of Europe's most controversial borderlands: the city of Melilla, a territory of 12 km[2] in north-eastern Morocco which has been under Spanish sovereignty since 1497. Along with the twin city of Ceuta, also in northern Morocco but on the west end, this is one of the only two EU land borders in Africa.

It is impossible to 'locate' the Mediterranean today without taking into consideration the changing dynamics of the EU border regime and how it has shaped the geopolitical landscape across the region. Melilla is a particularly interesting site to explore this question because of its unique position as a territory that is somehow 'out of place', neither here (Europe) nor there (Africa), or both here and there. Instead of thinking about Melilla as a 'margin' or a 'periphery' and considering how it interacts with the EU as a 'centre', I approach Melilla's condition of liminality as a distinctive topological combination between distance and proximity, between connection and disconnection.[3]

I build my argument around Ardener's concept of remote areas, which first appeared in a piece published in 1987 (reprinted in *HAU* in

2012). In the original text, Ardener presents a peculiar phenomenological account of remote areas that takes him from the Scottish High-
lands to the Cameroons. Contrary to what we may think, he tells us,
remote areas are constantly subject to change and intervention. They
are full of strangers and innovators, filled with rubbish and ruins of the
past, in permanent contact with the outside world and always obsessed
with communication. Distance is not necessarily the issue, for, even
when they are 'reached', remote areas continue to be remote.[4]

Ardener's argument is not just that remote places are not necessarily physically removed but rather that they constitute a distinct and
identifiable type of place. Remote areas are places that are identified as
singularities by dominant zones, and it is the nature of this relation that
defines them as remote. This is why not all geographical peripheries
are remote, and why remoteness is also not restricted to peripheries.
For remoteness is 'a condition not related to the periphery, but to the
fact that certain peripheries are by definition *not properly linked* to the
dominant zone' (1987, 532). Remoteness is simply, as Ardener puts it,
an empty formative to describe 'the interaction between the anthropologist and his field, the definer and the defined, the classifier and the
classified, the imagined and the realized' (530).

The text gives us some clues as to how we might identify remote
areas. It is a peculiarity of remote areas, he writes, that *events* are much
more frequent. Happenings that would hold little or no significance
elsewhere acquire in remote areas the significance of *an event*. Remoteness, he argues, is both internal and external; it is both a specification
or perception from the outside and an internal response to that specification, which works in the opposite direction. Another, related feature
is that people in remote areas are 'at least intermittently conscious of
the defining processes of others that might absorb them' (1987, 532).
The problem of identity is thus experienced with particular intensity in
these places, which may appear distant and unreachable from the outside but feel open, vulnerable, and unprotected from the inside (more
on this later).

Ardener's argument is deliberately elusive and it would do him no
justice to try to summarise it here. Instead, I draw on the many threads
he lays out to try to rethink the question of remoteness in the Mediterranean. In this, I hope to contribute to an ongoing discussion on
contemporary forms of remoteness inspired by the reprint of Ardener's
classic piece in 2012. Two collections are particularly significant in this

regard. Harms et al. (2014) pick up Ardener's thread in a special issue that explores cases from various parts of Asia, Africa, and Latin America to argue that remoteness should be understood not as a spatial concept but as a relational category and a 'way of being'. Geographical distance, in their view, is tangential to the concept. Saxer and Andersson (2019), by contrast, insist that it is unproductive to detach 'remoteness' from its geographical moorings, and that we must consider instead how remoteness 'is made and unmade in the current "world disorder" of shifting geopolitical and economic realignments' (2019, 142). They emphasise three aspects of remote areas: how they are made *through* connections and partial (dis)connections, how they can become economically productive, and how they are easily subject to various forms of 'remote' control.

The ideas I present in the following pages are inspired by this theoretical engagement, which I wish to push further in three directions. First, I want to go back to a point made by Ardener that has been overlooked in later discussions: the idea of remote areas as 'singularities'. Second, I wish to reflect on the ethnographic traces of remoteness in the field. And last, I want open up the discussion to reflect on the nature of connections and disconnections more generally, shifting the focus away from 'remote areas' as places (or localities, as discussed in Chapter 1) to 'remote areas' as locations, and focusing on how locations like Melilla can help us reimagine spatial hierarchies in the Mediterranean.

The Making of a Singularity

Arguably, Melilla has always been 'singular' in geopolitical terms.[5] The territory upon which it was built was seized by the Spanish in 1497, as part of a military effort to secure a number of small garrisons along the North African coast following the end of the Spanish 'Reconquista' of Al-Andalus (1492). For nearly four centuries, Melilla operated as a prison colony (*presidio*) where the Spanish crown disposed of political enemies and cast away the undesired. The citadel comprised a small cluster of buildings surrounded by fortified walls, accommodating a population of a few hundred soldiers, prisoners, and auxiliary personnel (Calderón Vázquez 2008). Initially, noble and rich men were sent there to perform military duties in what was often considered a form of deportation, but over time it became a penal settlement for the general criminal population.[6]

We can trace the beginnings of Melilla's economic and political transformation to the second half of the 19th century, when the territory under Spanish control grew from 1 to 12 km² in surface. At that time, Europe was immersed in the Scramble for Africa. The Alaouite dynasty had successfully kept Morocco out of the European race throughout the 18th century and most of the 19th, but pressure from both the French and the British was mounting. In 1844, Sultan Abd al-Rahman lost the Franco-Moroccan war and officially recognised Algeria as part of the French Empire. A few years later (1856), he agreed to make Great Britain Morocco's 'protector'. Armed confrontations between Spain and the Moroccan Sultanate broke out soon after, culminating in the War of Africa (*Guerra de Africa*) in 1859. Morocco lost the war, and as part of the peace treaty the sultan was forced to hand over a large stretch of land around Ceuta and Melilla (Ponce Gómez, 1988).

Soon after Melilla's enlargement, the citadel was declared a free port (1863). This was the first step towards the making of Melilla as a fiscal 'singularity'. Gradually, Melilla was incorporated into a regional network of weekly rural markets linking the presidio with Taza, in Morocco, and Oran and Algiers in Algeria. A few years earlier, in the late 1850s, a French shipping company had established regular lines linking the two Spanish territories to Marseille, the coast of Algeria, and the Atlantic coast of Morocco (Saro Gandarillas 1984). This, along with the establishment of the free port, opened up new trading opportunities. Caravans from French Algeria, sometimes travelling for as long as 16 days, came to Melilla to buy English products shipped in from Gibraltar (sugar, tea, cotton, and candles). Moroccan traders sold chickens, eggs, wax, vegetables, cattle, leather, and wool and bought manufactured products to be exported to the Moroccan hinterland. Jewish merchants from Tetouan, Tangiers, Gibraltar, and Oran arrived in Melilla, attracted by the new trading opportunities as middlemen, while Berbers became the main couriers of cross-border trade.[7]

The first half of the 20th century was a period of economic and urban expansion. Spain's colonial policies shifted from Central and South America towards the southern shore of the Mediterranean, and military campaigns in Morocco became increasingly common. In 1912, Spain was handed formal control over the northern strip of

Morocco to prevent French monopoly in the southern Mediterranean.[8] Not everyone in Spain favoured military intervention in Morocco, but the Spanish economy was in shambles, and the government faced mounting pressure from financial, industrial, and commercial interests that were seeking new markets in order to compensate the sudden fall in trade with the ex-colonies (Bunes Ibarra 1995).[9] The wars (1893, 1909, and 1921) brought tens of thousands of soldiers to Melilla in several waves, raising demand for produce, textiles, and other services, and leading to an increase in trade revenues on imports. Tax revenues were then reinvested in construction work and generated employment for thousands of migrants, both Spanish and Moroccan (see Bravo Nieto 1996). Engineers were brought in from mainland Spain to design a new urban plan for the city, and 14 local newspapers were launched. Melilla had its own Rotary Club, and a Chamber of Commerce to defend the interests of trading and banking houses (Castro Maestro 2003; Moga Romero 1988). It was a time of prosperity, and the population grew rapidly, from a little under 9,000 in the 1900 census to over 81,000 in 1949.[10]

Logically, Melilla was deeply affected by the loss of the Protectorate. The declaration of Moroccan independence in 1956 led to the first diplomatic rows over the sovereignty of the Spanish exclaves, revealing the vulnerability of their geopolitical position. Soon, the Spanish began to abandon their businesses in northern Morocco and return to mainland Spain. The mines were deserted and eventually shut down, and thousands of soldiers returned to mainland Spain. By the early 1980s, the population had reached a low point of 58,000 inhabitants. After that, Ceuta and Melilla fell into oblivion. In mainland Spain, the African territories came to be known as a popular destination for one of two things: performing the mandatory military service and buying cheap foreign goods. Save for the young men who were sent to there to perform the mandatory military service, or those who regularly made the trip down to 'el moro' (Morocco) to buy hashish, very few people in mainland Spain could point the location of the North African territories on a map. Melilla had one of the highest unemployment rates in the country. It lagged behind in basic infrastructure: tap water was not drinkable, there was no natural gas – bottled butane gas is still today shipped in from the mainland – the sewage system was deficient, and the electricity supply unstable. Muslim districts faced the worst conditions, and tensions between the Spanish and the Muslim communities were at an all-time high (Soto Bermant 2015).

Meanwhile, across the sea, the EEC was taking its first steps to consolidate Europe as a unified political and economic space. As Europe prepared to eliminate internal borders through the creation of the Schengen Area (1985), the porosity of the Spanish border became a problem. As Elbek argues in Chapter 2 of this volume, the Schengen Agreement did not simply remove the borders of the EU; rather, they were shifted to other locations. Like Italy, Spain found itself at the centre of this process of relocation. The Spanish government was required to pass a new immigration law, and the Spanish North African territories acquired unprecedented relevance in the national political scene.

This was the second turning point in the making of Melilla as a 'singularity'. Financed in large part by the EU, the process of legally and *materially* turning Melilla into Europe's gatekeeper was swift. After the arrival of the first group of sub-Saharan migrants in the late 1990s, the Spanish government built a perimetric fence around the city. Three years later, construction work began for the CETI, a temporary detention centre for asylum seekers and refugees. Continued assaults on the fence led in 2005 to the erection of second and third perimetral fences, raising six metres above the ground and equipped with infrared cameras, sound detectors, and watch posts. A road was built along the fence to allow regular border patrols, supplemented with a police helicopter at night. In addition, Morocco built a secondary fence covered in razor-wire across the other side. Spain increased border patrol personnel and special divisions were sent in from the mainland for rotating 'border shifts' lasting between two and three weeks. The Spanish territory became a buffer zone and a funnel, which both attracted and contained migrants from sub-Saharan Africa, the Middle East, and, in the first periods, even South Asia. Increased Frontex operations in the Mediterranean and in the Atlantic near the Canary Islands made this (and Ceuta's) route even more important.

Gradually, Melilla became an object of outside intervention, engulfed in EU visions of development for a new border regime, and increasingly dependent on funds from the European Union not only for border infrastructure but also for social and economic development. Through the European Regional Development Fund (ERDF) and the European Social Fund (ESF), the local government was able to finance development projects ranging from basic infrastructure (a water desalination plant, a refuse dumping ground, an industrial park, an incinerator plant and a ring road, to name only a few) to transport communications, the rehabilitation of new leisure spaces (most controversially, a golf course sitting across the temporary stay centre for migrants), and numerous training programmes to encourage the growth of the private sector in the city. These grand infrastructural projects generated employment opportunities for the local population, while attracting private companies specialised in construction, security, and general maintenance looking to catch a substantial government contract.

More generally, the influx of outside monies turned the local government into a gatekeeper with the power to decide, distribute, and allocate. The effect was a reconfiguration of the economy of the city, splitting it into two main fields: the public sector, which employs around 40 per cent of the population, commerce (comprising mostly informal trade across the border), and the services sector (also partly informal), which provides a livelihood to most of the remaining 60 per cent.[11]

But turning Melilla into an offshore borderland also required some 'border acrobatics'. This is the term Ferrer-Gallardo (2007) uses to describe the complex system of selective permeability that was put in place to ensure the safeguard the informal border economy. Closing of the border of Melilla completely would have been disastrous for the local economy, both in Melilla and across the border in Nador, which was one of the poorest and least 'developed' regions of Morocco. To avoid the dangers of cutting out all sources of income to those at the bottom of the ladder, and also to secure that Melilla could continue to profit from a reserve army of frontier workers willing to take on poorly paid jobs as domestics, cooks, cleaners, handymen, mechanics, and so forth, a series of regulatory exceptions were put in place. First, an agreement between Spain and Morocco eliminated visa restrictions for Moroccans who could prove residency in the provinces neighbouring the two Spanish territories, and allowed free movement across the border for local people. Second, the Spanish government negotiated a special clause with the EU to keep Ceuta and Melilla outside the European Free Trade Area, thus preserving their 'privileged' position as free ports and, with it, the continued influx of trade revenues and tax income levied on incoming merchandise from Asia, Europe, and America. The stakes were high, with the city pocketing up to 60 million euros annually in local taxes alone. Far from becoming an inexpungable fortress, then, Melilla was reconfigured as a space in between, located inside the European Union but outside the European Free Trade Area; and partly outside the Schengen Area, a 'layered border' carved out between Spain and Morocco where different categories of people had access to different spaces.[12]

Melilla thus entered into a very particular relationship with Europe, not only politically and economically but also symbolically. It was configured as a 'singularity' (in fact, Ceuta and Melilla are classified by the European Commission as 'special economic zones'[13]), in the sense of being, by definition, *not properly linked* to the dominant zone (Ardener 1987, 532), which is not the same as saying disconnected from or unlinked to. In the same way as the Spanish crown used Melilla's physical location as an instrument to cast away an undesired population, amid a wider process of reconfiguration of EU borders and externalisation of the border regime to the southern Mediterranean periphery, the EU found in Melilla the ideal location for an offshore border zone. A place cut off from the European continent but administratively linked to it, a magnet for migratory flows and a perfect site for their contention. At the same time, Melilla's geopolitical location at the interstices between the EU and Morocco (but also North Africa more generally) opened up important economic opportunities. To preserve its 'singularity' as a free port was to protect an economic circuit that was kept partly hidden in the shadows, apparently (but only apparently) disconnected from the visible routes of global capitalism.

To sum up, we can say that the twofold production of Melilla as an offshore borderland and as a special economic zone was the result of a series of turning points that brought together local and outside interests to reconfigure the legal, economic, and political structure of the city and thus transform its 'relative location' (Green 2012). In both cases, it was a reconfiguration of international alliances and interests beyond Melilla's control that made Melilla strategically significant. These conjunctural crossroads configured, layer after layer, the complex economic and political structure that we find in Melilla today. This begs the question how people living there became entangled in this process of resignifying Melilla and how the political work that went into turning it into Europe's sentinel fed into local visions of belonging and identity. In the following section, I turn to my ethnography to discuss how this was a double-edged sword, which appeared to bring Melilla closer to the centre of power but in fact made it more remote.

Remote Areas Are Full of Strangers

Let me begin with a personal observation about doing ethnography in 'remote areas'. When I first arrived in Melilla, in the summer of 2008, the six-metre-tall, triple security fence already surrounded the city. Melilla had made international headlines briefly in the late 1990s, when the first group of sub-Saharan migrants arrived seeking EU asylum, and again in 2005, when thousands of migrants attempted to enter Melilla in five coordinated break-ins in just over a week, leaving six migrants dead. These dramatic events were a wake-up call for the Spanish government, which decided to raise the fence from three to six metres in height. Nonetheless, even then, very few people outside Spain knew of the existence of the Spanish North African territories. And even Spaniards like me, who knew of its existence, would have had trouble pointing to it on a map.

As the years went by, Melilla's appearance in international news headlines became more and more frequent. The group 'jumps' (*saltos*) became more common, and Melilla quickly garnered attention from journalists and political activists. Images of migrants climbing over the fence made the covers of national and international news outlets several times in the years between 2005 and 2018, including a photograph taken in 2014 by local activist and NGO founder Jose Palazón that went viral online (Image 3.1). The photograph showed 11 men sitting atop the border fence as a police officer approaches, while two Melillans play golf below, on the Spanish side of the fence. The woman is in mid-swing while the man is turned toward the migrants, watching the dramatic scene.

The sudden proliferation of these images responded to the efforts of activists and journalists to show the outside world what was happening at Europe's back gate. But it also unwittingly served a local interest in overplaying the immigration drama. The images of dozens if not hundreds of black African bodies, their clothes torn, climbing makeshift ladders or tying hooks to their shoes to climb over the fence made the perfect pitch to apply for the EU's Emergency Fund. It was all part of what De Genova has termed 'the border spectacle', that is, the circulation of violent, spectacular and grotesque images in the media

Image 3.1: Migrants climbing over the border fence while two Melillans play golf.
Photo: José Palazón. Released under CC BY-SA 4.0.

that produce a vision of the border as a problem, and of the illegal migrant as a threat that needs to be managed, controlled, acted upon. In the case of Melilla, this was so obvious that even the journalists who covered some of these events in 2014 published an open letter in social media to publicly express their discomfort with the way in which their work was being used by the local government to create a social panic around the border.

At some point during this process of 'mediatisation', I started to notice that when I presented my work at conferences and workshops and mentioned Melilla, instead of the blank stare I had grown accustomed to in the first years of my research, I was met with a nod of acknowledgement. More and more people seemed to have heard about Melilla, and, even if they did not remember or could not pronounce the name, they certainly knew of its existence.

In the field, and at around the same time, I started to notice ethnographic traces of Melilla's remoteness. The number of 'strangers' started to grow exponentially. Activists, journalists, foreign scholars, even artists had something to say about Melilla, and would make the occasional pilgrimage to draw attention to the 'immigration drama'.[14] Things that happened in Melilla became *events* to be witnessed, reported, documented. Melillans became the protagonists of a story written elsewhere, permanently under the gaze of external visitors and critical observers.

The fact that, in a way, I was one of those strangers myself meant that their interactions with me were also mediated by this deeply ambivalent feeling of exposure. I remember with particular vividness one evening in April 2017. One of my friends and regular informants, a well-connected and very influential woman in her mid-fifties (let us call her Anna), had organised a group dinner for me and my guest, a French scholar who was involved in our research project. Anna took us to a fancy restaurant in the city centre, where we were introduced to our dinner companions, a man and a woman, both university professors. After exchanging the usual pleasantries, our hosts began to talk about Melilla. After a brief introduction to the city, the conversation turned, quite quickly, to two of Melillans' favourite topics at the time: the increased, and increasingly disruptive, presence of the MENA (a legal acronym that stands for *menores extranjeros no acompañados*, unaccompanied foreign minors) and the radicalisation of the local Muslim population that has taken place over the past few years. The general message conveyed was that Melilla had become more dangerous, that it was 'not what it used to be'.

This was hardly surprising to me, having grown accustomed to these kinds of conversations. But something was different this time, perhaps due to the presence of my colleague, whose foreignness was greater than mine. The whole evening was punctuated by a series of awkward interactions between our hosts and the restaurant staff, and in particular the waitress who was serving us, a young Muslim girl. It started with small gestures: calling the waitress *garçon*, as one would in a French restaurant, with a quick clap of the hands to draw her attention. And it slowly escalated as they complained about the food and, later, the bill. What was particularly interesting was that these scenes of disagreement were enacted not with anger or irritation but with an air of condescension. At one point, our host caressed the face of the waitress, telling me how 'lovely' she was, speaking about her in the third person as if she were not present. The girl looked manifestly uncomfortable, but kept silent and smiled. Our hosts' behaviour during these brief scenes was that of a colonial elite: a kind of patronising disdain meant to be seen by others, and particularly by us, foreigners. A power-wielding act that implicated us directly as accomplices and spectators.

On our way out of the restaurant, Anna told me about a friend of hers from Madrid, a judge, who, during a brief visit to Melilla, had joined a guided tour to visit the fence. These tours were organised by the local government in collaboration with the military and national police bodies, and were offered to journalists and scholars visiting the city. During the tour, she found a shoe with a hook tied to it (of the kind migrants use to climb over the fence). She took it home and hung it up on the wall of her living room in Madrid. 'You should see it!' my Melillan friend told me, full of admiration. 'How beautiful!' our dinner companion remarked. A few days later, I was able to book my own 'tour' of the fence, with my own private 'guide' from the Spanish military police.

The creation of this new terrain of 'cultural intimacy' (Herzfeld 2005), a terrain punctuated by what I call ethnographic traces of remoteness, has to be understood in context of the wider political process that turned Melilla into an object of intervention. The frequent media frenzies formed around Melilla's border spectacles put Melilla on a global stage. Every attempt by migrants to break into Melilla that was reported in the media set off a wave of criticism towards Spanish border policies in general and Melilla's border patrol officers in particular. In response, after every break-in, Melillans turned to social media to share their concerns and defend themselves from outside criticism, invoking their right to protect the city against intrusion, and denouncing (what they perceived to be) the irresponsible attitude of journalists, politicians, and activists who became 'experts' on Melilla after spending barely one week in the city. I lost count of the times I witnessed the same sequence of events: break-in attempt, followed by a critical piece published in a newspaper or on TV, followed by a heated discussion in one the several closed Facebook groups Melillans turn to to voice their concerns.

After a while, I realised that these virtual platforms had become a safe space where people felt free to speak their mind about all sorts of controversial issues, not only in relation to the border, but also cases of corruption, or issues to do with marginal neighbourhoods in the city, petty crime, unemployment, transportation, and so on and so forth. The things people would not say to me (or to each other) face to face in a cafeteria they voiced openly here. This was all the more surprising looking at the numbers: the largest of these groups numbered over 20,000 members (which, in a city of 80,000, amounts to 25 per cent of the population). Yet, the tone of the conversations was intimate, almost familiar. Reading the comments and posts in these groups, I had the sense of having gone behind the scenes and entered a sort of backstage, a space of social or cultural intimacy away from the public eye (Herzfeld 2005; Shryock 2004). And, indeed, the reason these virtual spaces were 'safe' was that they had been carefully removed from the gaze of external observers. This was achieved through a combination of very restrictive privacy settings and thorough background checks on members who wished to join in order to make sure that they were *genuine* Melillans.

I began to follow these groups closely, searching for further ethnographic clues and patterns. After some time, I noticed that, paradoxically, the more this place seemed to be connected to the outside world, the more people complained about feeling disconnected, isolated, and abandoned. And the more Melilla was 'securitised' and 'militarised', the more people seemed to feel vulnerable and exposed. The ethnographic question for me then became: how and why did this supposed increase in 'connectivity' make people feel more disconnected?

Living in a Caged City

To begin with, some topographical elements are relevant. Melilla can be said to be 'objectively' remote (in the sense of distant) from the rest of Spain. Being physically removed from the hinterland has material consequences. There are the frequent water cuts and electricity outages, for example, due to the fact that the Melilla's electricity and water desalination plants do not have the capacity to meet the demand of a rising local population. There is also the dependency on shipments from Spain for basic food supplies and potable water, for there is not enough land in Melilla for either farming or agriculture, and the water coming from the desalination plant is not drinkable. And there are problems with transportation. Reaching Melilla is not easy. Flights to mainland Spain are very expensive, even with the discount for Melillan residents. And the only alternative is the overnight ferries, which take around eight hours to reach the Spanish coast. When the weather is not optimal, especially if there are strong winds, both the ferries and the planes are grounded. And, if the bad weather persists, there may not be a way out of Melilla for a few days at a time. These material factors contribute to the perception of Melilla as a 'blank' area in the middle of nowhere, a space-in-between removed from the world.

Indeed, for Melillans, the problem of remoteness manifested itself principally as one of mobility, or lack thereof. One thing that caught my attention from the early days of my fieldwork was how often people complained about the difficulties in getting out of Melilla. First, there was the question of travelling to mainland Spain. At times, the journey seemed to take on Odyssean qualities. The cost, the length of the trip, the lack of destinations, the variable schedule, they all seemed to conspire to keep people in. Any interruption of regular transportation with mainland Spain, however brief, was experienced as a national crisis, reported in local newspapers and discussed at length in cafés and online forums. Then there was the problem of crossing the border in the other direction, out into Morocco. Almost everyone I met told me about the long lines of cars that form in both directions (going in and out of Melilla) due to the large volume of informal trade, and how this meant that driving out of the city could take up to two or three hours. This was perhaps one the most frequent complaints I heard during the time I spent in Melilla. Soon, I realised that these complaints always came coupled with nostalgic references to the past. 'It was different back then,' said the taxi driver on my first day in Melilla (2008), on a ride from the airport to the border crossing point of Beni Enzar:

> Back then crossing the border took only about twenty minutes. We all used to go to Morocco every Sunday for lunch, or to have Moroccan tea and pastries. But now, now it takes at least two or three hours with all the contraband! I used to take customers through the frontier at least four or five times a day, but now, now I won't do it for less than a hundred euros.

The paradox of living in a 'caged city' summed up the encounter with remoteness very well for Melillans, who seemed to experience this relocation as an implosion of their social space. Concerns were thus expressed in terms of a restriction of movement in classical narratives of structural nostalgia that evoked a shrinking social universe. This is hardly surprising if we consider that within a few decades Melilla had gone from being the centre of one social universe (Spanish Morocco) to becoming the periphery of another (Europe). This relocation was experienced in spatial terms. Thus, while stories about the past talk about expansion, about how easy it was to 'go out' into Morocco – in other words, about Melilla moving outwards – narratives about the present talk about implosion, about the outside creeping in. Indeed, as Ardener suggests, there is a heightened sense of vulnerability to exposure and intrusion. This vulnerability manifests in different ways, but the dominant image is that of a city under siege, always in danger of being invaded. There is an exaggerated sense of vulnerability and exposure, of ease of entry (the following quotes are taken from one of the Facebook groups I mentioned):

> I don't know how this is going to end, but there are hundreds and hundreds of them and we need to stop it.

> We need to end the 'calling effect' because they are entering the city with total impunity. This is not racism, just preoccupation for our city, we have Sub-Saharans, Algerians, Moroccans.

> Melilla is our home and we have to defend it, like we would defend our own homes if they were attacked. … We are alone in this battle and if we don't do anything nobody will.

To the outside observer, these may seem like the typical anti-immigrant rhetoric that can be heard in any city across Europe. But it is one thing to engage in this kind of discourse living in Paris, Madrid, or London, and quite a different matter if you are in a place like Melilla, surrounded by a six-metre-high fence, hearing the police helicopter patrol the skies every night, and waking up every morning to local news about a break-in attempt (perhaps even coming across a group of fleeing migrants yourself on the road). In these 'eventful' conditions, the 'threat' of migration has a distinctively material quality to it.

It is worth recalling Ardener's point: while they may look inaccessible from the outside, remote areas feel open and vulnerable from the inside. This is a theme that recurs in the most unexpected places. Once, I signed up for one of the guided tour to visit the catacombs of the old citadel. The tour ran on the same day of the week almost every week of the year and was offered, free of charge, by the Department of Tourism. I was interested in hearing how the story of the city was told in a semi-official context such as that one, and I was also curious to see who had signed up for the tour. I had noticed that there was an ample offer of guided visits and other leisure activities for foreign tourists in the city, but had failed to see a single tourist in over a year.

The visit began at the Museum of Sacred Art, a small museum built in a former Franciscan convent that had direct access to the underground tunnels. I arrived ten minutes early. The two receptionists were chatting lazily by the entrance with a security guard. Inside, a carefully arranged selection of objects collected dust. I walked in and looked around. The permanent collection featured several images of St Francis of Assisi, patron saint of Melilla, and over one hundred pieces of 'Christian art', mostly saintly figures, from the 17th to 21st centuries. A life-size statue of Christ carrying the cross presided over the room. One by one, a group of around ten people walked in. All of them were Spanish: around half were actually from Melilla, and the other half had either lived in Melilla in the past or had relatives living there. The audience was local, then. A few minutes later, a young girl dressed in a blue uniform with the logo of a private security company introduced herself as our guide. Following her lead, we began to walk down the stairs, towards the tunnels.

The entire visit lasted approximately one hour, and I was surprised to find out that the whole purpose of the tour was to 'relive' the infamous siege of 1774, when the troops of the Moroccan sultan besieged Melilla for over three months and Melillans took refuge in the tunnels built under the citadel. The passages were completely refurbished a few years ago, and some of the rooms have now been 'staged' to illustrate the siege: 'this is how they cooked', 'this is where they slept', 'these were their weapons', 'from these windows they could see the Spanish ships approaching', and so forth. The climax arrived at the end of the visit, as we entered the largest chamber. There, we were invited to watch a short film showing a re-enactment of the final days of the siege projected on the wall. We stood in the dark, huddled together, as epic music played in the background and a first-person voice-over recounted the dramatic final moments of the siege, as it had been recorded in the chronicles of the time.

I left the museum in a daze. After spending over an hour walking in single file through the entrails of the citadel and being told about the dangers faced by our 'forebears', the sense of vulnerability and exposure was genuine. I began to walk towards the city centre and passed by the 'Ethnographic Museum' and the 'Archaeological Museum', both housed in a beautifully refurbished 17th-century armoury. The two receptionists were chatting lazily by the entrance with the security guards. I kept walking and looked around. I noticed how everything in the old city had been replaced with a newer old-looking version of itself: the cobblestones on the road, the military watchtowers, the central square, the walls, even the old canons fired in the 19th century to determine the new limits of the city are replicas. Everything looked perfect and slightly unreal, like a life-sized model of itself.

I found myself wondering how many millions of euros were spent on this as I stopped at one of the viewpoints to take in the view of the entire city. I glanced across the horizon lost in my thoughts, until my eyes stopped at a group of around 20 young boys standing around in a parking lot some 20 metres below from where I was. I had seen them many times before. They were the MENA, Moroccan street children from Fes, Casablanca, and other big cities in Morocco who come to Melilla in the hopes that they may be able to sneak into one of the ships headed towards mainland Spain. During the day, they walked aimlessly around the city, begging for food from passers-by or rummaging in rubbish bins. In the evenings, they sought shelter by the cliffs, where they could hide from the rain and the police. Although some are as young as seven or eight, horror stories about them circulate widely in social media (they are violent, they are thieves, they are drug addicts, they do not want help, and so on), and the moral panic was so strong back then that there had been suggestions of creating vigilante groups to 'keep them at bay'.

Standing on that viewpoint, as I replayed in my head the stories I had just heard about the siege, I realised that the reason people were so terrified of these children was that they represented a visual 'glitch' in a carefully manufactured landscape. The 'spectacular' drama of African migrants climbing over the fence was but the narrowing tip of the iceberg. In the eyes of Melillans, the greatest dangers were less 'spectacular' and much more ordinary: street children roaming the streets of the city and begging for food, old men collecting plastic water carafes to sell in Morocco for five cents apiece, smugglers pushing the large, heavy bundles of clothes, heaps of rubble, discarded plastic wraps and cardboard boxes tossed on the pavement. To be Melillan was to be haunted by the materiality of those daily 'intrusions'.

Who Then Are We, *Really*?

In this chapter, I have tried to show how Melilla came into being as a particular kind of place through its connections to and disconnections from other locations. Instead of focusing on the question of identity and belonging (as is common in the anthropological literature of border areas), I focused on the idea of Melilla as a *location*. This led me to examine Melilla in relation to Edwin Ardener's notion of 'remote areas'. Ardener's argument is that remote areas constitute a distinct and identifiable type of place. These are places that have been marked as *singularities* by dominant zones, and it is the nature of this asymmetrical relation that defines them as remote. The problem of identity is experienced with particular force in these places, which appear isolated and unreachable from the outside, but feel vulnerable and exposed from the inside. Melilla, I have argued, is one such place. For all the performative work that goes into turning Melilla into a European space, the perception from the inside is that Africa is always lurking in the shadows, ready to absorb the city. To dismiss these concerns as mere 'racism' would be to miss the point. Something is known here about the material and symbolic conditions of Melilla's existence that cannot be explicitly articulated. That 'something' concerns precisely the relationship between Melilla and other locations elsewhere, across the northern shore of the Mediterranean.

By concentrating on the question of *where* Melilla is – that is, on how Melilla is positioned or 'located' in the Mediterranean region and how it is connected to and disconnected from other locations *elsewhere* – I hope to have made visible the multiplicity of 'trajectories' (Massey 2005), both synchronic and diachronic, that have come together to constitute Melilla as a particular kind of place. Like Lampedusa, Melilla embodies both a centre and a margin (see Elbek, Chapter 2 in this volume). It was thrust into the international limelight in the early days of the migration crisis, and quickly became a symbol for the tragedy of irregular migration, with images of black African bodies jumping over the border fence making headlines around the world. This relocation put Melilla at the centre of the EU's political agenda, but was locally experienced with a sense of increased detachment and isolation. The more connected Melilla was to Europe, the more remote it appeared to those living inside. This general experience of marginality, of being, as it were, on the outside looking in, evokes a larger constellation of relations, connections and separations across the Mediterranean region and beyond.

It is clear that to be 'somewhere in particular' in the Mediterranean is to be part of a wider definitional space shaped by the experience of colonialism and historically divided between Europe and Europe's southern 'neighbours'. North Africa occupies a special place in this cartographic landscape, being symbolically severed from the rest of Africa and connected – but only *selectively* – to Europe. Far from creating a homogenous political landscape, the 'rebordering' of the Mediterranean (Suárez Navas 2004) that began with the creation of the Schengen Area in the 1980s continues to metamorphose through the signing of new partnerships, neighbourhood policies, and bilateral agreements that outsource EU border control to third countries and generates zones of 'awkward engagement' (Tsing 2005) like Ceuta and Melilla.

Does this mean that we can consider the southern Mediterranean a vast, undifferentiated 'remote area'? Probably not. As Del Sarto (2010) has shown, the extension of governance patterns and functional regimes from the EU to its periphery is highly differentiated and the resulting political landscape is far from homogenous. Nonetheless, as more and more countries are recruited to defend and protect a privileged political, economic, and conceptual space (Europe) from which they themselves have historically been excluded (Soto Bermant 2017), we may wonder how these processes affect the zones of intimacy that flourish in the backstage of public culture.

Take the refugee crisis of 2015, for example, tellingly referred to in the media as the *European* migrant crisis. Turkey, Greece, Italy, Malta, and, to a lesser degree, Spain (but, significantly, not France) came under the spotlight for refusing to harbour refugees fleeing from Syria, Afghanistan, and Iraq. The intense media coverage of the crisis, with dramatic images of sinking boats, overcrowded camps, and detention centres, contrasted with the relative silence around the 'other' crisis happening in the war-torn countries where migrants came from, and created a moral narrative of guilt that placed the Mediterranean and its people (particularly those in 'remote' areas like Lampedusa, Lesvos, or, indeed, Ceuta and Melilla) under the permanent gaze of an audience, an 'external observer whose opinion is imagined, *and imagined to matter*' (Herzfeld 2005, 11, emphasis in original). When Herzfeld wrote those words, he was describing a wider phenomenon related to the creation of a new kind of social terrain, a shadow zone produced by the global stage of identity politics. But perhaps it is not a coincidence that he was writing about Greece. Reflecting on the Gaels and the Bretons, Ardener (1987) notes that it is an important feature of remote social spaces that the question of identity seems to impose itself, so that people living there keep on asking 'who then are we, *really*?' – as if 'they were indeed privileged enough to require to know something that no one can ever know' (526).

Notes

1 This chapter is based on material collected prior to the Covid-19 pandemic. In March 2020, the land border between Spain and Morocco located in Melilla was shut down completely, and remained closed until May of 2022.

2 My connection to the region dates back to my doctoral fieldwork, which I carried out in 2008 and 2009. I have been back to Melilla and Nador several times since, in 2013, 2017, and 2018.

3 For all its uniqueness, it is surprising how little attention Melilla has received from anthropologists working in the region. With the exception of H. Driessen's (1992) monograph, written in the early 1990s, the Spanish enclave has largely gone unnoticed. The neighbouring Moroccan province of Nador, by contrast, is an established fieldsite amongst Moroccan specialists. From David M. Hart's (1976) classical work on the Aith Waryaghar to David McMurray's (2001) more recent monograph on smuggling and migration, this classically 'remote', Berber-speaking region of Morocco was at the centre of heated debates on tribal structures and segmentary lineage in the 1980s and has featured frequently in anthropological debates on the relationship between 'tribes' and 'the state' in North Africa (see, for example, Seddon 1981 and Munson 1989). It was only very recently, when the rebordering of the EU turned it into one of the key migration hotspots in Africa, that Melilla attracted the interest of anthropologists (see, for example, Andersson 2014).

4 This is in many ways similar to Simmel's (1950) arguments on the unity of nearness and remoteness in the phenomenon of the stranger, which he saw as involving both distance at close range, and closeness at a distance.

5 This section is based on a multiplicity of primary and secondary historical sources, the majority written in Spanish. The history of Melilla is remarkably well documented, partly thanks to the painstaking work of local historians, both professional and amateur. The government of the city has financed the publication of many of these works, both directly, and indirectly through the work of the Asociacion de Estudios Melillenses (Society of Melillense Studies), which runs the publication of local history journal *Trapana* since 1987. I am grateful to Vicente Moga, director of the Society, for his help and guidance in looking through the historical and cartographical archives of the city during my research.

6 See Pike (1983, chapter 7) for a detailed history of the Spanish North African presidios in English. For Spanish sources, see Calderón Vázquez, F. J. (2008), Domínguez Llosá, S. and Rivas Ahuir, M. A. (1989).

7 Alongside trade, though, the 19th century was characterised by raiding and occasionally violent conflicts across the border, concerning especially smuggled goods. For a detailed account of some of these conflicts, and how they were mediated through the legal system, see Pennell 2002.

8 See Martín Corrales, E. (1999) for a historical account of the Spanish protectorate of Morocco, and Melilla's role in it.

9 For a full account of Spain's colonial venture in Morocco during the first half of the 20th century, see Balfour 2002.

10 Census data provided by the Instituto Nacional de Estadística (National statistics institute), available at https://www.ine.es.

11 For a good, though somewhat outdated, analysis of Melilla's informal economy, see Gómez Rodilla 2007.

12 Regarding the Schengen Area, Ceuta and Melilla were included in the 1991 Protocol of Accession of Spain to the Schengen Agreement as exceptions, where visa requirements could be waived on condition of imposing strict controls at the port and airport of the city to avoid migrants reaching the European continent. So, in practical terms, the Schengen Area begins at the port and airport of the North African enclaves. See Castan Pinos (2008) for more details.

13 For a detailed description of Melilla's peculiar tax regime and its history, see López-Guzmán and González Fernández 2009.

14 In 2015, for example, the Spanish circus company Kanbahiota put on a clown performance by the border fence (https://elpais.com/politica/2015/04/13/actualidad/1428929204_209704.html), and a year earlier, in 2014, actress Jil Love posed next to the fence in a white nightgown and covered in fake blood for a photoshoot to 'raise awareness' (https://elfarodemelilla.es/la-actriz-jil-love-exige-que-se-retire-la-concertina-de-la-valla-de-melilla).

References

Andersson, Ruben. 2014. *Illegality, Inc: Clandestine migration and the business of bordering Europe*. Oakland: University of California Press

Ardener, Edwin. 2012 [1987]. 'Remote Areas: Some Theoretical Considerations'. *HAU: Journal of Ethnographic Theory* 2 (1): 519–33. https://doi.org/10.14318/hau2.1.023

Aziza, Mimoun. 'Entre Nador et Melilla, une frontière européenne en terre marocaine: Analyse des relations transfrontalières'. Presentation at *Vivre et tracer les frontières dans les mondes contemporains,* Tangier, 31 January–2 February 2008.

Balfour, Sebastian. 2002. *Deadly Embrace*. Oxford: Oxford University Press.

Bravo Nieto, Antonio. 1996. *La construcción de una ciudad europea en el contexto norteafricano: Arquitectos e ingenieros en la Melilla contemporánea*. Melilla: Universidad de Málaga.

Bunes Ibarra, Miguel Angel de. 1995. 'La presencia española en el norte de África: Las diversas justificaciones de las conquistas del Maghreb'. *Aldaba: revista del Centro Asociado a la UNED de Melilla* 25: 13–35.

Calderón Vázquez, Francisco José. 2008. *Fronteras, identidad, conflicto e interacción. Los presidios españoles en el norte africano*. Electronic edition. www.eumed.net/libros/2008c/433.

Castan Pinos, Jaume. 2008. *Building Fortress Europe? Schengen and the Cases of Ceuta and Melilla*. CIBR-Working Papers in Border Studies/WP10. Belfast: Centre for International Border Research, Queen's University Belfast.

Castro Maestro, Angel. 2003. 'Melilla… Hacia la ciudad: Melilla en los albores del siglo XX'. *Akros* (2): 39–44.

Del Sarto, Raffaella A. 2010. 'Borderlands: The Middle East and North Africa as the EU's Southern Buffer Zone'. In *Mediterranean Frontiers: Borders, Conflict and Memory in a Transnational World*, edited by Dimitar Bechev and Kalypso Nicolaidis. London: IB Tauris.

Domínguez Llosá, Santiago, and Maria de los Angeles Rivas Ahuir. 1989. 'Notas sobre el Presidio de Melilla (mediados del siglo XVII a 1906)'. *Trápana: Revista de la Asociación de Estudios Melillenses* 3 (3–4): 21–26.

Driessen, Henk. 1992. *On the Spanish-Moroccan Frontier: A Study in Ritual, Power and Ethnicity*. Oxford: Berg.

Ferrer-Gallardo, Xavier. 2007. 'Border Acrobatics between the European Union and Africa. The Management of Sealed-off Permeability on the Borders of Ceuta and Melilla'. In *Borderlands: Comparing Border Security in North America and Europe*, edited by Emmanuel Brunet-Jailly, 75–93. Ottawa: University of Ottawa Press.

Gómez Rodilla, Israel, ed. 2007. *La Economía Sumergida en la Ciudad Autónoma de Melilla*. Salamanca: ZIES Investigación y Consultoría.

Green, Sarah F. 2012. 'A Sense of Border: The Story So Far'. In *A Companion to Border Studies*, edited by Thomas M. Wilson and Hastings Donnan. Chichester: Wiley Blackwell.

Harms, Erik, Shafqat Hussein, Sasha Newell, Charles Piot, Louisa Schein, Sara Shneiderman, Terence S. Turner, and Juan Zhang. 2014. 'Remote and Edgy: New Takes on Old Anthropological Themes'. *HAU: Journal of Ethnographic Theory* 4 (1): 361–81. https://doi.org/10.14318/hau4.1.020

Hart, David M. 1976. *The Aith Waryaghar of the Moroccan Rif: An Ethnography and History*. Tucson, AZ: University of Arizona Press.

Hauswedell, Tessa, Axel Körner, and Ulrich Tiedau. 2019. *Re-Mapping Centre and Periphery Asymmetrical Encounters in European and Global Contexts*. Los Angeles, CA: UCL Press.

Herzfeld, Michael. 2005. *Cultural Intimacy: Social Poetics in the Nation-State*. London: Routledge.

López-Guzmán, Tomás, and Virgilio González Fernández. 2009. 'Melilla: Fiscalidad Local y Actividad Comercial. Una Reflexión'. *Boletín Económico de ICE* (2958): 37–43.

Martín Corrales, Eloy. 1999. 'El Protectorado Español en Marruecos (1912–1956): Una perspectiva histórica'. In *España en Marruecos (1912–1956): Discursos geográficos e intervención territorial*, edited by Joan Nogué and José Luis Villanova, 145–58. Lleida: Editorial Milenio.

Massey, Doreen. 2005. *For Space*. London: Sage Publications.

McMurray, David A. 2001. *In and out of Morocco: Smuggling and Migration in a Frontier Boomtown*. Minneapolis, MN: University of Minnesota Press.

Moga Romero, Vicente. 1988. 'Datos para la historia del "Rotary Club" de Melilla (1933/1936)'. *Trápana: Revista de la Asociación de Estudios Melillenses* 2 (2): 62–68.

Munson, Henry. 1989. 'On the Irrelevance of the Segmentary Lineage Model in the Moroccan Rif'. *American Anthropologist*, New Series, 91 (2): 386–400.

Pennell, C.R. 2002. 'Law on a Wild Frontier: Moroccans in the Spanish Courts in Melilla in the Nineteenth Century'. *The Journal of North African Studies* 7 (3): 67–78. https://doi.org/10.1080/13629380208718474

Pike, Ruth. 1983. *Penal Servitude in Early Modern Spain*. Madison, WI: University of Wisconsin Press. http://libro.uca.edu/pservitude/pservitude.htm

Ponce Gómez, Adela A. 1988. 'El Término Jurisdiccional de Melilla'. *Trápana: Revista de la Asociación de Estudios Melillenses* 2 (2): 93–97.

Saro Gandarillas, Francisco. 1984. 'Municipalidad y Administración Local, antecedentes a la Constitución del Ayuntamiento de Melilla'. *Aldaba: revista del Centro Asociado de la UNED de Melilla* 3: 27–40.

Saxer, Martin, and Ruben Andersson. 2019. 'The Return of Remoteness: Insecurity, Isolation and Connectivity in the New World Disorder'. *Social Anthropology* 27 (2): 140–55. https://doi.org/10.1111/1469-8676.12652

Seddon, David. 1981. *Moroccan Peasants: A Century of Change in the Eastern Rif, 1870–1970*.Folkestone: Dawson.

Shryock, Andrew, ed. 2004. *Off Stage/On Display: Intimacy and Ethnography in the Age of Public Culture*. Stanford, CA: Stanford University Press.

Simmel, Georg. 1950. 'The Stranger'. In *The Sociology of Georg Simmel*, edited by Kurt Wolff. New York, NY: Free Press.

Soto Bermant, Laia. 2015. 'A Tale of Two Cities: The Production of Difference in a Mediterranean Border Enclave'. *Social Anthropology/Anthropologie Sociale* 23 (4): 450–64. https://doi.org/10.1111/1469-8676.12266

Soto Bermant, Laia. 2017. 'The Mediterranean Question: Europe and its Predicaments in the Southern Peripheries'. In *The Borders of 'Europe': Autonomy of Migration, Tactics of Bordering*, edited by Nicholas De Genova. Durham, NC: Duke University Press.

Suárez Navas, Liliana. 2004. *Rebordering the Mediterranean: Boundaries and Citizenship in Southern Europe*. Oxford: Berghahn Books.

Tsing, Anna L. 2005. *Friction. An Ethnography of Global Connection*. Princeton, NJ: Princeton University Press.

CHAPTER 4

The Mediterranean (A)bridged
A View from Nafpaktos, Also Known as Lepanto

Phaedra Douzina-Bakalaki

University of Helsinki

Abstract

The Battle of Lepanto took place in 1571, when the allied naval forces of the Holy League engaged the Ottoman fleet at the gulf of Corinth–Patras, near modern Nafpaktos, a western Greek town of 20,000 people. The Catholic victory resonated across Europe, to capture the imagination of Renaissance composers and poets, to inspire important artwork, and to leave an indelible mark on Miguel de Cervantes, whose left hand 'became useless at the Battle of Lepanto, to glorify the right one', as he is quoted to have said. Today, Lepanto holds a prominent place in Islamophobic discourses and alt-right formations across Europe and North America. Yet, unlike commemorators who rejoice in divisions between the enlightened Christian West and barbaric Rest, my Nafpaktian interlocutors are more ambiguously positioned vis-à-vis these binaries. In fact, rather than celebrating Lepanto's contemporary symbolism, Nafpaktos's claim to the battle is premised on location, and on the town's proximity to the site of the naval engage-

How to cite this book chapter:
Douzina-Bakalaki, Phaedra. 2022. 'The Mediterranean (A)bridged: A View from Nafpaktos, Also Known as Lepanto'. In *Locating the Mediterranean: Connections and Separations across Space and Time,* edited by Carl Rommel and Joseph John Viscomi, 77–101. Helsinki: Helsinki University Press. DOI: https://doi.org/10.33134/HUP-18-4.

ment. This chapter examines Nafpaktians' quests for a meaningful location-driven narrative on the Battle of Lepanto. Tracing the mutual co-production of relative location and historical event – Nafpaktos and Lepanto – the chapter draws attention to the different Mediterraneans afforded by such processes of creative synthesis.

Introduction

'For all the century of dreams that has gone into it, [the Rio–Antirio Bridge] looks a fine example of linking nowhere much to nowhere at all', wrote The Economist in July 2004.[1] The spectacular bridge crosses the Corinthian Gulf and connects the peninsula of the Peloponnese to mainland Greece. The bridge spans 2,880 metres and features a much-celebrated multi-span cable-stayed design – one of the longest of its kind in the world. Among the first to cross it were torchbearers of the 2004 Athens Olympics, including Otto Rehhagel, the German football coach who led Greece to the victorious final of the 2004 European Championship. The flamboyance of the early 2000s, however, soon gave way to relentless austerity, and national elation turned into fierce condemnation. Having cost the state a staggering €770 million, many considered the Rio–Antirio Bridge to be yet another culprit of the Greek economic crisis.

I first crossed the Rio–Antirio Bridge on 7 October 2017 on my way to Nafpaktos, into which the bridge opens. Nafpaktos, also known by its Venetian name Lepanto, is a town of 20,000 people. Its picturesque port features an impressive fortress, its central street is filled with shops, and its main square offers plenty of tavernas. Once outside the centre of the town, however, the sight of bankrupt businesses and decrepit buildings is common. Caught within the aftermath of the crisis, while also brimming with beauty, Nafpaktos resembles several other Greek coastal towns. And, yet, a large sign by the harbour leading to 'Cervantes Park' also gives sense of Nafpaktos's unlikeness. What brought the Spaniard to the 'land of nowhere' and what did he accomplish here to deserve an entire park in his honour? I followed the path indicated by the sign, and soon found myself in front of a statue of Miguel de Cervantes. His figure is slim and his posture proud. His left arm holds a sword, while his right arm is raised to the sky. The sign below reads:

To Cervantes (1547–1616), the universal literary spirit of Spain, who always carried with pride his wounds from the Battle of Lepanto.

To the eternal memory of the greatest battle in the history of the rowing navy, and the most solemn judgment of the Mediterranean people to reject war and collectively establish peace.

The Battle of Lepanto was the product of competing claims over the Mediterranean basin, at a time of westward Ottoman expansion and deep European divisions following the Protestant reformation. The Ottoman invasion of Venetian colonies in Cyprus in 1570 forced Venice to appeal for aid to the relentless reformer and inquisitor Pope Pius V. In spite of conflicting interests among parties, Pius V was eventually able to arrange a coalition for the protection of Catholic colonies and commercial hubs. The Holy League was a fragile alliance between the Republic of Venice, the Spanish Empire, the Papal States, the Republic of Genoa, and several other smaller states and military orders. It was led by Don Jon of Austria, half-brother of King Philip II. After an expedition past Naples, Messina, and Corfu, the allied Catholic fleet reached the island of Cephalonia on 4 October 1571, where they received news of the fall of the Venetian colony of Famagusta in Cyprus and of the Ottomans' movements in the Corinthian Gulf, near modern-day Nafpaktos, which at the time was under Ottoman occupation. Three days later, Sultan Selim II ordered Muezzinzade Ali Pasha and his fleet to leave their naval station in Lepanto. In the meantime, the Catholic armada had begun its journey eastwards. The two fleets met soon afterwards. The naval engagement resulted in the severe defeat of the Ottomans, as well as the death of some 40,000 soldiers and sailors from both sides.

The victory of the Holy League resonated across Catholic Europe, to capture the imagination of Renaissance composers and poets, to inspire artwork by Titian, Tintoretto, and Veronese, and to leave an indelible mark on Miguel de Cervantes, whose left hand 'became useless at the Battle of Lepanto, to glorify the right one', as he is quoted to have said. Despite this immediate climate of elation, however, the long-term impact of the battle has been controversial. In *The Mediterranean and the Mediterranean World in the Age of Philip II*, Fernand Braudel writes that 'historians have joined in an impressively unanimous chorus to say that Lepanto was a great spectacle, a glorious one even, but in the end leading nowhere' (1949, 1088). The weak and exhausted Catholic allies failed to repeat the triumph of Lepanto in the following year and eventually disintegrated. The Ottomans, on the other hand, were quick to restore their naval forces and continue their mostly uninterrupted raids across the Mediterranean for another decade. Yet Braudel sees the battle as having marked the end of Christendom's prolonged period of depression, driven by the Ottomans' supremacy (1949; cf. Hess 1972). In fact, Braudel writes that, 'if we look beneath the events, beneath that glittering layer on the surface of history, we shall find that the ripples of Lepanto spread silently, inconspicuously, far and wide' (1949, 1088).

In certain ways, the ripples of Lepanto continue to spread far and wide. A quick Google search leaves no doubt about Lepanto's contemporary symbolism and centrality in Islamophobic discourse (Betz and Meret 2009). The US invasion of Afghanistan is said to have taken place on 7 October 2001 in order to allude to the battle's stakes and outcomes. Matteo Salvini, leader of Italy's far-right League, often holds his press conferences against artwork that depicts the naval engagement. Plenty of alt-right and neofascist clubs across Europe and North America are named after the battle, as are several anti-Islamic mobilisations. The gathering of one million Catholics in Poland on 7 October 2017 to memorialise the event and protest against immigration is case in point (see also Buchowski 2017). In these commemorations, the Battle of Lepanto acquires mythological dimensions and features as a highly symbolic episode in the 'clash of civilisations' (Buttigieg 2007). Additionally, it draws a sharp division between the enlightened Christian West and barbaric Rest and allies the former against the latter in a war believed to be immemorial.

The material presented in this chapter also concerns the celebration of the Battle of Lepanto. Unlike commemorators who rejoice in cultural divisions and religious conflicts, however, my Nafpaktian interlocutors were more ambivalently positioned vis-à-vis these binaries. In fact, rather than celebrating the battle's contemporary political symbolism, Nafpaktos's claim to the battle is premised on location and, more specifically, on the town's geographical proximity to the site of the naval engagement. That the battle took place close to modern-day Nafpaktos, in the region that was once known as Lepanto, did not explain much on its own. I argue, instead, that it provided Nafpaktians with a riddle as to how the historical event was to be integrated within a meaningful narrative that took location both as a point of departure and a destination.

In *Corsican Fragments*, Matei Candea challenges the assumptions of expansion and complexity that lie in original formations of multisited ethnography, on the basis that the displacement of the delimited field site in favour of multisitedness merely recasts and upscales methodological convictions in holism and closure (2010, 9–39; see also Moore 2004). The concept of the 'arbitrary location', by contrast, recognises that even the most bounded of field sites are enmeshed in multisitedness, since they are always linked to a variety of 'wholes, elsewhens, and elsewheres' (Candea 2010, 36), and thus constitute 'relative locations' (Green 2005; see Chapter 1). Additionally, 'arbitrary location' allows one to move a step further, and to invert the dominant logic that has been treating place as a mere avenue towards the study of abstracted Weberian ideal types. In Candea's words,

> While the ideal type allows one to connect and compare separate instances, the arbitrary location allows one to reflect on and rethink conceptual entities, to challenge their coherence and their totalising aspirations. … If the ideal type is meaning that cuts through space, the arbitrary location is space that cuts through meaning. (2010, 34–35)

By Candea's logic, there is no reason to assume that any location is more multisited or arbitrary than the rest. Nonetheless, I suggest that the commemoration of the Battle of Lepanto in Nafpaktos is a case study into the (un)making of meaning by means of geographical contingency and, indeed, arbitrariness. Absent from official Greek historiography, mass education, and dominant narratives of nationhood and Orthodoxy, the Battle of Lepanto generated space that begged to be attached to meaning. In the story I recount here, therefore, the almighty event does not constitute a historical backdrop or a reservoir of fixed meanings. Rather, in what follows, I examine the mutual co-production of relative location and historical event, Nafpaktos and Lepanto, and I draw particular attention to the different Mediterraneans afforded by such processes of co-production.

Drawing on interviews, participant observation, and Nafpaktos's local press, I examine three different instantiations of this location-driven meaning-making process. First, I examine the institution of the battle's annual celebration in the late 1990s and I trace the emergence of two competing Marian icons that served to distil the relationship between town and battle, first in terms of divine causality and, second, in terms of secular retrospection. I then turn to 'Roads of Lepanto', an inter-town network that sought to frame the battle as cultural heritage, and I pay particular attention to tensions between evocations of pan-Mediterranean heritage and contemporary political configurations. Lastly, I examine the battle's re-enactment and, more specifically, the dressing-up of Nafpaktians into 16th-century Ottomans and Europeans. This, I suggest, offers snapshots into what arbitrariness, as performance and spectacle, might look like.

The tripartite equation that Nafpaktians have had to work through in their quest for a meaningful narrative on the Battle of Lepanto, made of location, region, and event, has yielded different solutions over the years. In whatever way these three elements have come to be joined and arranged, however, they have also transformed in themselves. When the battle's outcome is attributed to Nafpaktos's Orthodox patroness, the town transforms into a determining agent of European and Mediterranean history. When the battle comes to be tailored to cultural policy schemes, the town is envisioned as an important hub of Mediterranean heritage. Lastly, when the battle transforms into spectacle, Nafpaktos provides a vantage point from where the event can non-combatantly be observed and Mediterranean history can be put into perspective. In each case, the Battle of Lepanto, its stakes, and its legacy become arranged concentrically – their centre, of course, being Nafpaktos, while the Mediterranean emerges as a set of variously conceived (dis)connections between shifting parts and wholes.

Lepanto of Miracles and History

In *The Invention of Tradition*, Eric Hobsbawm (1983) writes of the invocation of factitious continuities with an (imagined) past. To invent a tradition, according to Hobsbawm, means to establish and ritualise historical perpetuity by way of repetition and invariance. The weekly newspaper Embros tells us a great deal about the tenacious efforts made toward the creation of what today constitutes Nafpaktos's trademark tradition. While the presidential decree that established the annual anniversary of the historical event was passed in 1981 (Decree 599/1981), the first official commemoration of the event was not held until 18 years later, in October 1999. In the months preceding the celebration, the local newspaper featured several articles dedicated to the event, its historical significance, and contemporary value. Translated excerpts from G. K. Chesterton's poem 'Lepanto' stood next to commentaries written by local connoisseurs, and copies of Renaissance artwork stood next to paintings made by some of Nafpaktos's elementary students.

Of particular interest is an article written by Yiannis Chalatsis, head of Nafpaktos's library, author of several books on the region's history, and invaluable interlocutor. The article, published on 30 April 1999 and titled 'Historical Void in Nafpaktos', elaborates on the dangers entailed in failing to pay due tribute to the landmark event.[2] Scrutinising local authorities, 'who are unable to grasp the magnitude of the battle and its significance for our town', Chalatsis makes a number of recommendations that will help fill this 'historical void'. Among others, he advocates the organisation of a scientific conference dedicated to the event, the installation of a monument, and the opening of a museum. Chalatsis concludes his article by noting that Nafpaktos's 'historical void' is so vast that others have been filling it to their advantage. It was the neighbouring town of Messolonghi, rather than Nafpaktos, that celebrated the Battle of Lepanto the year before, Chalatsis bitterly observes.

But, as it turned out, the first official commemoration was anything but a success. In the weeks following the event, Embros featured photographs of empty chairs accompanied by castigating commentaries on the absence of both residents and important local figures.[3] This climate of failure appears to have stemmed from the unavailability of convenient narratives that would connect place and event in meaningful terms and, more specifically, from the battle's discordance with culturally salient registers of nationhood and Orthodoxy. As Mr Chalatsis explained to me, 'people thought "Neither did Greece exist in 1571, nor were the conquerors Orthodox, so what is point?" People back then couldn't see beyond their noses'. In short, despite the legitimacy granted by the town's geographical proximity to the site of the naval engagement, it was not clear what this 'historical void' should be stuffed with and how this 'invented tradition' should re-envision Nafpaktos's past and present.

But, while this general sense of confusion appears to have deterred some, it most certainly propelled others, for soon Nafpaktos's annual celebration of the Battle of Lepanto transformed into an object of contentious debate and conflicting visions. The local press of the early 2000s is replete with references to the bifurcation of the commemoration and the emergence of two competing celebrations. 'The Municipality [celebrates] history ... the Monastery [celebrates] the miracle!' reads the title of an article published by Embros in September 2001.[4] The tension between 'miracle' and 'history' concerned two Marian icons, used in the respective events staged by the Municipality of Nafpaktos and the Orthodox Monastery of the Transfiguration of the Saviour (henceforth the Municipality and the Monastery). On a more general level, the tension reflects the creative labour that went towards weaving meaning into an historical event that had previously been nested in opacity and ambivalence.

The fact that two Marian icons were at the heart of the dispute between the Municipality and the Monastery is not surprising. The figure of the Virgin Mary is intricately linked with the Battle of Lepanto. In the days preceding the naval engagement, Pope Pius V is said to have asked Catholics to pray to the rosary and to have led rosary processions in Rome. After accrediting the unexpected victory of the Holy League to the divine intervention of the Virgin Mary, the Pope instituted the annual feast of Our Lady of the Rosary. The feast is celebrated up to date throughout the Roman Catholic world on 7 October. Links between the Battle of Lepanto and the Virgin Mary have also been established through a Marian icon that was carried by the mast of the galley led by Venetian admiral Sebastiano Venier. The origins and current location of the icon, known as Madonna di Lepanto, formed the topic of heated debate in Nafpaktos during the late 1990s and early 2000s. Additionally, they generated two competing narrativisations that distilled the Battle of Lepanto: first, as a matter of historiography and, second, as a deed of divine intervention, thus calling to mind Hirsch and Stewart's distinction between 'historicism' and 'historicity'. Whereas the former isolates the past and separates it from the present, the latter:

> is not concerned with objectivity, accuracy and factuality in local accounts of the past, but rather with recovering all of the social and cultural assumptions with which a people imbue these accounts. In short, the ethnographer investigates social ideologies of history/the past and substantive representations of the past as cultural forms to be understood in relation to the social life of the community. (Hirsch and Stewart 2005, 268)

So far, the events organised by the Municipality have included talks, art exhibitions, sailing races, chess tournaments, the re-enactment of the event, and an annual procession and memorial service for the Catholics killed in battle. The Monastery, on the other hand, holds a separate celebration. This consists of a vigil, mass, and litany on the 'day of the holy miracle'. At the centre of the events organised by the Municipality is the 'Icon of the Battle' (eikona tis Navmachias), depicting the Virgin Mary surrounded by angels and leaning over the Corinthian Gulf. The icon was commissioned by the mayor in the late 1990s and was partly funded by the concessionaires of the Rio–Antirio Bridge, who continue to sponsor the Municipality's cultural initiatives up to date. At the centre of the Monastery's celebration, on the other hand, is the 'Icon of the Virgin Mary of Nafpaktos', also known as eikona tis Panayias Nafpaktiotissas. Unlike the 'Icon of the Battle', which is often referred to as a 'modern-day synthesis', thus alluding to the retrospective addition of the Orthodox Mary in the scene of the battle, that of Panayia Nafpaktiotissa is claimed to have played a decisive role in the battle's very outcome.

According to the Monastery, the icon of Panayia Nafpaktiotissa is closely related to Sebastiano Venier's icon of Madonna di Lepanto. In some versions of the narrative, the two icons are claimed to be identical. In others, the latter is seen as a copy of the former.[5] In the Monastery's account of events, the Venetians only began to worship the Virgin Mary during their occupation of Nafpaktos between 1407 and 1499, when the area was a Venetian exclave in Ottoman territory. This was a decisive time for the Catholics not only because they were exposed to the Orthodox tradition, which places special importance on the Virgin Mary (e.g. Dubisch 1995; Hann 2011), but also because they were acquainted with the town's patroness, who is no other than Panayia Nafpaktiotissa. In short, it was thanks to Venetians' occupation of Nafpaktos that Admiral Venier decorated his galley mast with the Virgin Mary and the Pope attributed the Holy League's victory to Her.

The official articulation of this discourse can also be found in the Wikipedia entry for Panayia Nafpaktiotissa, where we read that 'the Virgin Mary of Nafpaktos became known not only in Italy, but also throughout Catholic Europe as Madonna di Lepanto'.[6] In this alternative account of events, Madonna di Lepanto is no other than an exported version of Panayia Nafpaktiotissa. Unlike the Municipality's icon, which constitutes an Orthodox interpretation of a Catholic event, the Monastery's icon collapses differences between the two Virgin Marys and attributes the battle's outcome to Orthodox intervention-cum-location (see also Baeva and Valtchinova 2009; Seraïdari 2009). In what may thus be seen as an inversion of the dominant narrative, Catholic Europe did not merely disembark in Nafpaktos in 1571 but was rather formed there in the 15th century and later exported to where it belongs today.

In their recent call for an 'anthropology of history', Palmié and Stewart (2016) note that Western notions of history were largely established in opposition to eschatological and scriptural understandings of the past. They emphasise, however, that this did not eradicate 'inspired' historicising practices or historical accounts that do not comply with standard historiography. The dispute between 'miracle' and 'history', however, is also suggestive of the assumed incompatibility that frames relationships between the two. Several articles written by local politicians and readers of Embros condemn the Monastery for manipulating history for the sake of false impressions and ultimately profit.[7] Some authors dissolve associations between Panayia Nafpaktiotissa and Venier's Madonna de Lepanto, by providing information on the icon's current location, which is speculated to be either the church of Santa Maria Formosa in Venice or the archaeological museum of Palermo. Others expose the fabrication of Panayia Nafpaktiotissa:

> Where are all those churches, chapels, hymns and doxologies in honour of 'Panayia Nafpaktiotissa'? Had anyone heard of Her before the Hegumen decided to expand his business ventures? Where are the songs and local tales that worship the Virgin Mary in question?[8]

In short, the recasting of geographical location and proximity in terms of divine causality amounted to fraud. Yet, a similar criticism was made against the icon used in the Municipality's events. In an open letter titled 'Copy?', a reader of Embros asks, 'How can an "Icon of the Battle" transform into a "Holy Icon" in procession? By this logic, we should all frame a picture of the battle and display it for worship. Or is this arbitrariness justified by the participation of the Catholic fleet in the Battle?'[9] The accusation directed against this icon is also one of fabrication, but here the opposite argument is in operation, namely that the location of the battle does not justify the Orthodoxisation of the event. The author concludes that 'these holy matters are not to be messed with'.

Whether seen from the perspective of the Municipality or that of the Monastery, the Battle of Lepanto appears to have animated a series of creative acts of bricolage (Shaw and Stewart 1994). Indeed, the Nafpaktian dispute of the two Virgin Marys is telling of the 'inventiveness' that went into what has since 1999 become an annual and unequivocal 'tradition', and the efforts made towards weaving meaning into location and geographical proximity. Insofar as the tension between 'history' and 'miracle' attached the battle to local concerns and wove the event within the symbolic universe of Orthodoxy, the battle had finally arrived home. Entangled with the deeds of local politicians, monastic authorities, and public figures, the battle had not simply taken place in Nafpaktos in 1571 but continued to unravel through its annual commemoration, its implication in competing histories, and contested representations. In this sense, inasmuch as Lepanto had been localised, location had been Lepantised, for place and event were now interlaced and joined in relations of mutuality and co-production.

Nafpaktos at the Forefront of Europe

My interlocutors' accounts of previous anniversaries were packed with cynical remarks about the squandering that took place in the so-called 'years of the fat-cows', or what Dalakoglou and Kallianos (2018) term the era of 'disjunctive modernisation'. This period lasted between the mid-1990s and the mid-2000s and was marked by mega projects and events coupled with imaginaries of Westernisation and progress. The Rio–Antirio Bridge that crosses the Corinthian Gulf, and the 2004 Athens Olympics during which the bridge was inaugurated arguably constitute epitomes of this 'golden era' (Traganou 2010; Yalouri 2010) and are telling of both the hopes that were nurtured by spectacular stagings of modernity and the fury and disappointment that ensued once these became attached to waste, scandals, and eventually austerity. The commemoration of the Battle of Lepanto appears to have followed suit both in terms of spectacle and spending. In 2000 the Municipality's ceremony was enhanced, first by the addition of a parade that takes place on the eve of the celebration, joined by locals dressed as members of the Holy League, and by the re-enactment of the battle, performed in Nafpaktos's harbour on the following evening.

Echoing these developments, the pages of Embros gradually stopped hosting controversies between 'history' and 'miracle', and reflected instead the growing ostentation of the event, suggested by an ever-increasing number of honourable guests and fireworks. According to Manos, a 50-year-old radio producer, Lepanto's celebration in the mid-2000s entailed a blend of kitsch aesthetics and corruption. Over coffee, Manos told me that the anniversary held in 2006 is rumoured to have cost an astonishing 500,000 euros. The money was spent on advanced lighting and sound technologies, a real-life-sized replica of a galley, and imported gondolas from Venice, which arrived with their gondoliers. It goes without saying, Manos added, that some of this money also found its way to organisers' pockets. Drawing a comparison between the Rio–Antirio Bridge, which entails 'a first world passage into the third world', Manos described the re-enactment as 'the one day in the calendar when Nafpaktos can spend like a Northern European town'.

Soon, however, the country's booming 'industry of spectacle' came to an abrupt halt. The celebration of the battle turned rather humble in the years following the official declaration of the Greek economic crisis in 2010, but did not cease to motivate symbolic investment. In the pages of Embros the battle features as an allegorical device in analyses of the 2004 Cypriot Annan Plan referendums, Turkey's European Union accession progress, and, later, the European debt crisis. In these publications, the events that unravelled in 1571 are shown to be pertinent to today's world. Additionally, these publications entertain the idea that, courtesy of the decisive event that it once hosted, Nafpaktos has in certain ways always been at 'at the forefront of European history', as the title of an article published in October 2014 states.[10] The article proceeds to inform readers of the foundation of an ambitious inter-town network named 'Roads of Lepanto'.

With the benefit of hindsight, one might say that the network has been more successful in producing headlines than in bringing concrete benefits. In charge of the initiative is Charis Batis, a long-standing local politician in his late sixties who describes himself as 'a guardian of Nafpaktos' history and culture'. Batis recounted the conception of 'Roads of Lepanto' over a long coffee we had in October 2019. After becoming deputy mayor of cultural affairs in 2014, Batis focused his energies on securing cultural funds and soon made two important discoveries. First, the Battle of Lepanto was celebrated throughout the world, from Costa Rica to Indonesia, and from Arkansas to the Canary Islands.

Second, the battle never failed to ignite awe in his European counter-parts. In short, Batis realised that the legacy of the 16th-century event would speak straight to EU policymakers' hearts, since 'there is no European official who does not get goosebumps at the mere sound of the word "Lepanto"'. In response, Batis began plotting a network that would connect several locations spread around the Mediterranean that would collectively commemorate the event, but also mobilise Euro-pean cultural heritage funds.

Cris Shore observes that, over the years, the European Union has undergone 'a shift in emphasis from integration, perceived as a rational by-product of economic prosperity and legal harmonisation, to more recent concerns about integration as a cultural process, and "culture" as a political instrument for furthering that construction process' (2000, 1). EU elites' efforts at inventing Europe as a common 'civilisa-tion' and constructing a shared European identity, took varied forms, ranging from the creation of new symbols to the dissemination of audio-visual materials, and the establishment of European-sponsored campaigns and events, such as public holidays, sporting competitions, and university exchange projects. Key to these endeavours was also the production of a robust body of EU historiography that sought both to combat divisive nationalist ideologies and to frame European culture in terms of 'shared heritage, moral ascendancy, and cultural continuity' (2000, 57). Shore's survey of related materials is illuminat-ing. The rewriting of history from a 'European perspective' essentially involved the articulation of a highly selective tale of evolutionary pro-gress and moral success that began with classical antiquity, narrated the spread of Christianity, the Renaissance, the Enlightenment, and the French Revolution, and concluded with the advent of liberal democ-racy. The end result, Shore argues, was a culturally racist reinvention of Europe as being 'set apart (and beyond) others by Christianity, sci-ence, the Caucasian race, and the Indo-European family of languages' (2000, 62), and as having successfully defended itself against variously defined significant Others, and most notably Islam.

The rationale behind the Roads of Lepanto, and Batis's faith that the historical event would bring Nafpaktos and other participating members a good fair of European resources, becomes all the more meaningful in light of Shore's analysis. As Batis remarked, pointing to the symbolic potency of the event, 'There exists no European city that hasn't named a square, a street, a station, or a museum after Lepanto.'

Indeed, the idea that others have been making better use of Lepanto was omnipresent throughout our conversations with Batis. Eager to show me celebrations from faraway places and to forward related articles published in the national newspapers of Spain, Italy, and Malta, Batis appeared convinced that Nafpaktos's Southern European counterparts were better at 'being' Lepanto than Lepanto itself. In addition, while Batis acknowledged that Nafpaktos had found itself at the centre of this (hi)story by mere chance, he also believed that the time to reclaim it had finally come.

The process of recasting Lepanto onto Nafpaktos, however, generated the need for a narrative that would be widely relevant, but also vehemently local (see also Papagaroufali 2008). In essence, this meant supplementing, if not dissolving, existing associations that obscure the location of the event. In short, for Lepanto to come home, the story needed to be retold and, rather than being a story about 'Europe' and the 'Ottomans', or Catholics and Muslims, it also needed to become one about Nafpaktos. In a triumphant article published in August 2016, Batis reports that dozens of Southern European towns, cities, and organisations expressed their interest in the Roads of Lepanto, as well as the cultural funds and tourist promotion the network promised to deliver. Batis concludes that 'it is of outmost importance that Nafpaktos, its culture, and needs extend beyond the borders of Rio-Antirio, to become known across the widths and lengths of the Mediterranean'.[11]

The popularity of 'Roads of Lepanto', however, came at a cost. The project, which had thus far been tailored to EU imaginaries of cultural heritage, soon became entangled in the 'politics of memory' and its tendency to conflate history and nation, and map the former onto the latter (Boyarin 1994; see also Wimmer and Glick Schiller 2002). First came a phone call from the ambassador of Croatia, who reminded Batis of Croatians' heroic participation in the battle, which has also been immortalised in the form of an honorary plaque that has been erected 'in memory of Croatian soldiers and sailors who fought in 1571'. The plaque, which sits next to several others spread throughout Nafpaktos's Venetian fortress, was put up in 2006. Although Batis was not directly involved in the negotiations, he remembered that the plaque's installation was met by state officials' resistance. The problem, he explained, lay with Greco-Serbian ties and Greece's support of Serbia during the Yugoslav Wars. In short, the recasting of the 1571 event onto today's political map proved to be complicated, for an event that predated the sovereign nation state had to accommodate to its logic and comply to contemporary alliances that, in Batis's view, did not reflect the associations of the past.

Then came phone calls, letters, and even visits from diplomats and ambassadors from Northern Macedonia, Albania, Bosnia and Herzegovina, Montenegro, and Ukraine, who provided proof of their countries' participation in the event and requested membership. Batis was instructed by state officials to avoid discussions with countries that do not belong in the EU, but struggled with this settlement; 'Can we reject these peoples only because they are not members of the EU?' he asked rhetorically. Batis was also approached by the 'representatives of the Ottomans', as he referred to ambassadors of Turkey, Lebanon, Morocco, Tunisia, Algeria, and Libya. His efforts to confine the network to EU Member States were met by the Egyptian ambassador's discontent: 'Can we have a conversation about the Second World War without the participation of the Germans? The defeated also deserve a place in the table.' Finally, Batis remembered being contacted by representatives of Marine Le Pen and Matteo Salvini, who 'were after a different, more dangerous message' that was undesirable not only because of its far-right and Islamophobic content but also because it did not serve the purpose of 'putting Nafpaktos on the map'. In short, Batis felt that what he had envisioned as an initiative premised on location had become co-opted by nationalist claims and religious fanaticism. The desired outcome, by contrast, would have been:

> A Euro-Mediterranean alliance among all those towns soaked by the Mediterranean Sea, all those people who in 1571, found themselves in Lepanto by whatever chance. But as it happens, even 450 years later the Battle of Lepanto continues to ignite passions.

After several negotiations with representatives of Ministry of Foreign Affairs and other state officials, Batis was forced to confine the network to EU member countries. From now on, the network would be called 'From the Battle of Lepanto to the European Union'. The mission statement was signed in August 2016 in Messina, while the statute was signed on 15 October 2016 in Nafpaktos. Members of the board included towns in Italy, Spain, Cyprus, Slovakia, and Germany. The presidency would always be held by Nafpaktos. Unsatisfied with this outcome, which obscured the pan-Mediterraneaness of Lepanto, Batis soon devised a new plan:

> I am now exploring new avenues. Imagine a virtual museum of the Battle of Lepanto, spread throughout the Mediterranean. The image will be identical, the event happened here in Nafpaktos, but the narrator will be a hologram. How can I dictate the events to an Arab or Turk? The holographic narrator will narrate the Battle in whatever way he wishes. After all, semiologically, the Battle of Lepanto means everything and anything you can imagine.

As metaphor, the 'hologram' forecloses closure, insofar as it constantly changes depending on where one stands in relation to it, and thus challenges monolithic narrativisations (Bunzl 2003; Johnston 2016). Location, in this sense, is crucial in holographic representations. Indeed, more than anything, Batis's envisioned holographic narrator appears to serve the purpose of showcasing location. If 'Roads of Lepanto' failed, then that was because the initiative was unable to outweigh dominant representations of the historical event and to detach it from European-cum-Christian imaginaries of cultural heritage and the logic of the nation state. By contrast, in Batis's holographic rendition of the event, interpretations of the historical event are allowed to multiply exponentially and thus lose their totalising aspirations. Seen from the perspective of Candea's 'arbitrary location', 'whose messiness, contingency, and lack of an overarching coherence or meaning serve as a "control" for a broader abstract object' (2010, 34), Batis's holographic vision can be understood as a manifesto of arbitrariness. The only fixed point in this otherwise deeply fragmentary story is the event's location, which is no other than Nafpaktos.

Performing Lepanto

By seven in the afternoon on Friday, 6 October 2017, the traffic of Nafpaktos had subsided and hundreds of people had gathered by the pavements of the empty streets. Half an hour later, the local philharmonic orchestra arrived at the Town Hall under the sound of pompous march. The orchestra was followed by a long parade of people dressed in what looked like a carnivalesque parody of 16th-century European apparel, featuring colourful corsets, farthingales, and capes, and holding all

Image 4.1: Members of Nafpaktos' annual parade, dressed as members of the Holy League.
Photo: Lena Malm.

sorts of torches, flags, and banners, adorned with Christian symbols (see Image 4.1). The members of the parade, mainly women of varying ages, had a mix of embarrassment and indulgence on their faces. When I got the opportunity to ask them about their participation, their responses pointed to a certain light-heartedness: 'I only participate for the dress,' said a teenage girl glowing with pride. Less pleased, her younger brother murmured that his mum dressed him like that. Three middle-aged women hurriedly stated that they participated only because they wanted to support the municipality's initiative, and then asked me to take a picture of them. A young man smirked and said, 'Greeks never miss a chance to party!' Once the parade reached the local authorities and visiting politicians standing by the Town Hall's entrance, one of its members left the crowd and opened an oversized papyrus:

> Hear hear! Tomorrow, 7 October, at the gulf of Nafpaktos, the United Christian forces of the Holy League and its 206 galleys, 6 galleasses, and 70 frigates, commanded by the Spanish admiral Don John of Austria, will encounter the Ottoman fleet, and its 200 galleys and 63 galliots,

commanded by Muezzinzade Ali Pasha. Tomorrow the future of Europe will be judged!

Two years later, in October 2019, I was introduced to Vassilis, the battle's crier since 2009. An actor of 50 years, Vassilis was eager to convey his left-wing convictions and activist past. He emphasised that he could not care less about the battle, or any other military event. When I probed him on his participation, he pointed that his only task was to announce the event. This, he said, made him a mere observer rather than an active participant in this 'kitsch and ahistorical fiesta'. He added that his training in acting had equipped him with a good understanding of the difference between performing and being. 'And anyway,' he added, 'we perform our liberators, not ourselves, since we did not even exist back then.' Vassilis's view was also shared by Andreas, a 30-year-old IT specialist, amateur photographer, actor, and enthusiastic participant in the battle's re-enactment. Andreas insisted that:

> The event is irrelevant to any national consciousness, since it is neither taught in school nor celebrated like in the rest of Europe. The Greeks fought on both sides, but the Greeks, as such, do not exist in this story. We connect the event to our geographical history, but not our national history. We say, 'it happened here geographically, not nationally' and we play out the battle. I don't know how else to put it.

Both Vassilis and Andreas pointed to the fact that in 1571 Nafpaktos was an Ottoman province. Hence, the apparel worn by members of the battle re-enactment not only turned them into people of other times but also aligned them with European invaders on the one hand and Ottoman rulers on the other. According to Michael Herzfeld (1987, 111), 'Greek identity is caught between two extreme poles, each derived from the image of a conquering Other'. At one end stand the Europeans and on the other the Orientals. This 'disemia', which Herzfeld (1997) later reframed under 'cultural intimacy', has given rise to the contrasting identities of the 'Hellene' and the 'Romios', which are internalised and deployed at will in acts of collective foreign-directed self-display on the one hand and intimate self-knowledge on the other. Seen from this perspective, the annual spectacle of Lepanto can be understood as a staged encounter between the two extreme poles that Herzfeld spoke of. Rather than stimulating identifications with either pole, however, I suggest that the performed altercations between the 'Ottomans' and the 'Europeans' merely provided a location, or a vantage point, from which disemia, now turned into masquerade, could be externally observed, and arbitrariness, now turned into geography-cum-history, could be viscerally guessed.

On Saturday, 5 October 2019, the fortress of Nafpaktos stood against a magnificent cloudy landscape. Some appeared concerned by the weather. 'If it rains the celebration will fail... All this money, all in vain,' I overheard a lady whispering to herself. Equipped with loud-speakers, headlights, and projectors, the port would serve as a theatrical scenery, and the grey tones in which it was embroiled made it all the more dramatic. By noon the boats and yachts moored at the port had sailed and only two remained. The one to the west was adorned with banners carrying Jesus Christ. The one to the east carried stars and crescents. By early afternoon, the main square was packed with people and street vendors, selling balloons and cotton candy. I made my way to the harbour to secure a good spot. Soon the two fleets would confront one another against a storm of fireworks and applause (see Image 4.2).

Image 4.2: The re-enactment of the Battle of Lepanto in Nafpaktos' harbour.
Photo: Lena Malm.

I sat at one of the harbour's benches, and was soon joined by group of elderly women, who had arrived to Nafpaktos from a village of Karditsa on a daily trip organised by the local women's association. Their trip was unrelated to the re-enactment and, evidently confused, the women started asking questions among themselves: 'What are they celebrating?' 'Will it be in Greek?' 'See, it's the Christians and the Turks, today must be Nafpaktos's liberation [from the Ottomans]!' Indeed, the observation that many people are ignorant of the historical event was common among my interlocutors and was often followed by remarks on the importance of educating Nafpaktians on their history and heritage. In an article published in Embros in 2000, an elementary teacher quotes one of his students: 'Sir, if the Ottomans were defeated at the Battle, then why wasn't [the] motherland liberated in 1571?'

At nine o'clock and just when the moon had made its appearance in the cloudy sky and a light drizzle had started to fall, the lights of the port went off. Accompanied by grandiose music, the welcome speech was given in Greek, Spanish, and Italian. The story, told in great detail and performed over the course of an hour, ended as follows:

> Ali Pasha fell. The sea was painted red. Forty thousand corpses; Europeans and Turks, Christians and Muslims. But the battle was over. What had happened was truly strange, almost metaphysical. The Christians had won. The battle was over. The sun set to the West. The Christians moored at the Greek coast.

Fireworks saturated the sky. One of the women turned to the rest and asked: 'And what is there to be celebrate? We had to put up with the [Ottomans] for another three hundred years,' she said, referring to the Greek War of Independence against the Ottoman Empire, which ended in 1829. 'At least we are now done with the Ottomans, now we only have the Europeans on our heads,' her friend responded. The women greeted me goodbye soon afterwards and, looking relieved that they would soon head back home, left.

Many Nafpaktians and those staying for the night stormed into the harbour's tavernas, or partied in some of Nafpaktos's bars until the early hours. I joined some of the actors, who, still wearing their flamboyant 16th-century costumes, departed from the official script. 'It's a good thing that the story was what it was, or else I would have destroyed you!' said Muezzinzade Ali Pasha to a sailor of the Holy League, to whom the latter responded, 'Go back to your byre, you yokel; this is Europe!' The celebration was finally over. The only reminder of Lepanto the following day was the dozens of visitors having a quick breakfast before returning to wherever they had come from, and the signs, statues, and plaques scattered across Nafpaktos's harbour, generously lending themselves to guesswork. 'And who did we say Miguel de Cervantes was? He was a great Philhellene, a Spaniard who fought in 1821, in the Greek War of Independence here in Nafpaktos,' a young man said didactically to his girlfriend, while getting the bill.

Conclusion

In 1971 the International Journal of Nautical Archaeology and Underwater Exploration published an article titled 'The Battle of Lepanto Search and Survey Mission (Greece), 1971–1972'. The authors concluded that:

> The purpose of the Lepanto search and survey project was to conduct a surface reconnaissance to locate the site of the Battle of Lepanto, using acoustic and magnetometer equipment. A map of 'targets' has been produced which showed promise as possible sites of wrecks from the battle. The next step is to go down to the bottom and investigate the cause of the signal. (Throckmorton, Edgerton, and Yalouris 1973, 129)

Traces, according to Sarah Green, evoke the passage of time and 'can be fragments of the whole entity, or a physical mark of it—the crumbs left from a loaf of bread that has been eaten, or footprints in the sand' and, in this capacity, they also 'leave much room for doubt, speculation, and interpretation' (2018, 70). Put differently, being mere fragments of what once existed, traces may be arranged variously, they may enable different connections and disconnections, and yield multiple parts and wholes.

In this chapter, I have attended to the various meanings that have been attached to Lepanto's traces, in the small town of Nafpaktos, and the different ways in which these have been envisioned to form parts of a whole. I have argued that the localisation of an event of considerable recognition in fields as varied as Mediterraneanist scholarship, Catholic belief, and Islamophobic discourse, has had important implications for what the event is taken to mean. In the commemorations examined, location and event, Nafpaktos and Lepanto, are shown to be mutually coproduced. Yet the terms of their co-production vary. The Battle of Lepanto, I suggest, has been framed by narratives of secular retrospection and divine causality, tailored to EU cultural policy schemes, and transformed into disemic spectacle and masquerade. Nafpaktos, on the other hand, has transformed into a locomotive of European ascendancy, a centre of pan-Mediterranean heritage, and a vantage point from which the battle can be observed. Each of these renditions of place and event, are premised on different logics and refract different Mediterraneans. I want to suggest, however, that this does not make them incompatible or any less real. If 'arbitrary location' is 'not an object to be explained, but a contingent window into complexity' (Candea 2010, 180), then Nafpaktos, also known as Lepanto, affords a contingent window into the multiple Mediterraneans that come to be (un)made and (re)worked through situated evocations of location.

Notes

1 AP. 2004. 'Construction: A Greek Lesson', 29 July 2004. Accessed 20 June 2020. https://www.economist.com/business/2004/07/29/a-greek-lesson.
2 Χαλάτσης Γιάννης. 1999. 'Ιστορικό κενό στη Ναύπακτο. Γιατί'. Εμπρός, 30 April, p. 13.
3 For example, Unknown Author. 1999. 'Ναυμαχία…ναυαγισμένη'. Εμπρός, 15 October, p. 8.
4 Unknown Author. 2001. 'Ο δήμος την ιστορία … η μονή το θαύμα'. Εμπρός, 28 September, p. 8.
5 The links that the Monastery of the Transfiguration of the Saviour identifies between Panayia Panfpaktiotissa and Madonna di Lepanto have changed over the time. In the early 2000s, several articles published in Embros scrutinised the Monastery's claim that the icon of Panayia Panfpaktiotissa is identical to the icon of Madonna di Lepanto, carried by Sebastiano Venier's mast. Later, however, the Monastery's account appears to have shifted its focus from the icon per se to the broader figure of the Virgin Mary, and its pervasive historical links to Nafpaktos. Today, the official website of the Monastery makes detailed reference to a byzantine parchment located in the archives of Regia Capella Palatina in Palermo, Sicily. The parchment carries a copy of an icon named 'Hyperayia Theotokos Nafpaktissis', which is claimed to have decorated an 11th-century monastery of central Greece, and a statute signed by members of a religious society that was established in 1048. The parchment is speculated to have been stolen from its original location during the Norman invasion of Thiva in 1147. In the Monastery's account, the parchment points to Panayia Panfpaktiotissa's widespread veneration prior to the 1571 Battle of Lepanto, and testifies to the

modelling of Madonna di Lepanto on Panayia Nafpaktiotissa. See also https://www.panagialepanto.gr. Accessed 21 June 2020.

6 Available at https://el.wikipedia.org/wiki/Παναγία Ναυπακτιώτισσα. Accessed 20 June 2020.

7 For example, Πελέκης Διονύσιος. 2000. ʻΟλίγα τινά περί Ναυμαχίαςʼ. Εμπρός, 27 October, p. 11; Μητροπολίτης Ιερόθεος. 2001. ʻΙερόθεος προς Σπυρίδωνα: Δεν μπορώ να συνεργήσω στο διχασμό … Καμία σχέση δεν έχει η «Παναγία Ναυπακτιώτισσα» με την «Madona de Lepanto»ʼ. Εμπρός, 5 October, p. 11; Ράπτης Γιάννης. 2001. ʻΗ σκοτεινή πλευρά του θαύματοςʼ. Εμπρός, 12 October, p. 12.

8 Τσούμας Πανος. 2001. ʻΚριτική στην εισήγηση του Νομάρχη για το "θαύμα"ʼ. Εμπρός, 19 October, p. 5.

9 Μαρία Φιλίππου. 2000. ʻΑντιγραφηʼ. Εμπρός, 13 October, p. 12.

10 Author Unknown. 2014. ʻΣτην αιχμή της Ευρωπαϊκής ιστορίαςʼ. Εμπρός, 3 October, pp. 12–13.

11 Ράπτης Γιάννης. 2016. ʻΑπό τη ναυμαχία στους «Δρόμους του Lepanto»ʼ. Εμπρός, 7 October, pp. 12–13.

References

Baeva, Vihra, and Galia Valtchinova. 2009. ʻA Women's Religious Organization in Southern Bulgaria: From Miracle Stories to Historyʼ. *History and Anthropology* 20 (3): 317–38. https://doi.org/10.1080/02757200903112503

Betz, Hans-Georg, and Susi Meret. 2009. ʻRevisiting Lepanto: The Political Mobilization against Islam in Contemporary Western Europeʼ. *Patterns of Prejudice* 43 (3–4): 313–34. https://doi.org/10.1080/00313220903109235

Braudel, Fernand. 1949. *The Mediterranean and the Mediterranean World in the Reign of Philip II*, 2 vols. London: Fontana.

Boyarin, Jonathan. 1994. ʻSpace, Time, and the Politics of Memoryʼ. In *Remapping Memory: The Politics of Timespace*, edited by Jonathan Boyarin, 1–37. Minnesota, MN: University of Minnesota Press.

Buchowski, Michał. 2017. ʻA New Tide of Racism, Xenophobia, and Islamophobia in Europe: Polish Anthropologists Swim against the Currentʼ. *American Anthropologist* 119 (3): 519–23. https://doi.org/10.1111/aman.12915

Bunzl, Matti. 2003. ʻOf Holograms and Storage Areas: Modernity and Postmodernity at Vienna's Jewish Museumʼ. Cultural Anthropology 18 (4): 435–68.

Buttigieg, Emanuel. 2007. ʻ"Clash of Civilizations", Crusades, Knights and Ottomans: An Analysis of Christian-Muslim Interaction in the Mediterraneanʼ. In *Religion and Power in Europe: Conflict and Convergence*, edited by Joaquim Cavalho: 203–20. Pisa: Pisa University Press.

Candea, Matei. 2010. *Corsican Fragments: Difference, Knowledge, and Fieldwork*. Bloomington, IN: Indiana University Press.

Dalakoglou, Dimitris, and Yannis Kallianos. 2018. ʻ"Eating Mountains" and "Eating Each Other": Disjunctive Modernization, Infrastructural Imaginaries and Crisis in Greeceʼ. *Political Geography* 67: 76–87. https://doi.org/10.1016/j.polgeo.2018.08.009

Dubisch, Jill. 1995. *In a Different Place: Pilgrimage, Gender, and Politics at a Greek Island Shrine* (Vol. 40). Princeton, NJ: Princeton University Press.

Green, Sarah. 2005. *Notes from the Balkans*. Princeton, NJ: Princeton University Press.

Green, Sarah. 2018. 'Lines, Borders, and Tidemarks: Further Reflections of Forms of Border'. In *The Political Materialities of Borders: New Theoretical Directions*, edited by Olga Demetriou and Rozita Dimova. Manchester: Manchester University Press.

Hann, Chris. 2011. *Eastern Christianity and Western Social Theory*. Erfurt: Universität Erfurt.

Herzfeld, Michael. 1987. *Anthropology through the Looking-Glass: Critical Ethnography in the Margins of Europe*. Cambridge: Cambridge University Press.

Herzfeld, Michael. 1997. *Cultural Intimacy: Social Poetics and the Real Life of States, Societies, and Institutions*. Oxon: Routledge.

Hess, Andrew C. 1972. 'The Battle of Lepanto and its Place in Mediterranean History'. *Past & Present* 57: 53–73.

Hirsch, Eric, and Charles Stewart. 2005. 'Introduction: Ethnographies of Historicity'. *History and Anthropology* 16 (3): 261–74. https://doi.org/10.1080/02757200500219289

Hobsbawm, Eric. 1983. 'Introduction: Inventing Traditions'. In *The Invention of Tradition*, edited by Eric Hobsbawm and Terrence Ranger, 1–14. Cambridge: Cambridge University Press.

Johnston, Sean. 2016. *Holograms: A Cultural History*. Oxford: Oxford University Press.

Moore, Henrietta L. 2004. 'Global Anxieties: Concept-Metaphors and Pre-Theoretical Commitments in Anthropology'. *Anthropological Theory* 4 (1): 71–88. https://doi.org/10.1177/1463499604040848

Palmié, Stephan, and Charles Stewart. 2016. 'Introduction: For an Anthropology of History'. *HAU: Journal of Ethnographic Theory* 6 (1): 207–36. https://doi.org/10.14318/hau6.1.014

Papagaroufali, Eleni. 2008. 'Of Euro-Symbols and Euro-Sentiments: The Case of Town and School Twinning'. *Historein* 8: 72–82. https://doi.org/10.12681/historein.39

Seraïdari, Katerina. 2009. 'Objects of Cult, Objects of Confrontation: Divine Interventions through Greek History'. *History and Anthropology* 21 (2): 139–57. https://doi.org/10.1080/02757200903112644

Shaw, Rosalind, and Charles Stewart, eds. 1994. *Syncretism/Anti-Syncretism: The Politics of Religious Synthesis*. London: Routledge.

Shore, Cris. 2000. *Building Europe: The Cultural Politics of European Integration*. London: Routledge.

Throckmorton, Peter, Harold E. Edgerton, and Eleftherios Yalouris. 1973. 'The Battle of Lepanto Search and Survey Mission (Greece), 1971–72'. *International Journal of Nautical Archaeology* 2 (1): 121–30. https://doi.org/10.1111/j.1095-9270.1973.tb00495.x

Traganou, Jilly. 2010. 'National Narratives in the Opening and Closing Ceremonies of the Athens 2004 Olympic Games'. *Journal of Sport and Social Issues* 34 (2): 236–51. https://doi.org/10.1177/0193723509360217

Wimmer, Andreas, and Nina Glick Schiller. 2002. 'Methodological Nationalism and beyond: Nation–State Building, Migration and the Social Sciences'. *Global Networks* 2 (4): 301–34. https://doi.org/10.1111/1471-0374.00043

Yalouri, Eleana. 2010. 'Fanning the Flame: Transformations of the 2004 Olympic Flame'. *The International Journal of the History of Sport* 27 (12): 2155–83. https://doi.org/10.1080/09523367.2010.495229

CHAPTER 5

Gentrified, Euro-Mediterranean, Arabic?
Situating Mediterranean Locations along a Street in Marseille

Claire Bullen

University of Tübingen, University Aix-Marseille

Abstract

In scientific literature and public discourse, Marseille is regularly depicted as fundamentally Mediterranean. While this is not grounds for assuming Marseille is Mediterranean, I argue that evocations of the Mediterranean in relation to Marseille need to be taken seriously. I suggest that examining urban dynamics in Marseille through a relational 'Mediterranean lens' can offer new perspectives on the production of socio-spatial difference in that city. To make my case, I draw on observations of three eateries situated along one long street that joins the docks to the city centre. By grounding the analysis along this diverse street, it is possible to move beyond sweeping generalisations about people or places, while allowing the processes shaping unequal socio-spatial relations in Marseille – including ones that can be associated with 'gentrifying', 'Euro-Mediterranean', and 'Arabic' Mediterranean identities – to come more sharply into focus.

How to cite this book chapter:
Bullen, Claire. 2022. 'Gentrified, Euro-Mediterranean, Arabic? Situating Mediterranean Locations along a Street in Marseille'. In *Locating the Mediterranean: Connections and Separations across Space and Time*, edited by Carl Rommel and Joseph John Viscomi, 103–27. Helsinki: Helsinki University Press. DOI: https://doi.org/10.33134/HUP-18-5.

Setting the scene

People who travel to Marseille on the Mediterranean line of the French high-speed TGV (*Train à Grande Vitesse*) arrive at the impressive terminus Gare Saint-Charles.[1] Built in the mid-19th century when Marseille was France's premier port of empire, the construction of the station was seen by some as transforming Marseille into a central pivot of a 'Mediterranean system' linking 'Europe' and 'the Orient' (Planchenault 2017, 21). Most leave the station by the front exit, generally stopping on the esplanade to absorb an arresting view of a dense urban landscape heading towards the Mediterranean Sea before heading down some monumental steps lined with statues to representing France's former colonies.

It is also possible to leave by the back entrance, taking a road that follows the railway lines, until one arrives at Boulevard National, a two-kilometre street laid out at the same time as Gare Saint-Charles (see Image 5.1). In one direction, Boulevard National cuts southeast through a dark, noisy, exhaust-fumed tunnel underneath the railway tracks and then continues until it joins the grand Boulevard Longchamp. This part of the street original formed part of Marseille's 'opulent quartiers' (Sewell 1985), as is reflected by its Hausmann-ian architecture built for and by a growing bourgeoisie with wealth closely linked to the city's colonial-based economy. Today, while there are some more recent buildings, a multi-storey car park and a huge gated residential complex, the 19th-century street layout is largely unchanged. The façades of the town houses have been recently cleaned and the retail units that line the street include recently-opened grocery stores selling organic goods, social enterprise co-working spaces, bars, and restaurants. Exchanges between pedestrians are generally quiet and restrained, reflecting an increasingly middle-class *bobo* (hipster) ambience.[2]

If instead one follows Boulevard National in a north-easterly direction the feel of the street is much more workaday. This part of the street was laid out to connect the docks and the station. As with the other side of the tunnel, commercial units line the street, but on this side, warehouses and offices of former shipping companies intersperse five and six-storey tenements. In the 2020s, a few shops have their shutters down. Aside from this, numerous bakeries, *snacks* (fast-food restaurants), cafés, bar *tabacs*, *shisha* bars, halal butchers and grocery stores,

Image 5.1: South Boulevard National.
Photo: Abed Abidat.

hairdressers, barbers and beauticians, internet cafés and mobile phone stores, car repair workshops and warehouses selling discounted furniture and household goods create a vibrant streetscape. Non-commercial activities include an overcrowded state primary school, an incessantly busy post office and a Catholic church. Along these pavements, Maghreb Arabic rivals French. This, and the visible presence of people from the Maghreb and Sub-Saharan Africa (identified by language, clothing, and appearance), as well as certain ways of occupying the street seen as *populaire*[3], contribute to pejorative descriptions of this section of Boulevard National from many Marseille dwellers and urban decision makers.

The street continues in the direction of the docks, overshadowed at one point by the towering columns of a motorway flyover built in the 1950s over the most impoverished, stigmatised neighbourhoods to the north of Marseille. Since the late 1990s, this part of Boulevard National has been strongly influenced by one of the biggest urban restructuring initiatives in Southern Europe: the state-led 'Euro-Mediterranean Urban Development Programme' (Euro-Med).[4] From the 2010s, a number of industrial and residential properties were knocked down; others are boarded up, awaiting demolition. Commercial activity continues to take place, yet the garages, convenience stores and Islamic bookshops operating out of the foot of pollution-stained 19th- and early 20th-century buildings seem increasingly out of place in the face of encroaching bright and 'modern' apartment blocks, office towers, and 'international' hotel chains. Official publicity campaigns that describe this Euro-Med programme do so in simple terms: the aim is to 'change Marseille'. A key focus has been to attract 'professional classes' to the city; in much policy discourse, there is a more or less overt desire/assumption that the new arrivals will be northern Europeans or Americans. Sometimes this urban repositioning effort has been described as making Marseille the 'capital of the Mediterranean' (see Bertoncello and Rodriquez-Malta 2003).

Locating Marseille, and the Mediterranean

This quick purview along Boulevard National serves to give a sense of some of the socio-spatial diversity present in Marseille in the 2020s, a place often represented as the most diverse city in France. It is in part because of this association with social diversity that Marseille has incited research interest over the last century, in ways that are comparable with Chicago (Bouillon and Sevin 2007). Like the US city, Marseille is regularly presented as *the* archetypal city of immigration in France and/or France's capital of numerous social problems (Roncayolo 1996). Both contentions are disputable (Peraldi, Duport, and Samson 2015). However, with poverty statistics regularly above the national average and with a reputation as a place with *particularly* high levels of immigration and an *especially* corrupt system of governance, Marseille continues to be researched and written about as the most ethnically mixed city in France, and France's urban *enfant terrible par excellence* (Biass and Fabiani 2011; Peraldi, Duport, and Samson 2015).

Research into socio-spatial difference in Marseille has tended to mirror issues problematised in the media or by policymakers (Zalio 1996),[5] with particular weight paid to marginalised or stigmatised groups associated with different immigration pathways, notably from France's former colonies. Many studies concentrate on the poor, *popu-*

laire, 'ethnically marked' and racialised *quartiers* (suburban districts) or *cités* (housing estates) in the impoverished city centre and to the north of the city.[6] And, as is common in urban ethnography more generally (Blokland 2012), the values, understandings, and interactions of individuals and groups in better-off parts of the city are often missing. Consequently, myriad connections within and *beyond* different groups and different parts of the city can be overlooked (see Glick Schiller and Çağlar 2013). A further consequence of treating Marseille as an exception within France (see Pinson 2006), is that the significance of multiscalar symbolic and material links and separations can escape analyse. For example, paying attention to specificities *within* particular neighbourhoods can elide the role of colonial, decolonialising and neocolonialising social systems in the production of diverse social-spatial relations in the city.[7] I argue that this is where a street like Boulevard National can be useful to think with.[8]

The 'street' has gained in popularity as an object of research in recent years. Sometimes serving as sites for micro-sociological analyses of urban socialities from civility and solidarity to fear and violence (Anderson 1999; Roulleau-Berger 2004), urban thoroughfares are also taken places from where to tease out the complexity of urban life without being bound to the official modes of carving up the city (e.g. administrative boundaries, housing tenure, census data or socio-economic profiling), helping thus to avoid getting lost in pinning down those slippery notions of 'neighbourhood' or 'community' (see Fournier and Mazzela 2004; Hall 2015; Miller 2005). Boulevard National certainly works in this respect. Intersecting two *arrondissements,* (urban districts) with distinct socio-spatial positions (the more 'central' 1st arrondissement and more 'marginalised' 3rd one), bordering six *quartiers* with varying socio-economic profiles, and with different sections managed by diverse urban policies, the two-kilometre length of Boulevard National helps challenge bounded socio-spatial thinking. While the long, dark tunnel under the railway tracks is often represented as a frontier between very different social places, this street has nevertheless operated as an infrastructure that has been connecting actors, spaces, and processes within and across diverse spatial scales for over 150 years. These have contributed to changing meanings and values accorded to some of the different social geographies along the street, some of which are couched in Mediterranean terms.

My attention to this Mediterranean idiom could seem misplaced. Notwithstanding the proliferation of 'Euro-Mediterranean' research programmes supported by EU and national funding programmes since the 1990s, relatively few studies have attempted to probe the meaning and value of the Mediterranean in Marseille (although see Berton-cello and Rodriguez-Malta 2003; Bullen 2012; Francez 2017b; Maisetti 2012). Reluctance to engage with this notion is perhaps understand-able. Definitions of the cultural characteristics and geographical limits of a Mediterranean region have been intricately wound up with pro-cesses of 19th-century European colonial expansion and subsequent neocolonial policies (see Chapter 1 in this volume). Four decades of critical scholarship has highlighted Eurocentric and essentialising assumptions often underlying analysis of social dynamics in these terms (Herzfeld 2005; Pina-Cabral 1989). But it is not sufficient to stop there. Much continues to be written about the 'Mediterranean region', and within this work 'Mediterranean cities' have a significant place.

As a rule, research on Mediterranean cities begins on the basis that these are *particularly* diverse milieu (Driessen 2005). This work tends to be inflected with a certain nostalgia for a supposed foregone cosmo-politanism, sometimes reifying and romanticising ethnic and cultural difference (Ben-Yehoyada 2014, 115–16). Alternatively, the Mediter-ranean qualifier connotes cities or parts of cities deemed *too* marked by immigration and associated with chaos, degradation, or dereliction. Both modes of framing are used in Marseille.

Whether understood as an expanse of water, an idea, an imagined social space, and/or a geopolitical system, the Mediterranean has and continues to play a significant role in how Marseille and different parts of Marseille have been valorised and/or stigmatised. Often depicted as fundamentally Mediterranean, in cultural terms, the city's social posi-tion – or relative location – can be represented as part of a region that is somewhere between Africa and Europe (see Soto Bermant, Chap-ter 3 in this volume). As in other places associated with the Mediterra-nean, the meaning and value accorded to this, shifts in and out of focus in Marseille, in relation to geopolitics and the situated location of the actor doing the evaluating (elhariry and Talbayev 2017). In Marseille, the trope has become increasingly buoyant in the city over the last 30 years, heard in the mouths of urban policymakers, within the media and 'ordinary' urban dwellers (Bullen 2012; Maisetti 2012). While not grounds for assuming Marseille *is* Mediterranean, this suggests that the use of the term needs to be taken seriously.

Drawing on critical regional studies, 'the Mediterranean' is explored here as a multiplicity of open, discontinuous social spaces, social systems and/or imaginaries situated differently within social, cultural, political, and economic spheres (Allen, Massey, and Cochrane 1998). Moreover, in this chapter, I borrow from scholarship on food studies in order to shed light on how these different social spaces, systems and imaginaries are produced within power relations (see Hyde 2014; Mintz and Du Bois 2002). Observations from three eateries found along Boulevard National serve as a means to think through both variations in socio-spatial value creation, and the diverse opportunities of different social actors whose paths cross this street to take part within city-making processes.[9]

Mediterranean Locations in/of Marseille

Gentrifying Mediterraneity?

The first eatery I focus on is a Syrian restaurant found along the southernmost section of Boulevard National, where Boulevard National joins the elegant Boulevard Longchamp. The restaurant facade comprises a stylishly designed signboard in black and white presenting the establishment's name, named after an ancient Assyrian Empire, and indicating that 'traditional Syrian food' is served. During opening hours, well-cared-for plants and small tables are set out on the pavement area. Inside, the dining area is furnished with wooden and brass tables. Posters on the wood-clad walls represent Syrian cities and regions and provide descriptions of various regional produce. The eating area is softly lit by ironwork lattice lamps and Arabic music plays quietly in the background.

On arrival, customers are greeted and shown to tables by waiters, all young men, with Arabic as their first language and varying degrees of competence in French. (Sometimes, during an interaction with customers, waiters would seek help from colleagues more fluent in French; an indication of their recent arrival to France.) Customers are brought leather-bound menus at their tables, with items including familiar exports from south and south-east Mediterranean shores (kebabs, falafels), along with less well known 'home-made' Syrian dishes and some vegetarian 'reinterpretations' of dishes from northern Mediterranean shores (such as 'ratatouille mousaka'). For customers unfamiliar with this fare, the waiters politely provide explanations; on one occasion, the dish of the day was shown on a smartphone. Both alcoholic beverages and halal meat are served, appealing to both practising Muslims and non-Muslim clientele. When it arrives, food is carefully presented, prioritising quality rather than quantity. Food is available to take away, presented in recycled brown paper bags, indicating a concern with sustainable business practices.

On TripAdvisor the restaurant is in the category 'Lebanese/Mediterranean/Middle Eastern/Arabic' and rated five out of five for quality of food, ambience, and services. Comments have been posed by customers from Syria, France, Europe, and North America, indicating the reach of this establishment within tourist circuits beyond the immediate locality. Observations at both midday and in the evening corroborate this. The majority of customers observed were Francophone, but some spoke with the waiters in Arabic or English. The smart and casual clothing styles and behaviour indicated most were highly-educated with relatively high social status. Prices are more expensive than the average eatery in Marseille (€15–20 for a main course).

In terms of appearances and manners, there is little to distinguish the waiters from the majority of their middle-class clients; the well-kempt beards of some male staff feel 'hipster' rather than 'Islamic'. The open-plan kitchen at the back of the restaurant also helps blurs the line between customers and staff. In contrast with the 'ethno-cultural' aesthetic front of house, the stand-alone island unit and grey work surfaces provides a middle-class 'modern' backdrop that could be found in the pages of a Sunday supplement or, one imagines, in some of the customers' homes. In combining imaginaries of an 'authentic' and 'modern' middle-class 'Mediterranean' lifestyle (Francez 2017b, 194–99), the restaurant owners distinguish this culinary experience from any association with 'populaire', 'Arabic' eateries further north along the street.

The antecedents for a growing attraction of a form of middle-class Mediterraneity can be dated back to the 1980s, when Marseille's urban systems and the city's relative location within local, national and transnational scales were undergoing tumultuous change. On the one hand, two decades of decolonisation and the restructuring of the global economy had deeply weakened the city's mainstream port-based economy, at a time of significant inward labour migration of workers from southern Europe, the Maghreb and West Africa and the arrival of '*Pied noirs*', European settlers who were 'repatriated' from Algeria in the early 60s around the time of Independence. Together, this surge in population exacerbated the city's existing housing crisis (Nasiali 2016, 90). On the other hand, impoverished city-centre neighbourhoods had become the hub of informal, essentially Maghreb commercial networks linking the southern, eastern, and northern shores of the Mediterranean (see Peraldi 1999; Tarrius 1987). This trade was estimated to generate millions, but in a context of growing racism and xenophobia across the country,[10] Marseille's local leadership sought to displace this 'foreign' 'Arabic' or 'North African' activity from the city centre, seen as driving away the 'real' (for which read 'white') Marseille population and putting off new residents of higher socio-economic profiles (ditto) (Manry 2002; Peraldi and Samson 2005).

Successive local and national state-led urban renewal initiatives floundered in attempts to renovate the 'historic' part of the city and to attract – and to keep – populations of higher socio-economic backgrounds. Many city-centre districts remain impoverished and associated with the individuals and groups who are ethnically and racially marked as 'of immigrant origin' or as 'Arabs' (Escobar 2017). But the combined on-going effects of major state-led policies since the 2000s has started to make their mark, notably the extension of the 'Mediterranean' line of the TGV in 2001 (making Paris accessible by train in three and a half hours), the laying out of new tramway across the city centre (including up Boulevard Longchamp), Marseille's designation as European Capital of Culture in 2013 and the Euro-Med waterfront regeneration which began in 1995 and was extended in 2007 to cover 480 hectares of the city centre. One consequence is the increased presence of the '*néo-Marseillais*' (neo-Marseille people) in certain city-centre districts.

Néo-Marseillais is a term that began to circulate in the early 2000s. It refers to recent arrivals to Marseille who are relatively young (under 40 years old), middle or upper middle class, and French or European, who might have a certain economic precarity but are generally more qualified and with greater cultural capital than the average city resident (Gasquet-Cyrus and Trimaille 2017).[11] In the study by Gasquet-Cyrus and Trimaille, the '*Mediterranean life-style*, social diversity and the cultural offer' of Marseille were considered significant factors affecting the choice to move to Marseille (84, my emphasis).[12] Some of those who fall within this neo-Marseille category have been active as volunteers and activists to support the arrival of other newcomers to Marseille, those categorised – and sometimes racialised - as '*migrants*' or '*primo-arrivants*'.[13] But, generally speaking, aspirations to the Mediterranean lifestyle tend to be associated with a vibrant café culture, with relatively little contact with ethnically marked, impoverished city-centre dwellers of visible migrant background (Francez 2017a; Gasquet-Cyrus and Trimaille 2017; Manry 2002). This end of Boulevard National is on the periphery of parts of city-centre districts popular with the *néo-Marseillais* demographic.

The restaurant in question was opened in 2017 by a family who left Syria following the onset of civil war. At that time, local authorities expressed concern that 'waves' of Syrians refugees would arrive in Marseille (Castelly 2015). Fewer arrived than expected, in part because of understandings and experiences of the restrictive immigration and asylum systems in France. Those who did make it to Marseille were faced with local public authorities unable or unwilling to meet the basic needs of the *primo-arrivants* (Dahdah, Audren, and Bouillon 2018). Those without private resources to draw upon had to struggle to access resources, often living hand-to-mouth in economically impoverished, racially stigmatised areas, associated with the Maghreb or 'the Arabs'.

In this case of the restaurant, the owners had the economic, social, and cultural resources to facilitate their incorporation into a part of the city undergoing upscaling in the last 20 years. With the choice of locality, in close vicinity to two bar/restaurants highly popular with Marseille's 'creative classes', just around the corner from an upmarket Egyptian café and cultural centre. Learning from the success of this Egyptian café, and benefiting from the relative upscale social position of urban location, the owners were able to present an aesthetic that is at once 'international', Syrian and 'Mediterranean'. Their culinary offer was able to attract high-status consumers who are environmentally and health conscious and interested in an 'alternative' yet 'high-quality' food experience. This, and their pricing policies, function as markers of difference from lower-status 'Arabic' eateries located further along the street.

Image 5.2: Café, central Boulevard National.
  Photo: Abed Abidat.

Populaire, 'Arabic' Mediterraneity?

Over a quarter of the small businesses located along the middle stretch of Boulevard National are eateries of some kind (see Image 5.2). Of these, approximately one fifth are bakeries, selling pizza slices and '*mahjouba*' (an Algerian flatbread filled with tomato and onion sauce) alongside baguettes and croissants. Most of the others are fast-food '*snacks*', with a growing number (four in a 200 metre stretch) offering 'Tunisian' specialities. Almost exclusively, they are run by people coming from the south and south-east Mediterranean, be they long-term French residents or more recent arrivals.

The restaurant I focus on was established by Turkish owners[14] and occupied the ground-floor of a block of late-20th-century flats, next to a discount furniture store and just up the street from a car repair workshop. As with other eateries here, this establishment was not on TripAdvisor. The restaurant was identified by a white, plastic, age-worn signboard with the name of a Turkish city alongside an image of a doner kebab. Custom was largely won in terms of proximity, rapidity of service, the lateness of opening hours, price, and, in this case, a large dining area at the back. Inside, the front area, lit by bright white overhead lighting, was functional in design. To one side was a glass-fronted counter behind which food was cooked and where orders and payment taken. Food choices and prices were simply displayed on a board behind the counter next to photographs of dishes; items no longer available were simply crossed out in pen. The menu was mainly meat-based (halal), grilled or cooked on a griddle, or sliced off the doner kebab. Behind the counter, industrial falafels lay touching the meat, a sign that little attention had been given to potential vegetarian clients. On the customer side of the counter, salads, rice, bulgur wheat, and the 'dish of the day' were displayed uncovered in a buffet unit and there was glass-fronted fridge, where customers could help themselves to cans of soda or bottles of water. No alcohol was sold.

Most of the time, the owner, dressed informally in jeans and a T-shirt, worked alone, or with one male colleague, preparing food, taking money, wrapping up the take away items in plastic bags, or carrying out plates of food to tables in the back. Sometimes the owner's wife and/or mother worked behind the counter, dressed in a dark-coloured kaftan dress and a headscarf. The women seemed less at ease at speaking French than the male workers, so worked mainly on non-customer focused tasks, packing up food to take away in polystyrene boxes and plastic bags, or clearing tables.[15]

During the day, the majority of customers were men, who came individually or in groups of two or three. Paint-splattered clothes or embroidered logos on sweatshirts and jackets indicated many were involved in manual labour in the construction sector. Sometimes groups of teenagers came in, using the restaurant served as a school canteen. In school holidays, long summer evenings and weekends, the restaurant was frequented by families of with young children. Generally, the majority of customers were of Maghreb, sub-Saharan African or Turkish origin. On weekday lunchtimes, however, the seating area at the back of the restaurant and the possibility of salad dishes and the falafel 'vegetarian' option in the falafel – enabled the restaurant to attract a more diverse customer base than other eateries down the street, including *néo-Marseillais* who lived in the city centre and came to this part of Boulevard National to work some of the social and cultural associations operating within the vicinity. This eatery thus offers as an interesting place from where to think through the relational production of material and symbolic social spaces here.

For a number of years now, several policies have sought to transform the social composition of this stretch of Boulevard National, to incorporate it within an expanding city centre (designated the *'hyper city centre'*). Initiatives include a short-term arts project funded through the European Capital of Culture programme where an international artist was paid to come up with a short-term installation in the dark tunnel; the opening of centre of contemporary dance further along the street, a number of different private student accommodation and a new cycle path (although often this is blocked by cars or rubbish bins) was painted along the pavements. The regular if minority presence of *néo-Marseille* pedestrians or bicyclists travelling up and down the street can be linked in part to these interventions.[16] However, relatively few stop to use the food services down the road. This restaurant was one of the few that was mentioned by those asked about their consumption choices.

When speaking to people about their decision about whether to purchase food along this part of the street, some jokingly spoke of the food on offer as *pourri,* literally 'rotten' or dirty. While said in jest, the association of the culinary offer with rottenness or dirt resonates symbolically with ideas of 'otherness' and 'foreignness'(Roulleau-Berger 2004, 96). Unlike the restaurant described above, the migration trajectory of the business owners and their *populaire* status robs these food establishments of their value, symbolic or otherwise, in classed and racialised terms.

Yet observations indicate the multiple values that eateries such as this one have in shaping possibilities for incorporation within diverse domains along the street. For example, in a part of the city that is revenue-poor, where a third of the population are under 20, the informal social norms, affordable meals, and space for pushchairs and children to move around make this restaurant accessible for lower socio-economic recent migrants with new aspirations to leisure practices.

Within economic terms, eateries along this stretch of Boulevard National change hands with great regularity. No doubt an indication of the toughness of the sector and often gruelling hours, this rapid turnover of business is also an indication that the catering sector is a relatively accessible mode of incorporation into the urban economy. This is a highly valuable opportunity structure in a neighbourhood where 40 per cent of the population are without formal employment in the neighbourhood (AGAM 2020). Further, in places, as here, where rental costs are relatively low and traffic is high, there is potential for considerable returns on time and financial investment (see Bouillon 2004). For the current owner who had previously worked in the construction industry, this recent new venture, which like many of the business owners was made possible because of resources transferred through kinship ties that stretch across the Mediterranean, was an opportunity for social advancement and more sociable hours.

In aesthetic terms, the look of this restaurant and other *snacks* down the street many not fit with the Western elite imaginary of the 'traditional' or 'middle-class' Mediterraneity, as offered by the Syrian establishment, neither, the form of café-culture desired by some urban planners in Marseille (see below). However, it could be argued that the 'modern' aesthetic (bright monochrome colours and lighting, loud music, or the presence of a television on the wall), the low-status fare and informal sociability of these establishments can be found in cities all around the Mediterranean Sea. Some establishments underscore such connections, choosing names that index themselves to urban places south and east of the Mediterranean (in Tunisia, Turkey, Algeria). In the Turkish restaurant, a form of Mediterranean modernity was valorised by the new owners through the commissioning of a huge fresco of Istanbul by night, depicting a glittering scene dominated by the dome of the Blue Mosque and a multitude of lit-up skyscrapers.

Without wishing to force this Mediterranean optic onto the street, I suggest that this part of the road can be usefully understood as offering a form of Mediterraneity often invisible for urban planners: an '*Arabic Mediterraneity*'. By choosing to describe this part of the street in terms of its 'Arabic-ness', I am influenced by recent scholarship on the 'Black Mediterranean' (Hawthorne 2021). The notion of Black Mediterranean was conceived as a way consider to at once explore the subjectivities of racialised immigrants seeking incorporation within Europe and to challenge Eurocentric accounts of Mediterranean crossings (Proglio 2018). Similarly, I suggest that by changing the gaze, and examining from the symbolic and physical spaces often stigmatised in Marseille as *populaire* and *Arabic*, from the perspectives of many of those shaping these spaces through their daily practices, we can better understand their use value, and can make visible a form of city-making often unseen or disparaged by urban elites with a Eurocentric vision of desirable forms of Mediterranean living.

Euro-Mediterraneity

The third and final outlet I examine is situated in huge 'mixed-use development' at the northernmost end of Boulevard National. Built on a 19th-century warehouse complex, it now consists of private and social flats, student accommodation, and an apartment-hotel, organised around a gated courtyard. It lies at the edge of the Euro-Med urban development area. During opening hours – 8am to 3pm on weekdays – bright pink tables are set out on the pavement, in front of plate-glass window and doors, which appear incongruous in one of the most impoverished neighbourhoods in France, 200 metres from one of the most highly stigmatised high-rise social housing estates in the city (see Image 5.3).

If the student accommodation over this eatery has been labelled with the 'Euro-Mediterranean' nomenclature, the minimalist décor

Image 5.3: Demolition and reconstruction, north Boulevard National.
Photo: Abed Abidat.

of this national food franchise feels placeless; there are no indications of any geographical anchorage. Inside, the décor is predominately in white and grey. Music played in the background is easy-listening Anglo-American pop. The menu in this establishment follows international trends of an environmental and health-conscious consumer. Food is promoted for its organic and health credentials (soups, quinoa salads, gluten-free muffins). Items are described with internationalising Anglicisms (*les* super foods, *les* poke bowls, etc.). A lunchtime menu costs over 11 euros and the coffee, which includes organic and decaffeinated options, is 50 cents more than the average coffee in nearby cafés, a steep economic barrier in a neighbourhood where most people live below the poverty threshold. Meat here is not halal, in a neighbourhood where the majority of residents are Muslim.

The café was staffed by two people, a middle-aged male manager and a younger female assistant, wearing a company T-shirt and jeans. Both are 'white' French, in a neighbourhood where official statistics give the percentage of foreigners as 20 per cent but observations suggest that the figure is much higher, the majority with origins in former French colonies. Likewise, the majority of customers were 'white'. Based on ID badges and snippets of conversation heard, most customers work for different urban and social services and associative structures operating in the neighbourhood. Most took their food back to the office in brown paper bags; a few used the café for meetings or working lunches. Some of those living in the student flats purchased food in the eatery on their way to or from their accommodation. From their accents, some came from the Maghreb. However, their sartorial style and behaviour identified them more as of 'international' middle-class backgrounds rather than 'ethnically marked' low-status migrants.

Overall, there is a marked separation between the majority of the clientele and the busy traffic of people walking between Métro National, the bus stop and the high-rise flats 200 yards away, although the tracksuit-wearing young men collecting food for Uber Eats-style delivery services could easily have come from the neighbouring housing estate. This social distance was starkly pointed out the first time I walked past the food outlet. As I stopped to take a photo of the 'Euro-Mediterranean' student apartments, one of the staff members who was folding up the terrace tables told me – in English – to be careful. When I asked why, he gestured in the direction of the high-rise subsidised housing.

This 'international', 'modern', rather 'placeless' site offers a good place to think about how the Mediterranean has been understood, produced and located within this part of the city. As mentioned above, Marseille's 'Euro-Mediterranean' antecedents date to the 1990s, when local and national leaders were casting around for solutions to deal with Marseille's different urban 'crises'. Different experts came up with propositions for a central business district along Marseille's waterfront that could reposition Marseille within the city region and internationally (Pinson 2002), drawing on well-used scripts for remodelling deindustrialised port cities (Baltimore, Barcelona, etc.). One specificity of Marseille's urban restructuring project was its designation as an Operation of National Interest and its 'Mediterranean' dimension, fitting in with French ambitions to keep a strategic presence in the Mediterranean basin, as negotiations were under way to establish a free trade zone around the Mediterranean (the 'Euro-Mediterranean partnership').

These national and transnational dimensions shifted how Marseille was understood for some national and local leaders. Marseille became reimagined as a base from where a 'Marshall Plan for Africa' could be launched by international organisations. The Euro-Med waterfront development was an overt part of state efforts to reposition Marseille as one 21st-century 'Mediterranean system'.[17] Yet, for some local partners of the Euro-Med programme, the 'Mediterranean' association added substance to Marseille's reputation as France's 'Arabic city'. This was seen as prejudicial for local voters and repelling middle-class residents and international investors from coming to the city. This helps to explain why the Mediterranean appellation was largely emptied of content in the first years of the programme (Tiano 2010). For Tiano, the 'Euro-Mediterranean theme could have been the bearer of values of contacts, contrasts, multiculturalism, etc ...' yet, in practice, little emerged from 'the project's speeches and actions apart from the very concrete value of property speculation'.

Ten years after this critical assessment, one staff member within the Euro-Med Development Agency noted that the Mediterranean was far from a *mot d'ordre* ('watchword') within the programme. Some of the young urban planners and architects I spoke to who worked on this or other urban restructuring programmes regretted this, asserting that Marseille's Euro-Med development is not 'Mediterranean enough'. Here Marseille was compared negatively with 'more Mediterranean' cities, such as Barcelona, Valencia, Rome, where there was a vibrant café-culture. New planning guidelines are being developed by staff within the Euromed agency have the objective to transform Marseille's Euro-Mediterranean district into the model 'sustainable Mediterranean city of tomorrow'. In these 'European' or 'international' aspirations to promote Mediterranean urbanity, the implication is that Marseille is not quite Mediterranean enough, or, alternatively, not Mediterranean in the right way. Somewhat ironically, the role-model cities presented within these guidelines hail from far away from the Mediterranean shore (Germany, Sweden, Singapore…).

Either way, policies that promote national chains, such as the food outlet evoked above, have undoubtedly displaced small, locally run businesses, displacing 'ethnically marked' residents and small businesses with direct links across the Mediterranean Sea (Borja et al. 2010) and contributing to create what Alain Tarrius (1992) evocatively described nearly 30 years ago as an identity for Marseille as 'international', *white and clean*. However, even a massive, state-led project like the Euro-Med development extending over three decades has not been completely successful in imposing a uniform vision on Marseille's urban form (Beauregard and Haila 1997). While huge amounts of money have been poured into making Marseille 'attractive' to certain populations, the numbers of *'néo-Marseillais'* arrivals has not met expectations, and a significant proportion of those who come do not settle (Escobar 2017). Buy-to-let owners continue to rent out property to low-income, often ethnically marked renters in the city centre at increasingly high rents. In the major Euro-Med housing developments like that at the bottom of Boulevard National, social accommodation is included alongside private apartments in lines with national housing regulations.[18]

This complex and sometimes contradictory entanglement of diverse projects and policies, and the relations and overlaps between different historically situated 'Mediterranean' locations in Marseille helps explain why today the socio-spatial configurations in this Euro-Mediterranean part of the street remain, for the moment, so diverse.

The Mediterranean as Epistemic Lens:
Some Concluding Thoughts

The material presented here comes from the early stages of a larger research project exploring social networks around the Mediterranean. The argument being made is that studying urban dynamics in Marseille with a relational 'Mediterranean lens' can shed light on the production of socio-spatial difference in ways that can transcend classic binaries (north/south, centre/periphery, migrant/non-migrant, rich/poor, etc.), notably in relation to the mesh of historically situated colonial, postcolonial, and neocolonial connections that stretch across and shape social spaces around the Mediterranean Sea. Drawing on some initial observations, this chapter sought to show how understandings of historically situated socio-spatial diversity in Marseille could be deepened by linking these to ideas of multiple Mediterranean systems. The first eatery offered an example of deliberate use of aesthetic representation of Mediterranean connections to feed into the discursive norms of middle-class *néo-Marseillais* urban dwellers. Here, restaurant owners with a recent south/north migration trajectory had the social status to permit them to transcend ethnic categorisation and to contribute alongside other recently arrived middle-classes entrepreneurs – though mainly from mainland France - to ongoing processes of gentrification in Marseille's city centre, supported by multi-scalar public policies. In the second case, the streetscape was produced materially and symbolically produced through the coming together of south/north symbolic, social and economic systems, particularly from the Maghreb. However, the social, cultural, aesthetic, and economic practices that make up this *populaire* Arabic Mediterraneity have been rendered invisible or actively discouraged from city-branding and repositioning policies over the last decades.[19] The last case speaks of the way that in this city the register of the Euro-Mediterranean has been wrapped up in state-led 'white' internationalisation and commodification of Marseille's former industrial docks, and the processes of social and spatial displacement that have ensued. The juxtaposition of these instances illustrates vividly how different Mediterranean imaginaries situated variously within social, cultural, political, and economic spheres affect opportunity structures for different people living and working in Marseille. As a case in point: at different times, the owners of the Syrian 'Lebanese/Mediterranean/Middle Eastern/Arabic' restaurant were invited to cater for events organised by the city's political and business elite. Conversely, restaurants such as the Turkish one are regularly pilloried by city officials for breaking hygiene standards, encouraging an undesirable customer base, and giving an 'Arabic colour' to the feel of the city (Bouillon 2004).

In methodological terms, these observations from the different eateries could be considered as going no further than 'apt illustrations'. However, when considered together – a gesture that is encouraged by considering the street as a whole – I suggest we can better seize some of how connections between the different parts shaped value-laden material and symbolic forms associated with the Mediterranean in Marseille in ways that could strengthen critical urban theory.

To date, most scholarship on the Mediterranean in Marseille comes from a policy perspective. There is surprisingly little understanding about how different understandings of the Mediterranean works within the contemporary vernacular in Marseille. Much of the analysis of Marseille separates the city into different sections or draws lines between *néo-Marseillais*, urban planners, and *populaire* populations, arguably obfuscating the multiplicity of relations involved in producing 'the urban' and 'the Mediterranean'. Beginning with an ethnographic analysis of different locations along this boulevard and tracing the social networks that extend beyond it allows us to capture the microsociology of interactions on pavements and to consider how the social positioning of different spaces in Marseille, and of Marseille within France and the world, are indexed in hierarchical relations of value. Locating this street ethnography within historically-situated Mediterranean spaces, systems and imaginaries, allows links between the colonial capitalism of Marseille's 19th century portside economy and efforts to reposition Marseille at the hub of a 21st-century 'Mediterranean system' to become more visible. In short, by starting from the street, and embedding and interpreting within these frames of gentrifying, Euro-Mediterranean and Arabic Mediterraneities, it becomes possible to point to unequal relations of class, culture, capital, and processes of colonisation without falling into sweeping generalisations about people or places.

Notes

1 My thanks to Carl Rommel and Joseph John Viscomi for their input and advice at various stages of this article, and to the anonymous reviewers for some good advice about how to make this stronger. This project has benefited from stimulating discussions with members of UNKUT at the University of Tübingen. I am also grateful to Abed Abidat, Heather Bullen, Othmane Djebbar, Muriel Girard, Franck Lamiot, Nadja Monnet, and Amel Zerourou, who have helped me to develop my ideas about the street as the research progresses.

2 *Bobo* is the abbreviate form of *bohemian-bourgeois*. As with 'hipster', it is a social category with very fuzzy edges (Authier et al. 2018) but can be taken as being more or less synonymous with those other very contingent social categories, 'hipsters' or the 'cultural classes'.

3 If, previously, cultural practices, social groups, or social spaces described by *populaire* in French could be translated in English by the term 'working class', this term is increasingly understood to mean areas or practices that are impoverished and ethnically marked (see Pasquier 2005).

4 https://euromediterranee.fr. Accessed 13 June 2020.

5 Of course as Wright Mills (1959) pointed out long ago, this is far from unique to Marseille.

6 In France, the debate about whether individuals and groups should be categorised in terms of ethnicity rages fiercely. Here the terms ethnically or racially marked to draw out hierarchical relations indexed against a privileged and unmarked 'white' Frenchness (see Mazouz 2017).

7 This is not to dismiss urban studies that do explore Marseille's position within broader political and economic systems (France, the European Union, the Euro-Mediterranean region, the world). However, this work tends to be quantitative and take the city as a whole. Less attention tends to given to how people negotiate and attribute meaning to these structures and systems in their everyday lives.

8 To date, Boulevard National has received very little scholarly attention. This could be because, although parts of it have 'central qualities' and parts of are often considered to match the characteristics of the part of the notorious *quartiers nord*, it is not *quite* central enough nor *north* enough to fit with research imaginaries.

9 These sections draw on observations that began in 2014 when I moved to Boulevard National. Since October 2021, these have been added to as part of a new project, 'Networks, Streets and Socio-spatial Difference: Comparing Social Relations in Urban Settings around the Mediterranean', funded by the Excellence Strategy of the German Federal and State Governments.

10 The 1980s was a period of increasingly visible and violent racism and xenophobia across France and Europe, when the presence of migrants from the former colonies was being blamed for growing unemployment. Racism was particularly vicious in the south of the country, where many '*pied noirs*' settled. Their presence has been linked to strong support for the extreme right-wing *Front National*.

11 People like me, in fact. I analyse my own social position within different social systems along Boulevard National elsewhere. Of note, following 'lockdown'

policies during 2020, this *néo-Marseille* category has been significantly reconfigured by the arrival of 'Parisians' seeking cheaper, more spacious accommodation.

12 These new arrivals added to artists and other archetypal 'figures' of urban gentrification who had begun moving to the city in the 1980s, profiting from industrial buildings available for low rents and new openings created by urban cultural policies, as urban leaders tried to reinvent the city.

13 Primo-arrivant is an administrative category that has emerged in the last decade to 'manage' newly arrived foreign immigrants who are assumed to be settling in France for the long-term, as part of governmental responses to manage the 'crisis' of integrating 'foreigners' (Goudeau 2018).

14 I use the past tense as the eatery has not opened its doors following the enforced closure as part of the anti-Covid-19 measures.

15 An in-depth discussion of the gendered production and division of socio-spatial relations along the street will be explored further, following the analysis semi-structured questionnaires carried out in 2021/2022. Initial observations suggest that the majority of business owners and workers in this stretch are men, but a growing number of food and retail businesses are headed up by women or by married couples, and women are often active in family-run businesses in this sector.

16 People fitting the néo-Marseille category do live along this section (including me), almost exclusively, those questioned during this research came to the boulevard during working hours and returned to residences south of the tunnel in the evening.

17 That Marseille was Europe's principal gateway for submarine communication cables from Africa and Asia increased its value within national and European international policies.

18 Law No. 2000-1208 of 13 December 2000 on urban solidarity and renewal.

19 Since June 2020, and the election of the left-wing *Printemps Marseille* party to the City Hall there has been a significant change to a far more inclusive narrative about the diversity of Marseille's population and connections with the southern Mediterranean shores. The fieldwork for this chapter predate this.

References

Allen, John, Doreen B. Massey, and Allan Cochrane. 1998. *Rethinking the Region*. London; New York: Routledge.

Anderson, Elijah. 1999. *Code of the Street: Decency, Violence, and the Moral Life of the Inner City*. 1st ed. New York, NY: W.W Norton.

Authier, Jean-Yves, Anaïs Collet, Colin Giraud, Matthieu Giroud, Edmond Préteceille, Jean Rivière, Sylvie Tissot, Jean-Yves Authier, Anaïs Collet, Colin Giraud, et al. 2018. *Les bobos n'existent pas*. Lyon: Presses universitaires de Lyon.

Beauregard, Robert A., and Anne Haila. 1997. 'The Unavoidable Incompleteness of the City'. *American Behavioral Scientist* 41 (3): 327–41. https://doi.org/10.1177/0002764297041003005

Ben-Yehoyada, Naor. 2017. *The Mediterranean Incarnate: Region Formation between Sicily and Tunisia Since World War II*. Chicago, IL: University of Chicago Press.

Bertoncello, Brigitte, and Rachel Rodrigues-Malta. 2003. 'Marseille versus Euromé-diterranée'. *Annales de Géographie* 632 (112): 424–36.

Biass, Sophie, and Jean-Louis Fabiani. 2011. 'Marseille, a City beyond Distinction'. *Nottingham French Studies* 50 (1): 83–94. https://doi.org/10.3366/nfs.2011.008

Blokland, Talja. 2012. 'Blaming Neither the Undeserving Poor Nor the Revanchist Middle Classes: A Relational Approach to Marginalization'. *Urban Geography* 33 (4): 488–507. https://doi.org/10.2747/0272-3638.33.4.488

Borja, Jean-Stéphane, Martine Derain, Véronique Manry, and Caroline Galmot. 2010. *Attention à la fermeture des portes! Citoyens et habitants au cœur des trans-formations urbaines. L'expérience de la rue de la République à Marseille.* Marseille: Editions commune.

Bouillon, Florence. 2004. 'Au Roi Du Kebab. Restauration à La Sauvette et Dynam-ique Commerciale Métissée'. In *Marseille, Entre Ville et Ports. Les Destins de La Rue de La République,* edited by Pierre Fournier and Sylvie Mazzella, 242–57. Paris: La Decouverte.

Bouillon, Florence, and Jean-Christophe Sevin. 2007. 'Introduction : migra-tions et patrimonialisation en débats'. ethnographiques.org. http://www.eth-nographiques.org/2007/Sevin- Bouillon.

Bullen, Claire. 2012. 'Marseille, ville méditerranéenne? Enjeux de pouvoir dans la construction des identités urbaines'. *Rives méditerranéennes* 42 (2): 157–71. https://doi.org/10.4000/rives.4211

Castelly, Lisa. 2005. 'Syriens en quête d'hospitalité'. *Marsactu,* 7 Nov 2005. https://marsactu.fr/syriens-en-quete-dhospitalite/

Dahdah, Assaf, Gwenaëlle Audren, and Florence Bouillon. 2018. 'La ville (in)hos-pitalière : parcours scolaire et résidentiel d'une famille syrienne à Marseille'. *Espaces et sociétés* 172–73 (1): 73. https://doi.org/10.3917/esp.172.0073

Driessen, Henk. 2005. 'Mediterranean Port Cities: Cosmopolitanism Recon-sidered'. *History and Anthropology* 16 (1): 129–41. https://doi.org/10.1080/0275720042000316669

DROS-PACA. 2013. *Atlas social de la région Provence-Alpes-Côte d'Azur 2013: Les aspects territoriaux de la pauvreté et de la précarité.* Dispositif Régional d'Observation Sociale Provence-Alpes-Côte d'Azur.

elhariry, yasser, and Edwige Tamalet Talbayev. 2018. *Critically Mediterranean: Tem-poralities, Aesthetics, and Deployments of a Sea in Crisis.* Cham: Springer.

Escobar, David Mateos. 2017. 'Le processus de gentrification rend-il compte des dynamiques de peuplement des quartiers centraux de Marseille ?' *Langage et societe* 162 (4): 47–51. https://doi.org/10.3917/ls.162.0047

Fournier, Pierre, and Sylvie Mazzela, eds. 2004. *Marseille, entre ville et ports : Les destins de la rue de la République.* Paris: La Découverte.

Francez, Émilie. 2017a. '(Re) Construire Un Patrimoine En Mobilité : Une Exposi-tion Sur Le Hammam à Marseille'. *Autrepart,* 21–37. https://doi.org/10.3917/autr.078.0021

Francez, Émilie. 2017b. *Politiques et représentations du hammam à Marseille : anthropologie d'un espace-frontière.* Aix-Marseille University.

Gasquet-Cyrus, Médéric, and Cyril Trimaille. 2017. 'Être néo quelque part : la gen-trification à Marseille et ses implications sociolinguistiques'. *Langage et societe* 162 (4): 81–105. https://doi.org/10.3917/ls.162.0081

Glick Schiller, Nina, and Ayşe Çağlar. 2013. 'Locating Migrant Pathways of Economic Emplacement: Thinking beyond the Ethnic Lens'. *Ethnicities* 13 (4): 494–514. https://doi.org/10.1177/1468796813483733

Hall, Suzanne M. 2015. 'Super-Diverse Street: A "Trans-ethnography" across Migrant Localities'. *Ethnic and Racial Studies* 38 (1): 22–37. https://doi.org/10.180/01419870.2013.858175

Hawthorne, Camilla. 2021. 'L'Italia Meticcia? The Black Mediterranean and the Racial Cartographies of Citizenship'. In *The Black Mediterranean*, edited by Gabriele Proglio, Camilla Hawthorne, Ida Danewid, P. Khalil Saucier, Giuseppe Grimaldi, Angelica Pesarini, Timothy Raeymaekers, Giulia Grechi, and Vivian Gerrand, 169–98. Cham: Springer International Publishing.

Herzfeld, Michael. 2005. 'Practical Mediterraneanisms: Excuses for Everything, from Epistemology to Eating'. In *Rethinking the Mediterranean*, edited by William V. Harris. Oxford: Oxford University Press.

Hyde, Zachary. 2014. 'Omnivorous gentrification: Restaurant reviews and neighborhood change in the downtown Eastside of Vancouver'. *City & Community* 13 (4): 341–59. https://doi.org/10.1111/cico.12088

Maisetti, Nicolas. 2012. *Marseille en Méditerranée: Récit politique territorial et sociologie de l'action publique locale internationale*. Paris: Université Paris I Panthéon-Sorbonne.

Manry, Véronique. 2002. 'Belsunce 2001: Chronique d'un cosmopolitisme annoncé?' *Revue Mediterraneans / Méditerranéennes* (13): 136–45. https://doi.org/10.34847/nkl.eef300jm

Mazouz, Sarah. 2017. *La République et ses autres: politiques de l'altérité dans la France des années 2000*. Lyon: ENS Éditions.

Miller, Daniel. 2005. 'Une rue du nord de Londres et ses magasins: Imaginaire et usages'. *Ethnologie française* 35 (1): 17–26. https://doi.org/10.3917/ethn.051.0017

Mintz, Sidney W., and Christine M. Du Bois. 2002. 'The anthropology of food and eating'. *Annual Review of Anthropology* 31 (1): 99–119. https://doi.org/10.1146/annurev.anthro.32.032702.131011

Nasiali, M. 2016. *Native to the Republic: Empire, Social Citizenship, and Everyday Life in Marseille since 1945*. Ithaca, NY: Cornell University Press.

Palomares, Élise. 2008. 'Itinéraire du credo de la « mixité sociale »'. *Revue Projet* 307 (6): 23–29. https://doi.org/10.3917/pro.307.0023

Pasquier, Dominique. 2005. 'La « culture populaire » à l'épreuve des débats sociologiques'. *Hermes, La Revue* 42 (2): 60–69. https://doi.org/10.4267/2042/8983

Peraldi, Michel. 1999. 'Marseille : réseaux migrants transfrontaliers, place marchande et économie de bazar'. *Cultures & Conflits* 33–34. https://doi.org/10.4000/conflits.232

Peraldi, Michel, Claire Duport, and Michel Samson. 2015. *Sociologie de Marseille*. Paris: La Découverte (Repères).

Peraldi, Michel, and Michel Samson. 2005. *Gouverner Marseille. Enquête sur Les Mondes Politiques Marseillais*. Paris: La Découverte.

Pina-Cabral, João de. 1989. 'The Mediterranean as a Category of Regional Comparison: A Critical View'. *Current Anthropology* 30 (3): 399–406.

Pinson, Gilles. 2002. *Projets et pouvoirs dans les villes europeennes. Une comparaison de Marseille, Venise, Nantes et Turin*. Rennes: CNRS/Université de Rennes I/ Institut d'Etudes Politiques de Rennes.

Pinson, Gilles. 2006. 'Michel Peraldi, Michel Samson: Gouverner Marseille. Enquête Sur Les Mondes Politiques Marseillais'. *Pôle Sud* 24: 164–66.

Planchenault, Gérard. 2008. *Marseille Saint-Charles: Histoire d'une Grande Gare 1847–2007. Parcours et labeurs*. Saint-Cyr-sur-Loire: Éditions Alain Sutton.

Proglio, Gabriele. 2018. 'Is the Mediterranean a White Italian–European Sea? The Multiplication of Borders in the Production of Historical Subjectivity'. *Interventions* 20 (3): 406–27. https://doi.org/10.1080/1369801X.2017.1421025

Roncayolo, Marcel. 1996. *Les grammaires d'une ville: essai sur la genèse des structures urbaines à Marseille*. Paris: Ecole des hautes études en sciences sociales.

Roulleau-Berger, Laurence. 2004. *La Rue, Miroir Des Peurs et Des Solidarités*. Paris: Presses universitaires de France.

Sant Cassia, Paul, and Isabel Schäfer. 2005. '"Mediterranean Conundrums": Pluridisciplinary Perspectives for Research in the Social Sciences'. *History and Anthropology* 16 (1): 1–23. https://doi.org/10.1080/02757200500103400

Sewell, William H. 1985. *Structure and Mobility: The Men and Women of Marseille, 1820–1870*. New York, NY: Cambridge University Press.

Shavit, Yaacov. 1988. 'The Mediterranean World and "Mediterraneanism": The Origins, Meaning, and Application of a Geo-Cultural Notion in Israel'. *Mediterranean Historical Review* 3 (2): 96–117. https://doi.org/10.1080/09518968808569552

Tarrius, Alain. 1987. 'L'entrée dans la ville: Migrations maghrébines et recompositions des tissus urbains à Tunis et à Marseille'. *Revue Européenne de Migrations Internationales* 3 (1–2): 131–48. https://doi.org/10.3406/remi.1987.1131

Tarrius, Alain. 1992. *Les Fourmis d'Europe. Migrants Riches, Migrants Pauvres et Nouvelles Villes Internationales*. Paris: Éditions L'Harmattan.

Tiano, Camille. 2010. 'Quelles Valeurs Pour Revaloriser Les Territoires Urbains?' *Cybergeo: European Journal of Geography*, 1–13.

Wright Mills, C. 1959. *The Sociological Imagination*. New York, NY: Oxford University Press.

Zalio, Pierre-Paul. 1996. 'Urbanités marseillaises: Marseille, terrain des sciences sociales'. *Enquête* (4): 191–210. https://doi.org/10.4000/enquete.903

CHAPTER 6

Virgin Mary of Trapani in La Goulette (Tunisia)
An Interreligious Crossing

Carmelo Russo

Sapienza University of Rome

Abstract

The Virgin Mary of Trapani in La Goulette (Tunisia) is an emblematic case for studying a Mediterranean crossing. Worship of Mary arrived in Tunis with Sicilian migrants, chiefly in the decades between the 19th and 20th centuries. During that period, La Goulette was a multi-ethnic and multi-religious town: Tunisians, Sicilians, French, and Maltese, and Christians, Jews, and Muslims lived there all together. Since 1885, in La Goulette, there has been a procession on 15 August in which both Jews and Muslims have participated. Tunisian independence disrupted this phenomenon: since 1962, the procession has been forbidden. On 15 August 2017, after 55 years, the Virgin Mary's procession returned to La Goulette, an event celebrated even by local Muslims. The 'new' Virgin Mary of Trapani in La Goulette is the symbol of secularity – in the sense of *laïcité* – who sustains the rights of religious minorities in the public sphere. Alongside other contemporary multi-faith sites, La Goulette, the Virgin Mary of Trapani, and her procession have become

How to cite this book chapter:
Russo, Carmelo. 2022. 'Virgin Mary of Trapani in La Goulette (Tunisia): An Interreligious Crossing'. In *Locating the Mediterranean: Connections and Separations
across Space and Time*, edited by Carl Rommel and Joseph John Viscomi, 129–51.
Helsinki: Helsinki University Press. DOI: https://doi.org/10.33134/HUP-18-6.

less of a movement of the people and is now a larger symbol of the state and society at large.

Introduction: The Virgin Mary, the Migration, and the Mediterranean

In European and North American cities, immigration and religious diversity are related topics (Vertovec 2007). Debates regarding inter-religious dialogue, peaceful coexistence, multi-faith sites, etc. have revitalised public discourse in recent years. Nevertheless, multi-faith sites are not only contemporary and Western issues: until the first half of the 20th century, the Mediterranean world 'hosted' many religious sites and places of worship that were shared by different monotheistic believers (Albera 2005; Albera and Couroucli 2009). The Mediterranean area was a peripheral territory in a political and religious sense, both in the early modern world and in the contemporary one, between continuity and rupture, among relations, trade, and conflicts. The towns and cities on its shores constitute a porous boundary between the Christian and Muslim worlds that even housed scattered Jewish communities. In particular, in the North African landscape there were 'mixed' monotheistic places of worship and religious shrines attended by adherents to different religious communities (Albera and Couroucli 2009).

Starting from these premises, the aim of this chapter is to examine the case of the cult of the Virgin Mary of Trapani in La Goulette, whose origins have their roots in a migration from Sicily to Tunisia.[1] Notre Dame de Trapani represents an example of how location and religious symbolism are deeply entangled with historical trajectories in the Mediterranean. Her worship is a case in point for studying religious interactions and multi-faith sites: between the 19th and 20th centuries, Christians, Jews, and Muslims were all devoted to her and attended her procession on 15 August, in La Goulette and broadly in Tunisia. Therefore, she is a means to explore how the religious locations functioned in the Mediterranean context, and her procession is a way of enacting or performing this pluralism. *Mutatis mutandis*, in recent years Mary's procession in La Goulette continues to preserve her plural feature. After the difficult years that followed the 'revolution' of 2011, the procession of the Virgin of Trapani occurred in La Goulette on 15 August 2017, after 55 years. It took place in 2018 and 2019 too.

This chapter demonstrates that the procession of 2017 was not a nostalgic process linked to the past but rather it was connected to the present and the future of Tunisia. The 'new' Notre Dame de Trapani in La Goulette is more 'Tunisian' than 'Sicilian', judging by the event in 2017. She is the symbol of secularity who guards against menaces of Islamic extremism and who supports the rights of religious minorities. Nevertheless, the historical mythology and the rhetorical pluralism of the community in La Goulette constitute the basis for the readoption and the contemporary relevance of the Virgin and her procession. They are locating La Goulette in space and time, placing the town on a Mediterranean map of tourism by connecting its past to the present.

Tunisia and La Goulette as a Plural Ambiguous Context (19th–20th Centuries)

The history of Tunisia has long involved 'ethnic' pluralism. This country has always been a point of encounter and exchange, of autonomy and subjecthood in the context of competing Mediterranean empires (Lewis 2014, 22). In ancient times, Tunisian pluralism was composed of Phoenicians, Romans, the Kingdom of the Vandals, the Byzantine Empire, and Arabs. Since the medieval period, it had been central to the struggles for hegemony in the Mediterranean Sea, especially those between Spain and the Ottoman Empire, which symbolised the encounter and clash between Christianity and Islam. After 1705, the country formally existed as a vassal of the Turks, yet the Bey, the monarchs at the head of the Regency of Tunis, had a great deal of autonomy (Bessis 2019; Chérif 2008). Between the 15th and 16th centuries, different foreign components settled in the country. Among them were the Genoese in Tabarka (Gourdin 2008; Pignon 1980); European Jews, mostly after the Spanish crown drove them out of the Iberian Peninsula; people captured in Southern Europe to trade as slaves by raids of corsairs, mostly from South Italy (Bono 2005); and other slaves coming from sub-Saharan Africa, Andalusia, and Libya (Speziale 2016, 35).

In 1881, the French state and the Bey signed the Bardo Agreement, making Tunisia a French protectorate; only in 1956 would Tunisia regain its independence. Historians identify public works meant to 'modernise' the country promoted by the French Protectorate as the reason for enticing a new wave of Italian immigration in Tunisia.[2] The French undertook major improvements and developments in several areas, including infrastructure, industry, transport, administration, public health and education, and the financial system (Kassab and Ounaïes 2010, 352–54). Maltese workers, and many Italian ones, the vast majority from neighbouring Sicily – arrived in Tunisia attracted by employment opportunities, especially in factories and mines (Pasotti 1971, 16–17; Pendola 2007, 56–58), in accordance with a stereotypical scheme of 'French capital and Italian labor' (Pasotti 1971, 52–54). In particular, the French Protectorate promoted the building of the 'cité nouvelle', the new European town – recognisable by its squared plan – east of the old Arab town, thus many Sicilians were employed as masons.

Certainly, there were poor, illiterate and proletarian Sicilians in Tunisia, who left the island because of the exploitation of workers, agricultural crisis, and political revolts of 1893–1894 (Renda 1963, 63–64). Others were rich landowners who preferred expatriation over the new political conditions after Italy's national unification in 1861. From that date, still more Sicilians came to Tunisia because the Sicilian Mafia persecuted them, and Tunisia represented an escape from persecution and reprisals. However, some Sicilians migrated to Tunisia because they worked for the Mafia, whose networks, trade, and business extended into that country (Loth 1905, 331). They settled along north-eastern coastal areas, in rural villages, and in urban settlements, in which Sicilian presence was more concentrated (Lupo 1996 [1992], 154; Melfa 2008, 230–31).

Table 6.1: European presence in Tunisia between 1881 and 1911.

Year	France	Italy	Malta	Other Europe	Total
1881	700	11,200	7,000	100	19,000
1886	3,500	16,750	9,000	750	30,000
1891	10,000	21,000	11,700	750	43,450
1896	16,000	55,000	10,200	800	82,000
1901	24,000	71,000	12,000	4,000	111,000
1906	34,000	81,000	10,000	2,400	127,400
1911	46,000	88,000	11,300	2,700	148,000

Source: Pasotti 1971, 50.

For many decades, a paradoxical condition emerged: despite Tunisia being a French protectorate, Italian subjects continuously outnumbered French subjects, as Table 6.1 shows (Pasotti 1971, 50).

The number of Italians surpassed 80,000 in 1906 and they stabilised around 90,000 until the Second World War (Passalacqua 2000, 218). The Italian presence was so significant that some scholars referred to Tunisia as 'an Italian colony administered by French functionaries' (Lewis 2016, 238). Sicilians were widely the majority. From 1891 until 1936, they ranged from 55 per cent to 75 per cent of the total population of Italians (Speziale 2016, 35). They represented themselves as proud of their origin, their culture, and their traditions, and attempted to bring with them many of the social institutions they had known in Sicily. Because of their numerousness, French right-wing politicians and newspapers soon began to spread the idea of the 'Italian danger', based on Sicilian 'characters', as dangerous for the daily life of other people. They depicted Sicilians as violent, rebellious, contrary to the Protectorate, and unfit for dignified work (Lewis 2014, 55; Pasotti 1971, 80; Loth 1905, 329–36).

Ordinary lives and sociality in Tunisia at the turn of the century were marked by ambiguity and an imbalance in power: French subjects against 'the others', because, according to a non-French perspective, the Protectorate pursued a discriminatory policy. The ambiguity also concerned ideas and perception of national and identitarian belonging. Nevertheless, people came from France, Italy – mostly from Sicily – Malta, Greece, Turkey, Albania, Spain, Portugal, and Russia. To a lesser degree, they came from Northern Europe and the Balkans, and other African areas. Under the Protectorate, plural sources of authority remained in the country. Not only the French and the Bey ones, but also those of Italy and Great Britain (Lewis 2014, 19–23). Therefore, people of different origins, nationalities and religions lived side by side with Tunisians and also among them, in some areas. This was especially true in the urbanised region around Tunis and coastal towns as Bizerte, Sfax, and Sousse, and on the Cap Bon Peninsula (Alexandropoulos and Cabanel 2000). In this respect, it should be noted that normally these ethnic and national communities all lived together not in cosmopolitan or pluralist harmony but rather with divisions in class and in space, through a multitude of connections and separations. For instance, different national groups lived in certain neighbourhoods of cities, and in specific rural areas (Clancy-Smith 2000, 2002). Concrete examples are the *Petite Siciles* (Little Sicilies), which were neighbour-hoods almost entirely populated by Sicilians in Tunis, La Goulette, Biz-erte, Ferryville, Hammam Lif, Grombalia, Saïda, Redeyef, Sousse, and Sfax (Melfa 2007).

La Goulette was a case in point. At the end of the 19th century, it was a small portal town near Tunis. It was a multi-ethnic and multi-religious place, in which Tunisian, Sicilian, French, Christians, Jews, and Muslims and others lived all together. Paul Sebag (1998, 451) dif-ferentiated *Goulettois* pluralism into the categories shown in Table 6.2:

Table 6.2: Population in La Goulette between 1921 and 1936.

Year	Tunisia (Muslim)	Tunisia (Jew)	France	Italy	Malta	Total
1921	778	1,540	772	2,449	381	5,920
1926	1,998	2,074	1,264	2,921	299	8,556
1931	2,274	843	2,233	3,476	332	9,158
1936	2,343	1,668	2,713	3,801	265	10,790

Source: Sebag 1998, 451.

Though these are just population numbers, an important feature of La Goulette was its concrete mixing in urban space. As opposed to other towns, in La Goulette, the *Petite Sicile* was not an 'ethnic ghetto'. Oral histories[3] confirmed that people of different origins and nationalities in La Goulette inhabited the same buildings and constructed a new collective identity, that of *Goulettois*. Faithfulness and disparate origins would be based on friendship and solidarity. Differences would be a strength and pluralism a pride (Darmon 1969, 43). As Joëlle Bahloul noted in her masterful *The Architecture of Memory* (1996), these issues were common to many French colonial societies and emphasised by their memory. Referring to her relatives' Algerian town of Sétif, the author's informants remembered a two-storey dwelling with many apartments surrounding a courtyard: the upstairs inhabited by Jews, the downstairs by Muslims, which gave birth to a complex intercul-tural and interreligious household. Although the peculiar case study proposed by Bahloul was specific, the focus was not unusual in French colonies. In a tension between past and memory, history and myth, those contexts reveal a multifaced situation in which both the 'local perspective' and the 'global' one are conversing (Bahloul 1996, 7–10). In La Goulette, Muslims and Jews also visited the Catholic church of the town, which was dedicated to Saints Augustine and Fidèle. Because of the visitors of different religions, the church was an important centre, a material point of encounter in the town for this pluralist community, and a sort of multi-faith site. The 'location' of the church – a town characterised by the *limen*, both a material place and a location that brought various communities together – created important conditions for the plurality. It is not only a container category since it is a location that enables and allows a meeting of differences, as it is stated in Chapter 1. Non-Catholic worshippers came in the church to pray to a statue of the Virgin Mary of Trapani, which was there. It is a 'copy' of the 'original statue' that is in the Basilica-Sanctuary of Maria Santissima Annunziata in Trapani. Most Sicilians in Tunisia had at least one ancestor that arrived from the Western Sicilian province of Trapani. As late as in 1959, more than half of the Italians of Tunisia originated from Trapani (Finzi 2016, 58). The provenance of the Virgin made the church a central point for Sicilians. Even more important is that, in La Goulette, Sicilians, Tunisians, *Goulettois* in general, Catholics, Muslims, and Jews gave different meaning to the Virgin Mary, as will be explained below. However, Notre Dame de Trapani was the focus of a peculiar interreligious practice, especially during the procession of the Assumption, 15 August, in which Muslims and Jews also participated. The Church of Saints Augustine and Fidèle and the statue of the Virgin Mary located there exemplify the particular collective identity of *Goulettois* (Russo 2020, 40–49).

The Mythical Arrival of the Virgin Mary of Trapani to La Goulette

While conducting oral historical research, I inquired about the beginning of the worship of the Virgin Mary of Trapani to La Goulette. Sicilian witnesses of Tunisia often confused and mixed the mythical arrival of the Virgin Mary in Trapani and the spread of the 'original' cult of the Virgin of that Sicilian town. The first statue, the 'original' one, has Cypriot roots. According to a well-known legend in Trapani, it was carved in Cyprus between 730 and 739. It remained in a castle in Famagusta. In 1191, Richard I of England defeated the island and sold it to the

Templar Knights. They brought the statue to Acre, in contemporary Israel, until the Mamelukes conquered that city. At the end of 13th century, then, the Templars carried the statue on a boat, and brought it to Trapani (Mondello 1878, 11–25).

The arrival of the Virgin Mary in La Goulette was fixed by the 1974 novel *Chronique des morts*, written by Adrien Salmieri, an Italian novelist and writer born in Tunisia in 1929. Even though it appears curious, only in the mid-1970s did the mythical Goulettoise origin of Mary of Trapani assume a shared form: after most departures of European people and after the south shore of the Mediterranean had changed dramatically from the point of view of these pluralist communities. Starting from the novel, collective memory became a historical mark while being written from an outsider's point of view, providing symbolic legitimisation to oral representations (Bahloul 1996, 8). The story was written in French. Although it was the language of the colonisers, it has been used as a *lingua franca* enhancing plural sharing and communication. These elements reveal important themes about the location of La Goulette. The novel was a kind of recording of the oral history of the icon and contributed to the spread of the myth about the arrival of the Virgin Mary, commonly accepted knowledge among Italians from La Goulette and Tunisia. According to Salmieri's novel, the founding myth tells us that the statue had been sculpted in Cyprus. Between 1569 and 1571, the Turks besieged Famagusta, and local Christians gave it to Sicilian fishermen who lived in La Goulette. It is worth noting that the statue did not actually pass through Trapani. The seeming contradiction leads back to the ability of Notre Dame de Trapani to be venerated beyond the borders of the island. The Sicilian Jesuit Ottavio Gaetani highlighted the penetration of the cult of the Virgin of Trapani in different geographical and national contexts. He supported the thesis with the discovery of numerous statues of the Virgin of Trapani in other Sicilian towns, in many Italian regions, in France, Spain, Germany, and Hungary, and in the Mediterranean and the Middle East, including regions occupied by the Ottoman Empire (Mondello 1878, 67–68). Quoting Gupta and Ferguson (1997), the spread of the statues of the Virgin Mary demonstrates the quality of a location of 'being somewhere in particular' through connections and separations to other locations elsewhere, and through the ability to refract in other places (see the Introduction). Nevertheless, her settlement in La Goulette is very different from the one of other places mentioned above.

In that Tunisian town the Virgin Mary created a powerful symbolic universe tied to the communities in/around La Goulette because of the proximity, geographic and social, with Trapani, due to the wide presence of Sicilian worshippers. The resonances elsewhere in the Mediterranean, Europe, or the Middle East was not similar, because many other statues were commissioned by noble families or members of the clergy (Mondello 1878, 134–41). Nowadays, different statues of the Virgin Mary of Trapani are still located in different churches in Trapani and other Sicilian places.

An article in a local newspaper explains that the first procession in La Goulette took place on 15 August 1885 (E 1959). Because of the increase in Sicilian presence, the statue probably arrived at La Goulette shortly before that year. At that time, an association of fishermen had been founded in what was then a small town. The Virgin immediately became 'the Virgin Mary of fishermen', reinforcing her connection with the sea. Progressively the worship of Mary expanded from La Goulette to other Tunisian towns, mostly on the coasts. In 1909 the first procession took place in Tunis. The spread of the Marian cult, retracing that of Trapani, supported a wide production and trade of simulacrums. Some of them were imported into the country from Sicily. In other cases, Sicilian artisan immigrants in Tunisia produced statues. The proliferation of the copies of a peculiar statue of Virgin Mary is a common occurrence. In the former French colonial North Africa, it often involved both the country of origin and the destination one. A masterful example is the Virgin Mary of Santa Cruz, whose cult spread in the city of Oran, Algeria (Slyomovics 2019, 5–10).

The meaning and signification of the Virgin Mary of Trapani changes when she is in the two different locations – one in which she is firmly rooted in local histories, Trapani; the other in which she is carried with communities and protects wider communities. In Trapani, Virgin Mary was the bastion against Islam: she defended Trapani against privateer raids from North Africa, in particular from Tunisia (Mondello 1878, 79, 116). The Virgin Mary was the protector of Sicilian slaves – especially of Trapani – who had been captured by Tunisian privateers and were living in Tunisia. Giuseppe Pitrè,[4] at the end of the 19th century (1978 [1900], XXIV–XXV, 335–36, 464–66), found numerous poems and short stories about struggles between the Virgin Mary and Muslims in which slaves of Trapani were freed by the Virgin. In 1535 an important event connected Trapani and Tunisia under the

Marian sign: Charles V reconquered Tunis and the Karraka fortress of La Goulette. The emperor went to Trapani to thank the Virgin Mary for her help and protection. He led 20,000 freed slaves back to Trapani (Mondello 1878, 79). These events tied the two places together, and together they form a narrative that binds both Muslim and Christian to this small Tunisian site.

The Reasons for an Interreligious Worship

After arriving in La Goulette, the Virgin Mary of Trapani's role was inverted. While in the Sicilian context Mary had protected people of Trapani from North African privateers, in La Goulette she became an interreligious symbol that protected every *Goulettois* welcoming Muslims and Jews. In the 19th and 20th centuries, various monotheistic worshippers, both Jews and Muslims next to Christians, attended the Church of Saints Augustine and Fidèle of La Goulette to pray to the Virgin Mary of Trapani (Salmieri 1996; Sebag 1998).

On the Catholic side, the polysemous nature of Notre Dame de Trapani was based on her skill to incorporate 'different Marys'. Although in the Italian diaspora of Tunisia many Marian figures were venerated, such as the Madonna of Pompei, the Lady of Mount Carmel and the Mary of the Rosary, the Virgin Mary of Trapani was the most important both for the large percentage of Sicilian people and for her miraculous power (see below). The main incorporation relates to the Lady of the Assumption, because of her popularity in Christianity. The one-day advance of the date of the procession is evidence: from the original day in Trapani, 16 August, to the Tunisian date, 15 August (Russo 2020, 138–48).

A crucial inquiry deals with the reasons for which Muslims and Jews venerated the Virgin Mary of Trapani in La Goulette. There were theological reasons: for both Muslims and Jews, Mary was not an extraneous symbol in their own religious panorama. She is a figure in the Qur'an, in which she appears in 11 suras. In particular, the ninth sura is called the sura of Mary and the third, the sura of the family of 'Imrān, is dedicated to Mary's genealogy and family[5] (Wensinck 1991, 613–15). Because of the problematic nature of Jesus, Jews do not consider Mary a holy woman. They do, however, appreciate her as a 'Jewish mother'. In some cases, there were biographical motivations for interreligious reception. Some worshippers were born to 'mixed couples' and developed a peculiar religious sensitivity for the multiple religious communities of La Goulette, both the mosque of Sidi Cherif and the Catholic church.

The multi-religiousness of the Virgin Mary of Trapani bears above all a political meaning. Both Sicilians and Tunisians felt discriminated against by the French government and French subjects in Tunisia. In their prevailing perception, France constructed their inferiority, perpetrating a policy of violence established on the imbalance in power and inequality of access to resources.[6] Sicilians considered the French Protectorate's decisions vexatious and malicious. In 1891, the French Protectorate forced Italian Capuchin monks to move to make way for French clergy (Pasotti 1971, 79; Russo 2017, 505). In 1908, a French band, Societé La Jeanne d'Arc, replaced the Stella d'Italia, an Italian orchestra, to play in the procession at the Virgin Mary of Trapani Feast. In 1910, there was the proclamation of Sainte Jeanne d'Arc as Patron of La Goulette, to replace Mary of Trapani (Dornier 2000, 53; Russo 2017, 505). All these events undermined the Sicilian presence and were due to French policies, which aimed to subvert Italian presence and strengthen the Protectorate's power through the naturalisation law (Lewis 2014, 137–38). During the fascist period, the conflict between Italians and French grew more pronounced. Many Italians interpreted the dictatorship as support for their national pride (Russo 2016, 86–87). There was also a larger anti-fascist population in Tunisia (compared to Libya, an official colony, or Egypt), whose protagonists were members of the liberal bourgeoisie, often of Masonic affiliation; militants of the anarchist movement; members of the working class organised in the Socialist and Communist parties; or adherents of Giustizia e Libertà (Justice and Freedom).[7] Furthermore, a Tunisian section of the LIDU (Italian League for Human Rights) played an important role against the regime. Therefore, Tunisia was a dynamic political laboratory animated by such young Italian-Tunisians as Maurizio Valenzi, Loris Gallico, Marco Vais, the brothers Bensasson, and the contribution of political figures such as Velio Spano and Giorgio Amendola sent by the PCI, the Italian Communist Party, to provide international scope to the anti-fascist movement in Tunisia (El Houssi 2014).

Therefore, Sicilians – some of whom also opted for French naturalisation – and Tunisians of every religion participated in the procession emphasising their position against the French Protectorate. Being set apart from French power, the Virgin Mary of Trapani became a symbol of discriminated people and was on the side of the weak. Oral histories narrate the procession as focused on subalternity, in accordance with Gramsci's terminology. Fishermen – Sicilians or Tunisians – were paradigmatic worshippers for their lowly state and modest background and in Tunisia Mary strengthened her role as fishermen's defender.

Through visions, voices, and dreams, the *Goulettoise* mother of Jesus carried out miracles in favour of oppressed people, which was a common character for both Sicilians and Tunisians, as non-French people (Russo 2017, 506–7; 2020, 107–26). This matter was strictly linked to the topic of popular religiosity,[8] thus people were devout followers of Virgin of Trapani for her apotropaic and thaumaturgical capability. The miracles dealt with health, wellness, wealth, and hope for the future, to which was added political redemption: the procession of 15 August became a political way for marginalised people to complain against French domination.

The procession was not only a religious manifestation but also a way to 'conquer' public places and affirm the 'right to exist'. There was a large 'popular' interreligious crowd, which connected faith with magical practices. It consisted of fishermen and poor, sick, and weak people. The subalterns were the protagonists of the religious festival. Worshippers relied on sacred objects such as candles, flowers, gold, necklaces, and bracelets offered to the Virgin Mary. They stroked the Marian statue, seeking her blessing. After official celebration, the worshippers put the Madonna statue on a bedrock near some braziers, so the Virgin Mary began to 'perspire'. Using a tissue, they took 'miraculous sweat' and brought it to sick relatives or friends (Darmon 1969, 27–28; Russo 2017, 501–2).

Independence disrupted this phenomenon. In 1958, the Tunisian government forbade the procession in Tunis. In 1962 in La Goulette, after a two-year ban, there was a symbolic procession in the courtyard of the church. It was the last one, because a definitive ban was promulgated. There were two main reasons for the prohibition: first, the Tunisian State interpreted the presence of the Catholic Church as a legacy of the French Protectorate; second, new institutions were based on secularity, according ambiguously to *laïcité française*. Although the Tunisian constitution of 1959 recognised Islam as the country's official religion, and the new personal status code borrowed elements from sharia law, unified law courts united Jews, Muslims, and Christians into a single, secular Tunisian legal system (Lewis 2014, 177).

Since the second half of the 1960s, many European citizens/subjects left Tunisia because of restrictive laws, which made it difficult to live and work in the country. Numbers constitute incontrovertible evidence: in 1964, 10,000 Italian people lived in Tunisia, showing an impressive decrease of more than 80 per cent since 1949 (Finzi 2016, 56). The year 1964 represented the peak of a series of injunctions that damaged the stability of foreign people. The government restricted their labour with laws in 1958 and 1961, and the requisition of their property with a law in 1964 (Pasotti 1971, 166–69). Because of these limitations, the majority of Europeans, even those who were born in Tunisia, left the country. After all, if Protectoral Tunisia's legal system had been divided between 'European' and 'Tunisian' jurisdictions (Lewis 2014, 65, 177), the new state led by the President Bourguiba maintained the division.[9]

Also in 1964, the Tunisian State and Holy See signed a new *modus vivendi* bilateral agreement, by which the Catholic Church renounced many privileges and accepted Tunisian jurisdiction and control. The daily life of Catholics changed, due to the decrease in their population and political influence, maintaining a role in education[10] (Russo 2020, 36–40, 176). However, the Virgin Mary of Trapani remained in the Church of Saints Augustine and Fidèle of La Goulette, even between 1984 and 1986, when an association of La Ciotat (Marseille) tried to bring the Mary statue to that French town. This was not a foregone conclusion, as documented by similar cases in which some Virgin Mary statues followed the migration from other former French colonies. A valid example regarding this is the translation of a peculiar statue of the Madonna from Oran to Nimes across the Mediterranean around 1964 (Slyomovics 2019, 9). The association of La Ciotat was composed of *Goulettois* of Sicilian origins who had migrated to La Ciotat. It was named Association des Goulettois de La Ciotat et de Provence Côte-d'Azur and its members requested the intervention of the mayor of the town, Louis Perrimond. He wrote to the Tunisian consulate general to inform him of the association, which 'counts more than a thousand returnees from La Goulette and would like to celebrate in our town, every year on August 15th, the religious ceremony of *Notre Dame de Trapani* who gathered in La Goulette nearly 40,000 people coming from all the regions of Tunisia' (Archive of Prelature of Tunis, file 'La Goulette', n. 2; 1985, 31 October). The surnames of the members revealed Sicilian origins, such as Sansone, Cannamela,

Pinna, Bertolino, Savalli, and Piccito. They identified their main aim as the 'repatriation' of the Madonna of Trapani. After their failure to provoke interest on behalf of the mayor, the group sought mediation through the permanent representative of France to UNESCO, Gisèle Halimi, who was herself born in La Goulette in 1927 of a Jewish mother and a Berber father. In February 1986, Michel Callens, prelate of Tunisia, definitively denied the relocation of the statue from La Goulette to La Ciotat: 'I have the honor to inform you that since the church of La Goulette is still in operation, there can be no question of transferring the statue that is venerated there' (Archive of Tunisian Prelature, file 'La Goulette', n. 2; 1985, 21 February).

The Return of a 'New' Virgin Mary

The revolution of 2011 brought the country in a climate of uncertainty. Nonetheless, the Virgin Mary returned to the Tunisian public debate. On 15 August 2017, the procession occurred in La Goulette after 55 years, an unexpected event that saw participation by local Muslims and Jews. In March of the same year, there had been an anticipation of the new procession: the realisation of a mural painting of the Virgin Mary of Trapani in the church of La Goulette by Collettivo FX. This is a group of muralist artists operating in Reggio Emilia (Italy)[11] that proposed a large project entitled 'La Madonna dell'adesso' (Virgin Mary of today). The focus of the project was to bring up-to-date representations of the Virgin Mary in Italian towns in which she has a strong role in relation to 'social identity'. The group programmed a series of tours through the Italian Peninsula to meet Catholic communities related to a specific Madonna and talk about a possible new role of Mary.

By chance, Collettivo FX knew the story of Virgin Mary of Trapani of La Goulette. In February, Paolo of Collettivo FX sent an e-mail to the director of the Institute for Italian Culture in Tunis to inform him of their project:

> Among the proposals we also received, there was that of a Sicilian girl who pointed out the Virgin Mary of Trapani who belongs to the Sicilian community of La Goulette, famous for a procession attended by all the people, Christians, Jews and Muslims. It seemed to me a significant story that acquires even more value in this particular historical moment:

the opportunity to make a project in Italy that goes beyond the Mediterranean sends a strong signal.

Therefore, Paolo planned to start his mural project from La Goulette, because of its peculiarity of being an Italian Catholic community abroad. The aim was to realise a contemporary image through a mural painting to describe current meanings of the Virgin Mary of Trapani in La Goulette. Nevertheless, by 2017 the Catholic community in La Goulette, and generally in Tunisia, had transformed from what it had been 50–60 years ago. The 2000s saw significant changes in both the national and social composition of the Catholic community in Tunisia. Sub-Saharan immigrants replaced Europeans. Most arrived in Tunisia as part of a more general movement of people from the Global South that aimed to eventually reach European destinations. One and a half thousand Ivorian Catholics settled in the country in 2003 following the displacement of the African Development Bank from Abidjan, caused by the Ivory Coast civil war. Nevertheless, a temporary Catholic population came from Europe to Tunisia for a limited working period (Russo 2020, 176–79). Finally, an important Catholic component is composed of Tunisian people who converted to Catholicism. Their paths ambiguously interweave with Tunisian conversions to Pentecostalism, which are more conspicuous than Catholic conversions (Boissevain 2006; 2014).

Because of these demographic changes, relatively few people took part in the meeting with Paolo to plan the mural project. Thus, the 'Catholic community' with which the artist collaborated consisted of ten Catholic sub-Saharan African youth (variously from the Ivory Coast, Cameroon, Nigeria, and the Democratic Republic of Congo) who had a failed migratory experience, the Parson Narcisse (who arrived in 2012 from Chad), two Tunisians – a Muslim and an atheist – and an old Sicilian man, Nicola.

In order to understand the meanings of Notre Dame de Trapani, in a room of the church there was a two-day debate (14 and 15 March) in which Catholic people were meant to tell Paolo their ideas. From the speeches, it became clear that these Catholics coming from sub-Saharan Africa lacked knowledge about the story of the Virgin Mary of Trapani. They considered her to be 'only' Virgin Mary the mother of Jesus, and ignored the peculiar characteristics of her arrival from Trapani and her Tunisian settlement. On the other hand, they spoke about topics such as neocolonialism, the exclusion of poor people by the 'rich world', discriminations in terms of mobility, and the lack of passports and documents. Therefore, the debate about the Virgin of Trapani turned into discussions about the lives of migrants. Most African Catholics ran into obstacles during their Tunisian experiences, which caused discouragement, fear of the future, and discrimination. They felt unsatisfied by their new Tunisian life, because of difficulties in finding work and exclusion from the local society. The frustration

Image 6.1: The mural of the 'new' Virgin Mary of Trapani, painted by Paolo of Collettivo FX in a room of the Church of Saints Augustine and Fidèle, La Goulette, Tunis. In dialogue with the new pluralist constellation of the city, Paolo of Collettivo FX decided to break from tradition and represented the Virgin in a new way, as the defender of migrants: in the painting they are under the coat of Mary, to be protected against their own passports and documents that are 'raining'.
Photo: Carmelo Russo

of sub-Saharan immigrants was such that they doubted the initial idea
to go to Europe.

In dialogue with the new pluralist constellation of the city, Paolo
of Collettivo FX decided to break from tradition and represented the
Virgin in a new way, as the defender of migrants: in the painting they
would be represented under the coat of Mary, to be protected against
their own passports and documents that are 'raining' (see Image 6.1).
Immigrant people strongly demand 'the rain of documents', because

Image 6.2: The 2017 procession of the Virgin Mary of Trapani in La Goulette, that has revived in the town after 55 years of prohibition. In the
foreground, sub-Saharan African men are carrying the Marian statue,
in order to confirm the leading position of subaltern people. The bishop
and other persons of the clergy, Tunisian and European people, Catholic,
Muslim, Jews and atheists, are participating together.
Photo: Carmelo Russo.

they symbolise the exclusion of poor black people from the equal access to the resources of the world. The early idea of Collettivo FX was to represent the mural on the external wall of the church. However, since Mary's mural outside could have triggered sensitivities about Muslims (such as the Parson Narcisse and other Catholic people scared of Islamic extremists), the parish priest chose to place the painting in a room of the church, the biggest one next to the hall of worship. On 17 March, Paolo completed the painting.

During the debate to decide the iconography, the Parson Narcisse – who had been in La Goulette since 2012 – discovered the story of the Virgin Mary of Trapani in La Goulette. He had always considered the statue of the Church of Saints Augustine and Fidèle as a 'normal' simulacrum of Mary. On that occasion, he reflected upon the historical role of the Virgin Mary of La Goulette for subaltern people. Thus, the procession was revived in the town on 15 August 2017 (see Image 6.2). Narcisse turned to the mayor of La Goulette, who authorised a symbolic procession in the courtyard of the church. According to his vision, the Parson Narcisse imagined this procession as the beginning of a new ritual: he wanted to assemble the largest crowd in the streets of La Goulette.

Conclusion: Mary as a Tunisian Symbol

The procession of 2017 was not a nostalgic process linked to the past, but rather connected to the present and the future of Tunisia. Despite the paradox, the 'new' Virgin Mary of Trapani at La Goulette is more Tunisian and less Catholic and Sicilian. During the mass of 15 August, the mayor of La Goulette, the archbishop of Tunis and Carthage, Ilario Antoniazzi, and the Tunisian police were all present. In front of the church, there were many Tunisian flags. Above all, many Tunisians took part in the celebration. About 200 people were in the church for the mass: 35–40 per cent sub-Saharan Africans, 20 per cent Tunisians (of which 5 per cent were Catholics and 15 per cent were Muslim or atheist), and the rest were 'classic' Europeans. Outside, at least 100 Tunisians awaited the procession. When the statue went out, they gave her a big round of applause and *yousyous* to welcome her. In 2017, the Virgin Mary of Trapani was part of the Tunisian cultural landscape.

Tunisian intellectuals played a key role. For several months before the new procession, through blogs, social media, and websites, they promoted the procession of the Virgin Mary of Trapani as a symbol of democratic expression and guaranty of minorities' rights. A relevant example is the dedication of Hatem Bourial. He is a Tunisian journalist, a writer, and an intellectual who is interested in the enhancement of cultural heritage, particularly about a plural Tunisian identity. Between 27 January and 16 August 2017, he wrote many posts on Webdo.tn.[12]

The return of the procession revisits a debate about defining Tunisian identity – is it an Arab and Muslim monolith, or a pluralistic Mediterranean identity? But there is something beyond the political background of 2017 procession: a new concept of tourism in the country. It provides for a shift from a seaside tourism – managed by foreign tour-operators – to a cultural one, in which the beach is not refused but combined with artistic, historic, folkloristic, and religious exploitation and development (Herzfeld 2005). These questions place La Goulette on a Mediterranean map of tourism by conjuring the pluralistic narrative of its past in the context of its differently pluralistic present. Some samples in the last years gained positive feedback: Sidi El Kantaoui zâwiya; Ghirba pilgrimage in Djerba; Aoussu Carnival in Sousse (reintroduced in 2015); the 'Festival du Poisson' in La Goulette; and cultural events such as the exhibition 'Lieux saints partagés', from November 2016 to February 2017, hosted by Bardo Museum, in which a section was focused on the Virgin Mary of Trapani in La Goulette. While the procession's closure in 1962 represented 'the end of an era', 2017 was the beginning of a new 'age'.

Paradoxically, the 'new' Virgin Mary of Trapani in La Goulette is the symbol of secularity – in the sense of laïcité – who guards against menaces of Islamic extremism and who sustains the rights of religious minorities in the public sphere. Both the mural and the return of the procession show that the Virgin Mary of Trapani in La Goulette has a political role in the present time, and is more than a nostalgic symbol of the past. She stands against those who want to instrumentalise post-revolutionary uneasiness in order to exclude non-Arabs and non-Muslims from rights and citizenship. She is still on the side of discriminated, weak, and subaltern people, not merely Christians in a Muslim context, but above all Tunisian people that stand for the plural origins of their own country and its involvement in Mediterranean relations.

Notes

1 Trapani is a town in the west of Sicily. The majority of Sicilian people who migrated to Tunisia came from that city and its surrounding area. Nevertheless, Sicilian people outside that area were also devoted to the Virgin Mary of Trapani. La Goulette is a coastal suburb of Tunis, 12 kilometres from the centre of the current capital.

2 Even before the establishment of the French Protectorate, the prime minister of the Regency, Khayr ad-Dīn, launched as early as 1870 a vast public works programme, because of progress on European models and the reform policy. Tunisian people were unable to satisfy a growing need for labour, which attracted many Italian workers (Melfa 2008, 66).

3 Marta Scialdone and I conducted two periods of fieldwork, in July–August 2012 and July–August 2013. We recorded 53 life stories of Sicilians of Tunisia. Since October 2014, audio and video, transcriptions, and photographs collected are stored at the 'Diego Carpitella' Laboratory of Anthropology of Images and Sounds at Sapienza University of Rome. Subsequently I conducted a second field research between 2014 and 2017 for my PhD program.

4 Giuseppe Pitrè (1841–1916) was a Sicilian medical doctor and senator for Sicily. He taught at the University of Palermo (Sicily) and wrote the first scientific studies on south Italian popular culture, pioneering ethnographic studies in his country.

5 'Imrān is the father of Mary, Joachim in Christian sources.

6 The history of Tunisia from the 1880s to the 1930s proves that the everyday manoeuvrings of colonised people posed obstacles to French administrators and forced them to react in ways that altered colonial governance considerably (Lewis 2014, 9).

7 A liberal–socialist political movement founded in Paris in August 1929 by a group of anti-fascist exiles, among whom emerged as leader Carlo Rosselli. His brother Nello, Emilio Lussu, and others, also played a prominent role.

8 The idea of popular religiosity/religion is well known in Italian anthropology and historiography thanks to Ernesto De Martino (1908–1965). In the 1940s and 1950s he conducted a series of field studies among poor and underschooled people of rural south Italy – the 'people without history' – focusing on the idea of their 'crisis of the presence and religious reintegration'. Other scholars followed his perspectives. De Martino's theories were based on the approach of Italian intellectual Antonio Gramsci (1891–1937), who was one of the founders of the Italian Communist Party. Gramsci reflected on the fundamental character of societies based on class divisions. He focused on the colonial and semi-colonial people, as well as proletarians and peasants in the hegemonic nations, in relation to the dominant class: the bourgeoisie (Gutherz 2017).

9 After independence, the Tunisian state passed a law allowing Europeans born in Tunisia, with fathers and paternal grandfathers born in Tunisia, to acquire Tunisian citizenship. There were few people who opted for this choice (Russo 2016, 87).

10 In 2016–2017, there were nine Catholic schools in Tunisia, five of them in the capital and others in Aïn Draham, Bizerte, Menzel Bourguiba, and Sousse.

There are about 6,000 students – the majority Muslims – and 600 employees, including teachers, office workers, etc. (Russo 2020, 176).

11 Some muralist artists of Reggio Emilia formed Collettivo FX in 2010. They are involved in programmes between Italy and Spain, but are also politically active in cultural and social enhancement of Emilia-Romagna.

12 Their titles are eloquent: 'Voici Notre-Dame de Trapani, la Madone de la Goulette!' (27 January 2017); 'La Goulette: La procession du 15 août pourrait reprendre en 2017' (6 July 2017); 'La procession de la Madone aura lieu le 15 août à La Goulette' (10 August 2017); 'Document: La procession de la Madone de Trapani par la photo' (16 August 2019).

References

Albera, Dionigi. 2005. 'Pèlerinages mixtes et sanctuaires 'ambigus' en Méditerranée'. In *Les pèlerinages au Moyen-Orient: espaces public, espaces du public*, edited by Sylvia Chiffoleau and Anna Madoeuf, 347–68. Damas: Institut Français du Proche-Orient.

Albera, Dionigi, and Maria Couroucli, eds. 2009. *Religions traversées: Lieux saints partagés entre chrétiens, musulmans et juifs en Méditerranée*. Arles: Éditions Actes Sud.

Alexandropoulos, Jacques, and Patrick Cabanel, eds. 2000. *La Tunisie mosaïque. Diasporas, cosmopolitisme, archéologies de l'identité*. Toulouse: Presses Universitaires Mirail.

Bahloul, Joëlle. 1996 [1992]. *The Architecture of Memory: A Jewish-Muslim Household in Colonial Algeria, 1937–1962*. Cambridge: Cambridge University Press.

Bessis, Sophie. 2019. *Histoire de la Tunisie. De Carthage à nos jours*. Paris: Tallandier.

Boissevain, Katia. 2006. *Sainte parmi les saints. Sayyda Mannûbiya ou les recompositions cultuelles dans la Tunisie contemporaine*. Paris: Maisonneuve & Larose. Accessed 6 September 2019. http://books.openedition.org/irmc/497.

Boissevain, Katia. 2014. 'Le baptême adulte de chrétiens tunisiens: rituel public d'un engagement privé'. *Cahier d'Étude du Religieux, Numéro spécial: Les conversions religieuses en Méditerranée*. https://doi.org/10.4000/cerri.1408

Bono, Salvatore. 2005. *Lumi e corsari. Europa e Maghreb nel Settecento*. Perugia: Morlacchi.

Chérif, Mohamed Hédi. 2008. *Histoire de la Tunisie. De la préhistoire à l'indépendance*. Tunis: Cérès.

Clancy-Smith, Julia. 2000. 'Gender in the City: The Medina of Tunis'. In *Africa's Urban Past*, edited by David Anderson and Richard Rathbone, 189–204. Oxford: Currey.

Clancy-Smith, Julia. 2002. 'Marginality and Migration: Europe's Social Outcasts in Pre-Colonial Tunisia, 1830–81'. In *Outside In: On the Margins of the Modern Middle East*, edited by Eugene L. Rogan, 149–82. London: Tauris.

Darmon, Raoul. 1969. *La Goulette... et les Goulettois*. Sidi Bou Said: Alyssa Editions.

Dornier, François. 2000. *La vie des catholiques en Tunisie au fil des ans*. Tunis: Finzi.

E, V. '1959 15 agosto. Assunzione in Cielo della S.S. Vergine Maria'. *Il Corriere di Tunisi*, 15 August, p. 2.

El Houssi, Leila. 2014. *L'urlo contro il regime. Gli antifascisti italiani in Tunisia tra le due guerre*. Rome: Carocci.

Finzi, Silvia. 2016. 'Oltre i mestieri. Memorie, identità politica e rappresentazioni sociali dei lavoratori italiani in Tunisia'. In *Non più a sud di Lampedusa. Italiani in Tunisia tra passato e presente*, edited by Laura Faranda, 43–68. Rome: Armando.

Gourdin, Philippe. 2008. *Tabarka. Histoire et archéologie d'un préside espagnol et d'un comptoir génois en terre africaine (XVe-XVIIIe siècle)*. Tunis: Institut National du Patrimoine.

Gupta, Akhil, and James Ferguson, eds. 1997. *Anthropological Locations: Boundaries and Grounds of a Field Science*. Berkeley, CA: University of California Press.

Gutherz, David. 2017. 'Ernesto de Martino and the Drama of Presence'. *Chicago Review* 60/61 (4/1): 55–61.

Herzfeld, Michael. 2005. 'Practical Mediterraneanism: Excuses for Everything, from Epistemology to Eating'. In *Rethinking the Mediterranean*, edited by William V. Harris, 45–63. Oxford: Oxford University Press.

Kassab, Ahmed, and Ahmed Ounaïes. 2010. *L'Époque Contemporaine 1881–1956*. Tunis: Sud Editions.

Lewis, Mary D. 2014. *Divided Rule: Sovereignty and Empire in French Tunisia, 1881–1938*. Berkeley, CA: University of California Press.

Lewis, Mary D. 2016. 'Europeans before Europe? The Mediterranean Prehistory of European Integration and Exclusion'. In *French Mediterraneans: Transnational and Imperial Histories*, edited by Patricia M.E. Lorcin and Todd Shepard, 232–61. Lincoln, NE: University of Nebraska Press.

Loth, Gaston. 1905. *Le peuplement italien en Tunisie et Algérie*. Paris: Colin.

Lupo, Salvatore. 1996 [1992]. *Storia della mafia dalle origini ai nostri giorni*. Rome: Donzelli.

Melfa, Daniela. 2007. 'Regards italiens sur les Petites Siciles de Tunisie'. *Ibla* 199 (1): 3–27.

Melfa, Daniela. 2008. *Migrando a sud. Coloni italiani in Tunisia (1881–1939)*. Rome: Aracne.

Mondello, Fortunato. 1878. *La Madonna di Trapani. Memorie patrio-storico-artistiche*. Palermo: Tipografia di Pietro Montaina e Comp.

Pasotti, Nullo. 1971. *Italiani e Italia in Tunisia dalle origini al 1970*. Tunis: Finzi.

Passalacqua, Daniele. 2000. 'Cenni sommari sulla vita culturale a Tunisi nel XIX e nella prima metà del XX secolo'. In *Memorie italiane di Tunisia*, edited by Silvia Finzi, 213–18. Tunis: Finzi.

Pendola, Marinette. 2007. *Gli italiani di Tunisia. Storia di una comunità (XIX-XX secolo)*. Foligno: Editoriale Umbra.

Perkins, Kenneth J. 1986. *Tunisia: Crossroads of the Islamic and European Worlds*. Boulder, CO: Westview.

Pignon, Jean. 1980. *Gênes et Tabarque au XVIIème siècle*. Tunis: Université de Tunis.

Pitrè, Giuseppe. 1978 [1900]. *Feste patronali in Sicilia*. Palermo: Il Vespro.

Renda, Francesco. 1963. *L'emigrazione in Sicilia*. Palermo: Sicilia al Lavoro.

Russo, Carmelo. 2016. 'Sangue italiano, mente francese, cuore tunisino. Nazionalità tra percezioni e appartenenze'. In *Non più a sud di Lampedusa. Italiani in Tunisia tra passato e presente*, edited by Laura Faranda, 85–111. Rome: Armando.

Russo, Carmelo. 2017. 'La Madonna di Trapani a La Goulette. Rappresentazioni identitarie e pluralismo religioso tra pratiche, retoriche, politiche'. In *La Storia delle religioni e la sfida dei pluralismi*, edited by Sergio Botta, Marianna Ferrara and Alessandro Saggioro, 496–507. Brescia: Morcelliana.

Russo, Carmelo. 2020. *Nostra Signora del limite. L'efficacia interreligiosa della Madonna di Trapani in Tunisia*. Brescia: Morcelliana

Salmieri, Adrien. 1996. 'Notes sur la colonie sicilienne de Tunisie entre 19e et 20e siècles'. In *Ailleurs, d'ailleurs*, edited by Jean-Charles Vegliante, 31–68. Paris: Presses de la Sorbonne Nouvelle.

Sebag, Paul. 1998. *Tunis. Histoire d'une ville*. Paris: L'Harmattan.

Slyomovics, Susan. 2019. 'The Virgin Mary of Algeria: French Mediterraneans'. *En Miroir, History and Anthropology*: 1–21. https://doi.org/10.1080/02757206.2019.1684912.

Speziale, Salvatore. 2016. 'Gli italiani di Tunisia tra età moderna e contemporanea: diacronia di un'emigrazione multiforme'. In *Non più a sud di Lampedusa: Italiani in Tunisia tra passato e presente*, edited by Laura Faranda, 17–42. Rome: Armando.

Vertovec, Steven. 2007. 'Super-diversity and Its Implications'. *Ethnic and Racial Studies* 30 (6): 1024–54. https://doi.org/https://doi.org/10.1080/01419870701599465.

Wensinck, Arent Jan. 1991. 'Maryam'. In *Encyclopédie de l'Islam*, vol. VI, edited by Clifford Edmund Bosworth, Charles Pellat and Emeri Johannes van Donzel, 613–17. Paris: Maisonneuve & Larose.

CHAPTER 7

A Line in the Sand
Colonial Traces on Beirut's Mediterranean Coastline

Samuli Lähteenaho
University of Helsinki

Abstract

A line drawn in the sand became significant in the late 2010s at a public beach on the Mediterranean coastline of Lebanon. This line, originally drawn by the French mandatory authority governing Lebanon at the time as part of a land registry reform in the late 1920s, gathered new-found significance in current day Lebanon. The chapter starts by outlining the historical shift from the Ottoman-era land registry and property regime in Beirut to the new regime instituted by the French colonial authorities. Then, the chapter discusses how contemporary urban politics such as public space campaigning has engaged the traces of the mandate-era reform, in relation to a widely shared propertied understanding of space on the Lebanese littoral. It further examines how the line in the sand became poetically dense, a locus for claiming space as public or private. Through these discussions, the chapter asks how the public beach (and the coastline at large) became located at the intersection of different spatial logics, including that of the land regis-

How to cite this book chapter:
Lähteenaho, Samuli. 2022. 'A Line in the Sand: Colonial Traces on Beirut's Mediterranean Coastline'. In *Locating the Mediterranean: Connections and Separations
across Space and Time*, edited by Carl Rommel and Joseph John Viscomi, 153–75.
Helsinki: Helsinki University Press. DOI: https://doi.org/10.33134/HUP-18-7.

try reform. The connections and disconnections implied in these logics were derived in part through the significance of the Mediterranean for the Lebanese coastline, but also composed it in the contemporary moment as a constitutive part of regional constellations.

Introduction

In the summer of 2019, on the public beach of Beirut, a line drawn in the sand became significant. The white sands of the beach, often spoken of as the last public beach in Beirut, had existed there for ages. Over the years, other such coastal spots around it had been closed off due to urbanisation and privatisation. Frequented by people from all walks of society, albeit with a rather working-class reputation, the narrow stretch of sand spread for around a kilometre and half between the Mediterranean Sea and a coastal boulevard. This was the place where I had carried out fieldwork since early 2018, following the work of an NGO responsible for the beach. As always, other lines had been carved in the sand by the waves and tides of the gushing sea, receding in the summer and reaching towards the elevated coastal boulevard during the storms of winter. The particular line followed in this chapter was instead a trace of a land registry reform carried out by the French during their colonial mandate in the 1920s.

The public beach, Ramlet el-Bayda, had come to play a central part in a discussion on Lebanon's privatised coastline (see Image 7.1). As space across the coast was increasingly fenced off for private resorts, the 'remaining' public beaches gained in significance. Although it was by no means the only public beach in the country, it remained the last free and managed sands in the immediate vicinity of the capital. Set on the southern edge of municipal Beirut, it was located next to a relatively well-off neighbourhood named after the sands.

Since at least the early 2000s, the beach had been officially consigned as a public beach, managed by a local environmental NGO on behalf of the Lebanese Ministry of Transportation. Over the almost 20 years of managing the beach, the older generation of environmentalists and younger volunteers from the NGO had made it their place, assembling infrastructure, providing services, safeguarding turtle nests, and spending endless cool evenings and scorching days on the sands. One summer Saturday morning, without previous warning, municipal employees descended on the beach and proceeded to

Image 7.1: The Ramlet al-Bayda beach.
Photo: Lena Malm.

trash everything put up by the NGO. Citing a lack of permits, they dismantled shacks for a kiosk, administration, and a snack restaurant, in addition to a large veranda. The infrastructure that had been painstakingly built over months and years, used by the group maintaining the beach for their day-to-day operation, was demolished in a mere half an hour with a bulldozer. The environmentalists were left in shock. Years and months of their work had gone down the drain. Some expressed defiance, vowing to rebuild and not let the municipality privatise the beach; one of my interlocutors said he had had enough of the country, and decided to look for work opportunities elsewhere.

A conflict over management of the beach was at stake. The municipality of Beirut had taken a negative perception on the existing arrangement between the NGO and the Ministry of Transportation. Publicly, the municipality claimed their new stance was related to a campaign for improving and beautifying the coastline of Beirut, but my interlocutors in the local NGO suggested that the reason was their staunch opposition to the beach being privatised. The real issue, they argued, was their vocal condemnation of a hotel that had recently been constructed on parts of the beach. The owner of the hotel happened to be a businessman well connected to political circles of the country.

Intense negotiations ensued. Whereas the NGO tried to reach their backers in the Ministry of Transportation, the municipal officers insisted that the group should vacate their operation on the beach. Before long, a kind of tense status quo was reached. The NGO relocated its equipment midway down the beach, paying respect to an invisible line in the sand. Meanwhile, municipal police made sure the environmentalists would not move their things above the line.

I was perplexed by this situation. Who drew this line in the sand? The NGO was allowed to store their equipment on the seaward side of the line, but they could not be moved above it. What exactly was going on? After all, the sands in their entirety were called the public beach of Beirut and had been designated as such by state authorities.

It took me a while to realise I had indeed seen this line in some maps before, and my interlocutors confirmed as much. The beach, a volatile stretch of white sands between a coastal boulevard and the sea, was legally divided in two. The upper part was surveyed[1] land, mapped in the land registry and owned mostly by private families and entrepreneurs, in addition to a plot owned by the municipality of Beirut. The part towards the sea, by contrast, was public land, designated as maritime public domain. The maritime public domain was originally legislated by French colonial authorities in the 1920s, stating that the reach of waves in the winter set the upper limit of this domain. Consequently, come autumn, my interlocutors were anxiously eyeing at the approaching winter, their equipment still located on the public domain, below which they certainly knew the winter storms would cover.

In this chapter I examine how the line in the sand, along with other traces of past spatial logics, gained in importance for contemporary politics of the coastline in Lebanon. I should note that it is not my intention to specifically interrogate the meaning of the public/private binary or the concept of public space in Beirut. I treat the concept of public space as emic, as it is used by my interlocutors in Beirut, and I refer to public or private as they are presented in the context of the Lebanese land registry, property regime, and general discourse on public space. I argue that, through focusing on the line in the sand, we can understand how the beach (and the coastline) becomes located (Green 2005, 2019) at the intersection of different spatial logics. I suggest that the intersection should be understood both as synchronic, in the sense of a simultaneity of different spatial logics, but also as dia-chronic in the sense of ghosts of past spatial logics haunting the pre-sent (Bou Akar 2019; see also Navaro-Yashin 2009). The connections and disconnections (Strathern 1996) these logics implied were derived through the place of the Lebanese coastline on the Mediterranean, but also composed it in the contemporary moment as a constitutive part of the regional constellations.

This chapter consists of three sections. First, I outline the shift from the land registry and property regime in Beirut as part of the late Ottoman Empire to the new regime instituted by the French colonial authorities, introduce the notion of spatial logics, and lay the ground for how reforms from the 1920s became crucial for the location of coastal places today. In the second part, I present some ways in which urban politics and public space campaigning in present-day Beirut has engaged the traces of the cadastral regime instituted nearly 100 years ago. I discuss how propertied understandings of the coastline (Fawaz and Moumtaz 2020) form a basis for contemporary urban politics, and how some activists went hunting for traces of past spatial logics as a political intervention. In the third part, I look at how the cadastral lines were contested and challenged both by fencing off the public for private use, and by sneaking onto the 'private' to claim it as public, and return to examine this dynamic at the public beach. I suggest that these contestations were grounded in the way locations become poetically dense (Stasch 2013), understood as carrying significance for a coastal politics.

A Cadastral Reform in Colonial Times

I was sitting in eastern Beirut, waiting on a restaurant windowsill, when I saw him walk up the street. He waved his hand and smiled, but kept talking on the phone for several minutes. When my interlocu-tor, the older-generation urbanist activist, stopped, he greeted me with another courteous smile. We walked inside the now-closed-down halal butcher's shop across the street, where he spread out several maps he had printed on a dusty table, and began explaining to me, outlining the task at hand. He needed to have photos of the neighbourhood, to pre-pare for a presentation about safeguarding a number of 1950s 'French-style' buildings under threat of demolition, as part of a campaign for saving architectural heritage in Beirut. He walked the pen (which I had kindly borrowed) along the map and outlined edges to form the area for our scrutiny, circling certain plots and crossing others over. Distracted from the issue being explained to me, my attention was drawn to the map. Black lines on white paper, squares with numbers in them. I was not looking at a touristic map but something that I slowly recognised as a cadastral map. Later on, as I was pondering on this encounter and others I had involving maps or other information related to the land registry, it dawned on me that such spatial imagination formed a central way of relating to urban space and effecting change in it for bureaucrats and officials, but also for urban activists looking to make positive change in heritage protection or issues of public space.

Maps are something of a taken-for-granted in urban politics. The way they outline streets, plots of land, and buildings, forms a backdrop and an essential tool for formulating and executing an urban politics in relation to judicial regimes of land ownership. The political importance of colonial land registry and mapping has raised some relatively recent scholarly interest. Giselle Byrnes (2002, 40), a historian of colonial New Zealand, has famously stated that the gaze of the colonial land surveyor was the gaze of the empire. In the context of the Levant, Robert Home (2006) has looked at the British institution of cadastral surveying in the Mandate for Palestine and suggested that colonial cadastral reforms had significant political outcomes, including facilitating transfers of land from Arabs to Jews. In relation to colonial mapping beyond the cadastral survey, recent work by Asher Kaufman (2015) has examined the extent to which colonial-era maps played a larger geopolitical role, constituting arguments for the state boundaries we see in the contemporary Middle East. As Mark Neocleous (2003) has argued, the power of maps is based on how author and interest are marginalised and done away with, allowing for the map to present a supposedly neutral depiction of reality. And, crucially for my understanding, Hatim el-Hibri (2009) has argued that traces of past cartographic practices continue to shape the space of Beirut today.

Building on the importance of spatial logics and imaginations embedded in mapping and the land registry, I propose an argument about the way the cadastral reform continues to haunt the urban politics of the present. Specifically, I argue that the historical institution and reform of land registry in Lebanon constituted a certain spatial logic that has become significant for the urban politics of today. The coastline becomes located diachronically in what the anthropologist of

Lebanon Heba Bou Akar has described in her discussion of contemporary spatial politics of sectarianism in relation to historical master plans as 'The fight over the shadows of old planning schemes' (Bou Akar 2019, 96): how spatial logics of past ages continue to haunt the present condition.

A short discussion of the history of the land registry and property regime in Beirut serves to ground this argument. The contemporary cadastral regime differs from the one upheld during late Ottoman times by the imperial administration in Beirut.[2] In those days, property ownership was not premised on precise identification and mapping of plots. Instead, the Ottoman land registry recorded sales of land between persons. In order to prove your ownership of land you would refer to the sales contract passing ownership of the land to you. Another important aspect of the Ottoman system, cutting some corners and without delving into the details of the legal framework, was differentiation between the categories of *mulk* and *miri*. While *mulk*, land in absolute ownership, was somewhat close to European notions of private property, *miri* was state-owned agricultural land, 'rented out' on permanent leases to individual farmers. However, in the late Ottoman system, *miri* lands could also be inherited and sold with only the symbolic approval of the relevant authorities, thus diminishing in practice the distinction between *miri* and the French notion of private property. According to Ziadeh (1993), this could be seen as part of a longer process of privatisation of state lands stretching back to the modernisation reforms of the Ottoman Empire in the mid-19th century.

With the breakdown of the Ottoman Empire after the Treaty of Lausanne in 1922, which ended the Great War, the French colonial regime assumed control over the territory of Greater Syria. The French mandatory administration instituted wide-ranging administrative reforms. One of these was a reform of the cadastral system in the newly formed State of Greater Lebanon, later to become the Republic of Lebanon. During the 1920s, the French mandatory administration undertook surveying work, registration of titles, and institution of a number of decrees establishing the Land Registry and the relevant administrative framework. In 1930, a new property law by administrative decree established principles for ownership rights, immovable property, and so on. As Hatem el-Hibri notes (2009, 122–23), the cadastral survey itself was commissioned to M. Camille Durraffourd, who hired Russian engineers with recent experience in cadastral surveys in Yugoslavia, and utilised new technologies such as aerial photography to achieve accuracy. Their work aimed at replacing the former Ottoman *Defter Khane* system with the Napoleonic *cadastre* and the Torrens land-title registration system, to foster agricultural reform in the countryside and urban planning especially in Beirut.(See Image 7.2.)

Centralised and reified knowledge of land ownership was unsurprisingly appreciated by the 21st-century land registry bureaucrats. As the official website of the Land Registry of Lebanon noted at the time of my fieldwork on the colonial-era reform, '[a]s a result of the implementation of the works related to surveying and land registry, estates appeared clearer and more accurate with regards to their area, ownership, or relevant rights'. From the perspective of the spatial logic of the land registry bureaucracy in contemporary Beirut, increased accuracy and clarity were still considered central outcomes of the 1920s reforms. In a related vein, the historian Elizabeth Williams (2015, 172) has argued that the French mapping of the *cadastre* in Syria implied a shift in ways of knowing and governing, producing centralised and reified knowledge of land ownership.

One summer 2018 afternoon in Beirut over a coffee on the busy Hamra street I was discussing the history and current state of Lebanese *cadastre* with a former employee of the Land Registry. The former employee noted to me that the French administration responsible for Lebanon had a very experimental approach to administration of the colonies, where they were free to test and use innovative administrative approaches. Thus, the system implemented in Lebanon was not the same as used in most of France but a Franco-German system found in Alsace during German times and up until today.[3]

Later, I interviewed a director of the Beirut Land Registry in his office on the top floor of a decaying concrete building close to downtown Beirut. The director, a respectful and enthusiastic man, also stressed the Alsace connection, and joyfully noted how he had recently enjoyed an interesting trip to Alsace due to it. He further emphasised that, although there are slight differences between the systems currently in use in Alsace and Lebanon, they are based on similar principles. It is based on unique identification of the plot with reference to a map based on surveying work, and includes a history of all sales of the plot. This contrasts with the standard French system in which the registry does not show the precise boundaries between properties.

Image 7.2: Cut from the cadastral map for the city of Beirut depicting the Ramlet al-Bayda area.

Source: Edited by DAGG, based on compilation of cadastral documents and field survey in 1964. Drawn by GAL Engineers. Updated in January 2004 by the Municipality of the City of Beirut. Drawn by the Kozhaya Sfeir Office of Topography. Image is in the public domain.

According to my land registry interlocutors, the significant feature of this French–Alsatian cadastral system is the identification of
plots with clearly defined borders. In terms of land ownership, and
importantly for the argument of this chapter, one change in the new
property law was a reshuffling of the public/private distinction. On
the one hand, the French colonial administration allowed *miri* lands to
be registered in the name of their former renters. On the other, public

ownership of land was divided between the public domain, meaning non-surveyed public lands, and so-called 'government private property', i.e. publicly owned surveyed land.

Another point of importance I leaned from my interlocutors at the land registry related to cuts in flows of information. As part of the passage of time from mandate Lebanon to our current age, in addition to numerous legal shifts and adjustments, Lebanon underwent a period of civil strife (1975–1990). Extended wars pose risks to archives and government institutions, yet according to my interlocutor the land registry survived the war relatively well. The documents containing the deeds survived the war well, yet the cadastral maps suffered some wear during the time. One of the measures taken by the registry's bureaucrats during the war was a freeze on registering changes to ownership with absentee owners. This was in order to prevent forgeries in a situation where many landowners had fled the country, and thus preserve ownership. My interlocutors noted that obviously there was still some forgery, but it was very limited in scale.

For our consideration, a crucial part of the French land registry reforms was the institution in 1925 of a decree on maritime public domain. This is the law that, accompanied by surveying work, effectively drew the line in the sand along the Lebanese coastline, separating public domain from surveyed land. As Beiruti activists often quoted from the law:

> The maritime public domain consists of the seashore extending to the farthest distance that the waves reach in winter, as well as sand and gravel beaches … and then, those coastal grounds, and waters connected to the sea that do not form part of the natural cadastred land of the country.[4]

The decree states that the land falling under the 'winter waves', the maritime public domain, cannot be recorded in the registry as property, nor can it be sold or acquired as property over time. From the outset, the decree came with exceptions. It allowed for a temporary occupation in exchange for a fee and meeting some conditions (see Legal Agenda 2016). The decree was later amended multiple times, specifying the details for such occupancy to the systematic benefit of investors and the real estate industry. Nonetheless, mapping the maritime public domain into cadastral maps produced a line running along the coastline, below which land is not surveyed and separated into plots.

This notion of 'public' implicit in the 1925 maritime public domain continues to carry a central importance in contemporary discussions around the coastline of Beirut.

The significance of the colonial law that instituted the coastline as public domain was not lost on urban activists in early 21st-century Beirut. During my fieldwork, mentions of the domain were circulating widely in activist publications and journalistic texts, and utilised in campaigns and protests (e.g. Dictaphone 2013). As part of the general becoming-significant of the land registry for both institutions and activists, the line that delineates the maritime public domain was part of a very active knowledge cultivated by campaigners and scholar-activists[5] in Beirut engaging with the privatisation of the city's coastline. This was the very same line in the sand we started this chapter with.

Engaging the *Cadastre*

Urban politics and activism in Beirut during my fieldwork pivoted to a large degree around issues of land and land ownership. In this context, the colonial reform of the land registry by the French mandate authorities in 1920s Lebanon emerged as important for contemporary urban politics. As the entanglement of urban space, the waves of the Mediterranean, and the spatial tools of the colonial land surveyor had brought about a demarcation of the coastline, lines drawn in 1920s Beirut became important again in the context of the 2010s. And not only in the sense of 'setting the stage' for privatisation of the coastline and opposition to it. What is more, the lines drawn by the cadastral regime became blurry and contested, through history.

The resurgent relevance of the line in the sand was related to how the coastline had come to be seen and acted upon as propertied landscapes. Anthropologist Nada Moumtaz and urbanist Mona Fawaz have suggested that urban actors in Beirut tend to see neighbourhoods as propertied landscapes, an approach to space that reduces 'alternative forms of claiming, ultimately limiting the imaginary of possible collectives and forms of being together to those imposed by the imperatives of project designers' and strips spaces of their communal, social, and religious meaning (Fawaz and Moumtaz 2020). In a somewhat similar vein, in the context of Singapore, urbanist Anne Haila (2017) has explored 'the property mind': the propensity of people to be acutely aware of issues and prices related to the property market. Such propertied understandings of coastal space in Beirut constitute a spatial logic central to the way politics of the coastline are carried out in Beirut. The perception of coastal space as propertied led some activists to go chasing after the shadows of past spatial logics, the paper traces of the French land registry reform.

As knowledge of the cadastral landscape in coastal Beirut became important for engaging in urban politics, it should be stressed that cuts, uncertainties, and controversies in knowledge became equally important. Even as perceiving the coastline as propertied was central, the knowledge of who exactly owns what, and where exactly the lines are drawn, was the constant subject of debate and circulation of contradictory information. Such uncertainties and cuts in knowledge were not merely a matter of knowing what exactly the bureaucratic record states, as 'true' relations of ownership could be hidden behind shady business arrangements or closed doors of archives. History and law were always and already hazy and subject to different claims and unearthings of hidden connections.

A prominent case of contestation around the public/private divide on the coastline in the 2010s was that of Dalieh el-Raouche, a small rocky peninsula extending to the sea next to the famous Pigeon Rocks of Beirut, located about a kilometre along the coastline from the public beach. In 2013, a proposed construction project that threatened to enclose this bit of openly accessible coastline from the public attracted the attention of large parts of Beirut's civil society and activist circles. Different groups and organisations sprung to action around the cause of defending Dalieh, and many activists, being from academic backgrounds including urban studies and architecture, began researching the history and current status of the site.

As part of this work the activists dug into local cultural history of the site and reclaimed a lost name for the site, *dalieh*,[6] meaning grapevine, coming likely from the historical use of the site as peri-urban farmland. The activists savvily connected this name to the name of the neighbourhood and the neighbouring famous 'Pigeon Rocks', Raouche, thus giving the place the name it is known by today: Dalieh of Raouche. This move can be seen as typical of a certain mode of history in the present practised by urban activists in Beirut, where connecting with local history provides tools for urban space advocacy. In giving the previously somewhat ignored coastal area a name and a history, the activists were thus making it knowable in new ways for the wider public. Accordingly, the booklet produced by a campaign for preservation of the area starts with the words:

> In Arabic, Dalieh refers to any plant that hangs down, typically used to roof terraces where families, neighbors and friends gather to mark the end of the workday. In Beirut, Dalieh refers to a vast terrain that extends from the city's emblematic Sakhret el-Raouche, and slopes gently towards the sea. (Dalieh Campaign 2015)

One of the issues that arose in the ensuing discussion and advocacy work was the legal status of land ownership in Dalieh. The campaigners wanted to protect the site as a public space. The problem, however, was that the land, according to the land registry, was privately owned. One activist in the campaign noted to me that in public discussions they often encountered the argument questioning how they can claim this place as public when it is private property. Under the Ottoman land registry regime, the lands of Dalieh had been state property, falling under the category of *miri*. The Ottoman state had leased these lands for use by some prominent Beiruti families as agricultural land. As part of the above-discussed land registry reform after the French took colonial possession of Lebanon, the rentier families of Dalieh were given title to the lands. Fast forward 60 years or so, to the 1990s, and a lot of these titles had been bought by the family of the late Lebanese prime minister and real estate businessman Rafiq Hariri (see Baumann 2017). Whereas the lands of Dalieh had previously been separated into multiple small plots and owned by different families, they were now mostly concentrated in the hands of a family with real estate business interests and the means to pursue them. In this way, the political and economic changes in post-civil war Lebanon had afforded the announcement of development in the lands of Dalieh.

During the debates about the status and future of Dalieh el-Raouche, around the year 2013, Beiruti activist-scholars encountered these traces of administrative reforms from nearly 100 years ago. Trying to unravel the history of land ownership and negotiate the juridical public/private distinction took the activist-researchers across the temporal separation.

As the activists were researching the legal status and history of Dalieh, they encountered a thorny issue. With regard to the law on maritime public domain mentioned earlier, some of the lands of Dalieh, low rocks descending to the sea that have been surveyed and separated into plots, fall currently under the 'winter waves'. According to the specific wording of the law, this apparently should not be possible. This apparent paradox is a good example of the vagueness and uncertainty of the knowledge circulating about the law. The former land registry employee mentioned earlier was strict on the topic: no one can have a deed or title to the coastal land falling under definition of the maritime public domain. One Beirut-based journalist, who had looked into this issue, told me that the best answer he got from the cadastral officials was speculation that perhaps climate change made the sea levels rise from a hundred years ago, and thus creep up the maritime public domain to the surveyed plots.

The urban activists decided to look to the archive, and try to locate the original cadastral map drawn by the French in the 1920s. According to el-Hibri (2009, 123), the original cadastral maps had either been lost during the collapse of the Mandate or had been taken back to France. In the archive, the activists indeed found something seemingly supportive of their claims. Let me quote at length from a 2015 publication by the activist coalition:

> Theft of Public Land - Historical and contemporary property records and maps (such as the French Plan Danger de Beyrouth) demonstrate that property boundaries in Dalieh have been modified to encroach on the maritime public domain, in contravention of the law. In other words, a large section of Dalieh has been illegally privatized, including the fishermen's port that until recently secured the livelihood of over 75 families. The official French 1926 cadastral map was not found in the official land registry in Beirut. If revealed, this document would act as an ultimate proof to the theft of public property and cadastral forging. (Dalieh Campaign 2015, 8)

In quite literal terms, then, the campaigners had come to the conclusion that the French colonial reforms in the 1920s set the stage for a politics of coastline that continues until today. Since there was a significant suspicion that the property boundaries had been modified, gaining access to an artefact from the 1920s that could be understood as trace[7] would help prove this falsification of property. The activists remained cut off from this knowledge, however, as the *ultimate proof* was not to be found in the archive, as I explain below. The trace not obtained still carried definite weight in its absence.

I had heard narrations of this story in slightly different versions,[8] but the one I present here is as told to me by one long-term activist in the spring of 2018, about events that had happened several years earlier. When beginning to look for the original cadastral map, the group of urban activists shortly realised that neither the land registry of Beirut nor the municipality had a copy of it. The first step after this realisation was to look in the other archives in Beirut. The first destination was the archives of the IFPO, the French Institute of the Near East. Browsing through the archives of IFPO from the colonial times, some materials were found: there were drafts of cadastral maps, yet no finalised, official version. The next direction was the central archive, administered by the Central Bank. Here, they were met with a closed door. Some sections of the archives were not to be accessed by the activist-researchers, although it is unclear whether they would have held something relevant to their search. Finally, some of the activists headed to France to search in the colonial archives, hoping they might hold an answer to the search. And there they indeed did find something interesting. Not a map, but a summary written by the French surveyor to the administration outlining what he will present to them as the result of the surveying work. Nonetheless, the all-important map was nowhere to be found. When I presented my interlocutor with the surprised question 'Wow, did you really go to all this trouble to find an old map?' he replied: 'Of course. If we had the documents, that would be it. Khalas.'

To sum up: connecting backwards through time by the mediation of the archive allowed the urban activists to stake claims about propertied space and the public/private divide in the contemporary urban landscape. The coming together of the underlying logic of understanding the littoral as propertied landscapes and the connection with the colonial-era cadastral maps proved significant for the contemporary coastline. Even though the vaunted original cadastral map was never found, tapping into history allowed the activists to contest the legality of the private ownership of the lands in Dalieh. Moreover, the colonial link became significant for the Beiruti activists in a quite literal sense. Chasing after the traces of a past spatial logic required them to take their search first to the archives of the IFPO, and beyond that across the Mediterranean Sea to the archives in France.

The image of public/private that emerges from this discussion presents itself in the multiple: while contemporary cadastral maps and records quite clearly delineate the plots and their ownership from the maritime public domain, the claimed likeliness of a historical falsification of the property record allows for a contestation of the registry. Thus, even if the spatial logic of the land registry in principle works according to the colonial logic of clear delineation, as it becomes historicised an uncanny complexity for the value of locations emerges. While the bureaucratic and legal logic of the *cadastre* was by no means the only regime in which the meaning of the coastline was being contested, the contestation was potent not least due to the moral and juridical power of the Lebanese state backing the distinction of public and private domain. The connections and disconnections relevant for even this particular location were thus not answerable in a clear yes/no manner, but through history they became fuzzy and layered.

Poetics of Spatial Logics, or Sneaking onto Beaches

What we could call a cartographic or cadastral imagination forms grounds for a poetic understanding of urban politics, where lines originally drawn on maps by French bureaucrats come to ground understandings of leisure and politics of space in contemporary Beirut. As discussed above, popular and academic understandings of the *cadastre* and the maritime public domain became important nodes for perceiving 'propertied landscapes' (Fawaz and Moumtaz 2020) and thus a central part for understanding the notions of public and private for my interlocutors. While I have argued that spatial logics calibrate the relative location of coastal places in Beirut, I would add that they become part of a poetic understanding of space. In discussing poetics of space, I follow anthropologist Rupert Stasch, who defines spatial poetics by the capacity of spatial forms to 'hold special historical power because of the multiplicity of relational connections they mediate … space's capacity to be poetically dense with a multiplicity of qualities and relational connections' (Stasch 2013, 556).[9] In ethnographic terms, I suggest that paying attention to poetics of space on the Lebanese coastline allows us to see how spatial arrangements and logics became rich with meaning and relationality for my interlocutors engaging with the coastline.

Law and bureaucracy were not merely statist forms of knowledge, but could be argued to form a tradition or history of spatialised understanding. Narratives and information about the legislation were widely circulated among civil society groups interested in questions of public space, and taken up and discussed even beyond activist circles. Especially among young politically aware adults, the notion that the coastline is public domain was keenly remembered, and the numerous exceptions made to the legislation later on were either dismissed as dubious or just not remarked on. My interlocutors from different backgrounds frequently reiterated to me the widely shared understanding that all attempts to fence off the coastline were illegal.

Since fencing off the coastline was a common practice among the leisure businesses and private beach clubs that proliferated along the Lebanese coastline, the tension was palpable and reflected in people's practices. Many beachgoers sought to relate to the colonial-era line in the sand where the waves hit highest in the winter by combining their leisurely practice with a political edge.[10] On multiple occasions, I heard people sharing the point that, even if a beach club has taken over a part of the beach, as a Lebanese citizen you have the right to utilise the sands they preside over: just walk along the coastline wherever you want, bring your towel, bypass any fence if necessary, and settle on the seaside to enjoy the Mediterranean. If the employees or security of the relevant beach club come up to you, inform them that this is your legal right and they will leave you alone. Some people who narrated this information would at the same time confess they had never engaged in such activity, yet others told me accounts of how they had entered sands in this manner. This sneaking onto private beaches was always framed as a righteous political act of reclaiming the public from those who had unrightfully enclosed and fenced it off. Even though the narratives of such reclaiming were likely more commonly circulating than actually carried out, they reinforced a common understanding of what should rightfully be public space.

This practice was contested. For example, during the summer after its opening, the newly built hotel on the public beach mentioned earlier in this chapter positioned a guard on the sands in order to prevent users of the public beach from entering and enjoying their time in front of the hotel. Similarly, most private beach restaurants and resorts would employ staff and security personnel to monitor and restrict non-paying beachgoers. With different modes of controlling access to the coastline and tactics and knowledges by beachgoers to challenge and circumvent these restrictions, the spatial logic of the maritime public domain had become a lively and symbolically rich part of the configuration of the Lebanese littoral. A similar narrative of negotiating the public domain and politics of access was utilised by the research and performance collective Dictaphone in their influential 2012 performance 'This Sea Is Mine', where participants were shipped on fishing boats for a tour of the privatised Beirut coastline, and performance artist Tanya El Khoury (2016) would swim across the enclosures of private beach clubs to underline how what should be public domain had been privatised illegally.

As the spatial logics of the colonial-era land registry reform encountered the contemporary perception of coastal landscapes as propertied, the line in the sand became rich with a multiplicity of qualities for those engaging with the Lebanese littoral. As the youth sneaking onto beaches knew, the line carried political and poetical weight for understanding the contemporary Lebanese society and real neo-liberal policy on its coastline. Understanding the significance of the line drawn in cadastral maps in the 1920s allowed for my interlocutors to strike a pose, rhetorical or practical, for their preferred understanding of the coastline as common space.

Conclusion

And then there was the public beach and the salience of the colonial line in the sand. As stated in the beginning of this chapter, the destruction by the municipality of Beirut of the equipment and infrastructure of the NGO managing the beach had ended in a kind of status quo, with the NGO moving their equipment below an invisible line dividing the beach into two parts. As I have explained, this line was likely drawn by a French surveyor in the 1920s. Even though the entirety of the beach was designated as a public beach by the Ministry of Transportation, in the land registry it was still demarcated into private and public parts. The municipal officials thus used their understanding of the configuration of public/private to chase the NGO from a privately held plot of land. Meanwhile the Ministry of Transportation, presiding over the maritime public domain, guaranteed the NGO could not be chased away from the seaward part of the beach.

This colonial line in the sand thus traced the different claims to the right to manage the beach, on the one hand by the municipality of Beirut and the owners of private property, and on the other hand by the NGO and the Ministry of Transportation. During summer 2019, the line separating the part of the beach designated as maritime public domain from the surveyed part got entangled with the way urban politics in Beirut is pursued through a propertied understanding of space. And it was never merely a matter of a simple application of the legislation on property in accordance with the cadastral record. For all sides taking part in the discussion, the propertied landscape became part of a wider understanding of space and for tactics and claims related to space and history in a situation of contestation.

But the story did not end there. In the summer of 2019 the municipality stationed some policemen at the beach entrance, effectively banning the NGO from engaging in any activity regardless of the line in the sand, such as renting chairs or tables, or selling things from their kiosk: this was explained to me by my interlocutors as trying to make them run dry of funds and thus drive them away from the beach for good. Consequently, as the autumn arrived, with the winter approaching and the waves reaching higher, my increasingly distressed interlocutors were wondering about the change of season. Soon their equipment was to fall under the rising waves, with uncertainty about where they could relocate their things.

In this chapter, I have given a perspective on how Mediterranean constellations, in this case embodied in colonial-era connections across the Mediterranean Sea, become reactivated and relevant in contemporary urban politics in Beirut. The way a propertied understanding of space in the context of urban politics forms the ground for contesting notions of public and private illustrates how the origins of the system for registering such property have become relevant again. For some actors, to make claims about public and private in 2010s Beirut necessitated reconnecting with the 1920s. For others, colonial lines in the sand became important only in their presence, and not through explicit knowledge of their history.

The way urban space in Beirut is understood as propertied and cadastral space is only one of the many ways the relative location of coastal places in Beirut is composed. While the juridical property-based understanding of the public/private distinction was an important feature of the discussions about urban space, it was by no means the only axis on which the concepts of public and private were understood. Thus, while the public beach was separated into the maritime public domain, privately owned plots of land, and municipally owned plots of land, these distinctions were only one part of a wider overlap of different spatial logics. The beach as a whole was claimed as public, and even designated as such by some state bodies. It was definitely defended as public by Beirut civil society. What becomes evident is thus that the way places become significant, and become located, is a process of multiple overlapping spatial logics. The beach becomes not one but many, differing on the connections and separations active in giving it meaning.

The chapter has also shown not only how the ghosts of past spatial logics, such as the one informing French bureaucrats in the 1920s, haunt the present condition but how some have gone hunting for their traces to make political interventions on the coastline. I have discussed how the bureaucratic logic of separating space into clearly delineated plots publicly or privately owned on the one hand, and into surveyed land and non-surveyed public domain on the other, has become entangled in a logic of perception of coastal space as propertied. Finally, I have examined how such entanglements come to be poetically dense, as they carry a wider significance for a politics of the coastline. In the synchronic and diachronic intersection of spatial logics, the beach becomes multiply located, but the ways it is located are simultaneously setting the ground for contesting the way public and private are divided and acted upon. For some of my interlocutors, working against the neo-liberal privatisation of the Lebanese coastline included hunting for traces of the past, while for some it implied the gesture of sneaking onto private beaches that were properly perceived as public.

I would like to point out one further aspect of the narrative: the fact that these colonial traces across the Mediterranean tie into the discussion in Beirut about the relationship of the city with the Mediterranean Sea, as it currently stands. The relationship of Beirut to the sea ties intimately into the urban politics of the city today, as was noted to me by people ranging from scholar-activists to a municipal council member. For many, overdevelopment of the coastline in Beirut and the resulting lack of publicly accessible coastal spaces is working to sever the connection of the city and the sea. Therefore, the engagement with the history of land registry I have narrated in this chapter could also be understood as a navigation of Beirut to the sea by activists involved in campaigns for public spaces, changing its location in the constellations composing the Mediterranean region. In this work, the bureaucratic ghosts of the colonial encounter still abound.

Notes

1 Surveyed land is land that has been mapped and recorded in the land registry and given plot identities and clear boundaries, as opposed to the public domain (i.e. streets, maritime public domain), which has no plot identity in the registry. When using the term 'surveyed land' in this text, I refer to this precise meaning. *Cadastre* means land registry, the system for storing information on land ownership and demarcation. As Ruth Kark (1997) has stated, 'Cadastre is a French word originating in the latin capitastrum, meaning a register of poll tax. Later it came to mean "an official register of the ownership, extent, and value of real property in a given area, used as a basis for taxation" or "survey ... showing or including boundaries, property lines, etc." The cadastre was thus the means used by rulers to collect data on the division of landed property.'

2 For details about land registration in the Lebanese context, see for example Lewis (1979) on changes in land tenure during the Ottoman era, and Ziadeh (1993), who looks at the transition from Ottoman to French property rights legal regime, including in Lebanon.

3 See for example Jean-Francoise Blanchette's *Burdens of Proof* (2012, 148–54) for a discussion of the computerization of the Alsace-Moselle land registry.

4 This English translation and the information below are derived from a slideshow by Tony Assaf from the Ministry of Public Works and Transport from 2009. The law in question is the decision no. 144 from 10/06/1925 by the French High Commissioner.

5 See anthropologist Alice Stefanelli's article 'Beyond the Organic Intellectual' (2020) for a detailed discussion of the intertwining of expert knowledges and urban space campaigning in the context of a campaign opposing the construction of a motorway bridge across a historical Beirut neighbourhood.

6 Note, according to the Hans Wehr *Dictionary for Modern Standard Arabic*, *dalieh* means the trellis used for supporting vines.

7 As Walter Benjamin wrote, 'The trace is appearance of a nearness, however far removed the thing that left it behind may be. The aura is appearance of a distance, however close the thing that calls it forth. In the trace, we gain possession of the thing; in the aura, it takes possession of us' (Benjamin 2002, 477). In his study of mapping in the history of Beirut, Hatim el-Hibri wrote: 'Maps are material traces of the operation of power, which tell us about the *how* of power' (El-Hibri 2009, 120).

8 See also Alice Stefanelli's (2017, 188–89) dissertation for a detailed treatment of the legal history of Dalieh and another narration of the hunt for the original cadastral maps.

9 See also Herzfeld's use of social poetics as analysis of essentialism in everyday life (Herzfeld 2005) and Gaston Bachelard's classic *Poetics of Space* (Bachelard 2014).

10 This could be understood as a mode of Asef Bayat's (2013, 46) *encroachment of the ordinary,* 'the silent, protracted, but pervasive advancement of the ordinary people on the propertied'.

References

Bachelard, Gaston. 2014 [1964]. *The Poetics of Space.* Translated by Maria Jolas. New York, NY: Penguin Books.

Baumann, Hannes. 2017. *Citizen Hariri.* London: Hurst Publishers.

Bayat, Asef. 2013. *Life as Politics: How Ordinary People Change the Middle East.* 2nd ed. Stanford, CA: Stanford University Press.

Benjamin, Walter. 2002. *The Arcades Project.* Translated by Howard Eiland and Kevin McLaughlin. Cambridge, MA: Belknap Press of Harvard University Press.

Bou Akar, Hiba. 2019. *For the War Yet to Come: Planning Beirut's Frontiers.* Stanford, CA: Stanford University Press.

Blanchette, Jean-François. 2012. *Burdens of Proof: Cryptographic Culture and Evidence Law in the Age of Electronic Documents.* Cambridge, MA: MIT Press.

Byrnes, Giselle. 2002. *Boundary Markers: Land Surveying and the Colonisation of New Zealand.* Wellington: Bridget Williams Books.

Dalieh Campaign. 2015. *Dalieh Campaign Booklet.* Accessed 25 January 2021. https://dalieh.org/assets/booklet-en.pdf

Dictaphone. 2013. *This Sea Is Mine.* Accessed 25 January 2021. http://www.dictaphonegroup.com/wp/wp-content/uploads/2013/11/SIM-booklet-compressed.pdf

El-Hibri, Hatem. 2009. 'Mapping Beirut: Toward a History of the Translation of Space from the French Mandate through the Civil War (1920–91)'. *The Arab World Geographer* 12 (3–4): 119–35. https://doi.org/10.5555/arwg.12.3-4.t923868061464973

El Khoury, Tania. 2016. 'Swimming in Sewage: Political Performances in the Mediterranean'. *Performance Research* 21 (2): 138–40.

Fawaz, Mona, and Nada Moumtaz. 2020. 'Neighborhoods as Propertied Landscapes: Lessons from Beirut's Reconstructions'. *TRAFO – Blog for Transregional Research.* Accessed 25 January 2021. https://trafo.hypotheses.org/21850

Green, Sarah. 2005. *Notes from the Balkans: Locating Marginality and Ambiguity on the Greek-Albanian Border.* Princeton, NJ: Princeton University Press.

Green, Sarah. 2019. 'Entangled Borders'. *Archivio Antropologico Mediterraneo* 21 (2). https://doi.org/10.4000/aam.1749

Haila, Anne. 2017. 'Institutionalization of "The Property Mind"'. *International Journal of Urban and Regional Research* 41 (3): 500–07. https://doi.org/10.1111/1468-2427.12495

Herzfeld, Michael. 2005. *Cultural Intimacy: Social Poetics in the Nation-State.* New York, NY: Routledge.

Home, Robert. 2006. 'Scientific Survey and Land Settlement in British Colonialism, with Particular Reference to Land Tenure Reform in the Middle East 1920–50'. *Planning Perspectives* 21 (1): 1–22. https://doi.org/10.1080/02665430500397048

Kark, Ruth. 1997. 'Mamlūk and Ottoman Cadastral Surveys and Early Mapping of Landed Properties in Palestine'. *Agricultural History* 71 (1): 46–70.

Kaufman, Asher. 2015. 'Colonial Cartography and the Making of Palestine, Lebanon, and Syria'. In *The Routledge Handbook of the History of the Middle East Mandates*, edited by Cyrus Schayegh and Andrew Arsan. New York, NY: Routledge.

Legal Agenda. 2016. 'The Legal Course of the Loss of Lebanon's Shoreline'. *The Legal Agenda*, October 6, 2016. https://www.legal-agenda.com/en/article.php?id=1766.

Lewis, Bernard. 1979. 'Ottoman Land Tenure and Taxation in Syria'. *Studia Islamica* 50: 109–24. https://doi.org/10.2307/1595560

Navaro-Yashin, Yael. 2009. 'Affective Spaces, Melancholic Objects: Ruination and the Production of Anthropological Knowledge'. *Journal of the Royal Anthropological Institute* 15 (1): 1–18.

Neocleous, Mark. 2003. 'Off the Map: On Violence and Cartography'. *European Journal of Social Theory* 6 (4): 409–25. https://doi.org/10.1177/13684310030064003

Stasch, Rupert. 2013. 'The Poetics of Village Space When Villages Are New: Settlement Form as History Making in Papua, Indonesia'. *American Ethnologist* 40 (3): 555–70. https://doi.org/10.1111/amet.12039

Stefanelli, Alice. 2017. 'Who Is the City for – Civic Advocacy, Private Interest and Statecraft in Contemporary Beirut'. PhD thesis. Manchester: University of Manchester.

Stefanelli, Alice. 2020. 'Beyond the Organic Intellectual: Politics and Contestation in the Planning Practice'. *City & Society* 32 (3): 649–69. https://doi.org/10.1111/ciso.12340

Strathern, Marilyn. 1996. 'Cutting the Network'. *The Journal of the Royal Anthropological Institute* 2 (3): 517–35. https://doi.org/10.2307/3034901

Williams, Elizabeth. 2015. 'Mapping the Cadastre, Producing the Fellah: Technologies and Discourses of Rule in French Mandate Syria and Lebanon'. In *The Routledge Handbook of the History of the Middle East Mandates*, edited by Cyrus Schayegh and Andrew Arsan. New York, NY: Routledge.

Ziadeh, Farhat. 1993. 'Property Rights in the Middle East: From Traditional Law to Modern Codes'. *Arab Law Quarterly* 8 (1): 3–12. https://doi.org/10.2307/3381489

CHAPTER 8

'The Exception Which Proves the Rule'
Gurbet and Historical Constellations of Mobility in Istanbul's Old City[1]

Janine Su
University College London

Abstract

Regimes of relative location in much of the former Ottoman Mediterranean position migrating from one's hometown or village as 'going to *gurbet*' – a term that best translates as 'exile' (Said 2000) – and those who leave are expected to perform exile in various ways. In contemporary Turkey, this expectation is particularly upheld among those who lack the social and institutional capital to navigate strict international visa schemes. In the Ottoman era, other mobile trajectories were available to peasants wishing to see more of the world, but these were lost in the structural upheavals of the transition to the modern nation-state era. However, the phenomenological descendants of mobile figures like bandits did not go extinct with the societal structures that begat them. Drawing on more than 18 months of ethnographic fieldwork in Istanbul's touristic Sultanahmet district, this chapter identifies the disconnect between historical and modern constellations of socio-spatial movement, and explores how it renders the subjectivities of some

How to cite this book chapter:
Su, Janine. 2022. "'The Exception Which Proves the Rule'": *Gurbet* and Historical Constellations of Mobility in Istanbul's Old City'. In *Locating the Mediterranean: Connections and Separations across Space and Time*, edited by Carl Rommel and Joseph John Viscomi, 177–98. Helsinki: Helsinki University Press. DOI: https://doi.org/10.33134/HUP-18-8.

young men 'unintelligible' (Butler 2009) to normative sociability today. These subjectivities are distinct for their affective detachment from *gurbet*, so their efforts to self-actualise mobile aspirations initially go unrecognised. Those who exhibit sufficient 'performative excellence' (Herzfeld 1985) to enact these aspirations, however, are then disparaged as upstarts and explained away as 'exceptions'.

On Being an Exception: Introducing Kaan[2]

You can't use Kaan as a sample of an experience of young males in Turkey. Kaan is an *exception*, a bastard who is young and good-looking and lucky all the time. Whenever I am trying to close in on my prey, Kaan shows up and then the girls forget about me. (my emphasis)[3]

This was Lemi's response when I tried to describe my doctoral research to him and he misunderstood that my aim was to construct a profile for the average or archetypal young man of Turkey. Lemi, a state-licensed tour guide, 'hates' (his own word choice) Kaan, in part because, despite the educational and professional disparity between the two that should have rendered him socially untouchable to the eighth-grade dropout working a low-end job at a backpacker hostel, Kaan's performative self impinged on his own masculine selfhood in key symbolic ways. For example, while Lemi professionally frequented the historic Sultanahmet district – the imperial district of Constantinople during the Byzantine and most of the Ottoman period – he returned each evening to his flat in the hip Cihangir neighbourhood across the Golden Horn and in the contemporary city centre. Kaan, meanwhile, bunked with three other young men in staff quarters behind the hostel. Indeed, this is how the two crossed paths in the first place: part of Kaan's job was to fetch and deliver food and drink orders to the hostel's manager whenever he and his friends like Lemi would retire at the end of the workday to its rooftop terrace to enjoy the view across the Marmara Sea, or to catch a Beşiktaş football match on the hostel's large communal television.

The formal contrasts between the two were stark: in addition to being fluent in English, Lemi held a degree in Italian literature from a highly regarded university, and was regularly under contract with the state's tourism board to lead groups all over the country in Turkish,

English, or Italian. Kaan, meanwhile, had little training in any foreign language but happened to have a talent for them. His English grammar wasn't as polished as Lemi's, nor his vocabulary as sophisticated, but the point is that tourists couldn't tell the difference. The other major zone of antagonism, as evidenced in Lemi's declaration above, was interactions with visiting foreign women, which often occurred in the onsite bars of Sultanahmet hotels and hostels. Kaan, for his part, was not only aware of Lemi's disdain, he took a personal delight in challenging the social order. On one occasion he even announced his intentions first, leaning in conspiratorially to whisper, 'Watch this: Lemi is over there talking with [a woman visiting from Italy]. He thinks he is charming but I'm going to take her away. It will be so funny!' He then got up from our booth and, from an almost cinematic vantage I watched as he crossed the room to join Lemi and the woman by the bar, then found his moment to interject something into the conversation (I wish I could report what he said but it was too noisy in the bar to eavesdrop). A moment later, the woman shifted her body language toward Kaan, turning her back on a fuming Lemi. Most awkward for me as a spectator was how long Lemi continued to stand there trying to look nonchalant while the other two huddled together in conversation next to him.

Years later, after we'd both left Turkey, Kaan and I had a good laugh over all this via online chat from our respective homes in the EU and US: 'Hahaha he was trying to be so intellectual … women liked me because I was more pure and spontaneous.'

***

The following is not an ethnography of flirting with tourists; or, it is one only insofar as the fact of my informants' choice to base themselves in Sultanahmet, and their eagerness to interact with visiting foreigners – and how both figure into the way they imagine their futures – are features of their 'masculine trajectories' (Ghannam 2013). And this is why it is worth including the ethnographic coda that Kaan no longer lives in Turkey. Based on 18 months of fieldwork in Istanbul, this study instead explores the intersection of mobility and manhood through historically charged concepts related to place and 'place identity' (Mills 2008). More specifically, I will show ethnographically how a disconnect between historical and modern constellations of relative location have rendered unintelligible the subjectivities of young men like Kaan, with 'intelligibility' defined by Judith Butler as 'readability in social space and time' (2009, 10–11).

I will also show that the unintelligibility of my informants' subjectivities from the normative perspective is mirrored in the unintelligibility of Sultanahmet itself. These young men may indeed be attracted to the district because of factors relating to its 'non-placeness' on the contemporary Turkish landscape, where 'non-place' is defined as 'a space which cannot be identified as relational, or historical, or concerned with identity' (Augé 1995 [1992], 77–78). This is a product of the district's own peculiar trajectory, as it long struggled to recover a sense of itself after, first, the Ottoman imperial epicentre was moved to another district, and then the Turkish republican capital was moved to another city altogether. By the mid-20th century Sultanahmet had been reduced to little more than a backwater of incongruous architectural grandeur. The obfuscation of its place identity was exacerbated with the rise of mass tourism later that century, and these days the district is considered to have been wholly given over to the industry, with most Istanbul residents preferring to avoid it.

Given a societal context wherein people and place are mutually and affectively defined, the fact of these young men's association with a non-place is a factor in their unintelligibility. And it is important to clarify that affiliation with a non-place does not suggest an *absence* of place identity but a 'non-place identity'. Indeed, my informants are generically referred to as 'Sultanahmet boys', a term whose construction follows both the convention of labelling individuals according to location affiliation and that of referring to any unmarried male as 'boy' (*çocuk*) regardless of age. I note this for clarity since my informants ranged from their late teens into their thirties, but the term 'boy' also signals rootlessness, as evidenced when contrasted against the Turkish word for 'married' (*evli*), which translates literally as 'of a home' (in the sense of house). Association with a non-place amplifies this, projecting Istanbulites' sense of malaise about the district onto its denizens. This scenario, though, also fosters new possibilities, as we saw above, wherein a combination of Sultanahmet's liminal non-placeness and tourists' lack of cultural baggage levelled the playing field between Lemi and Kaan. The latter's 'performative excellence' (Herzfeld 1985), in turn, was bitterly explained away by the former as an 'exception'. Such outcomes help illustrate why unintelligible people would be attracted to unintelligible place.

The project of portraying Sultanahmet boys' unintelligibility to the normative gaze has many layers, and over the course of this chapter I will establish who they are by subtracting who they are *not*, exploring points of slippage between the two with respect to the notion of socio-spatial movement. I argue that young men like my informants are defined by their non-normative 'affective bonds with place' (Gustafson 2001, 669), and will explore this in the next section through the indigenous concepts *sıla* and *gurbet*, which give shape to the affective relationship between person and place. *Gurbet* is a term common across much of the former Ottoman Mediterranean that most closely translates as 'exile', and is commonly invoked to describe both the location and experience of migration. I show the distinctiveness of these young men's affective distance from *gurbet* in normative context, and go on to link this disposition to an old social type that can be captured in the term *garip yiğit*. I elaborate on this by differentiating between the concepts of 'migration' and 'mobility' in ways not consistent with the literature but that are salient to the case of contemporary Turkey. I then extend these concepts diachronically in the subsequent section, contrasting the notion of migration-as-right-of-passage against the introduced term manhood-via-mobility with reference to the extant literature on the former. This is in order to connect these young men's subjectivities to their actions, and leads to the argument that, while migration-as-rite-of-passage is part of the normative process of intergenerational community propagation, manhood-via-mobility remains centred around individual subjectivity, with the result that life courses come to resemble 'trajectories' rather than 'cycles'.

Rather than young men like Kaan being an 'exception which proves the rule' (Hobsbawm 1981/1969; see next section for the quote in context), this chapter aims to show that they embody *another* rule, one that can be understood through historically encoded spatiotemporal constellations of place and place attachment common around the former Ottoman Mediterranean. Expressed ethnographically, 'Sultanahmet boys'-to-be originally leave their home towns and villages citing a sense of social constraint, as opposed to the economic or political push factors characteristic of classic migration literature. They would tell me that even as youngsters they could not envision themselves inhabiting the lives that had been modelled for them, and complained about the insular attitudes of those they grew up around, whom they found gallingly non-curious about the world. So they head to the big city, typically as teens, whereupon they gravitate toward the district of Sultan-ahmet at the heart of Istanbul's Old City (see Image 8.1). With Turkey consistently ranked among the most visited destinations worldwide,[4] this choice of positioning at the inside–outside frontier via interna-tional tourism – where the world comes to them rather than the other way around – is as near as they can get to freedom of movement in the near term, since Turkish citizens are subject to strict visa regulations for travel to most countries. This we can think of as an adaptation in the nation-state era to the trajectories of the *garip yiğitler* (plural), who roamed the 'borderless' Ottoman Empire. After a period of adventure, though, the impinging quality of the normative gaze eventually creeps back into their awareness. They sense that their aspirational subjec-tivities are misunderstood and/or looked down upon by other Istanbul residents, and they come to believe they will not ultimately be able to lead the lives they imagine for themselves if they remain in Tur-key. By this point, however, having intentionally not maintained the

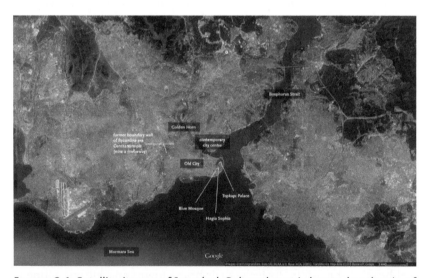

Image 8.1: Satellite image of Istanbul. Sultanahmet is located at the tip of the Old City peninsula, whose boundaries correspond to those of Byz-antine-era Constantinople. The city's unique geography, concentrated around three converging peninsulas, helps make the phenomenon of multiple urban centres that do not interact with one another plausible.
Source: Adapted by author from Google Maps: https://www.google.com/maps/@41.0276337 .28.9719445.24163m/data=!3m1!1e3. Imagery ©2015 DigitalGlobe, Data SIO, NOAA, U.S. Navy, NGA, GEBCO, TerraMetrics. Map data ©2015 Basarsoft, Google (retrieved 29 August 2015).

usual familial or hometown networks that could have been mobilised to help them move abroad (e.g. via chain migration), they endeavour instead to cultivate their own such networks, which in Sultanahmet often become centred around visiting foreign women.

Finally, I introduce another iteration of the normative perspective. This will be the migrant gaze of the Bitlis boys, as I call them, and the discordant ways in which their inwardly directed socio-spatial orientation interacted with the lived reality of liminal touristic space vividly portrays the difference between migrant and mobile subjectivities as these concepts are used here. The revelation that theirs is the expected disposition among those 'in *gurbet*' contrasts the subjectivities of Sultanahmet boys in ways that help to render the latter intelligible.

Mobility and Migration: A Turkish Case

Migration has been Istanbul's defining demographic trend since the mid-20th century, when a series of economic transformations (later also political developments) triggered successive waves of arrivals to Turkey's major cities, mostly from the Anatolian countryside. Istanbul in particular has received such a volume of migrants that today only a small minority of residents can claim roots in the city prior to 1960.[5] Unsurprisingly, this has been perceived by the now-outnumbered urbanites of old as a peasant invasion, and it is common to hear residents complaining that the city these days feels like 'a big village' (see also Demirtaş and Şen 2007; Keyder 2005; White 2010).

Settlement patterns reflect the persistence of what Sema Erder labelled 'relations of localism' (1999, 166), such that many urban neighbourhoods function as satellites of towns and villages around the country. The persistence of hometown attachments in the migration context can be illuminated through 'the dichotomous terms *gurbet* and *sıla* [which] are popularly employed to portray socio-spatial dimensions of migration' (Zırh 2012, 1780). *Sıla* means 'home' (in the sense of homeland), but is a Turkish adaptation of an Arabic word that translates as 'connection', 'convergence', or 'coming together', and so circumscribes the concept of home as both a spatial and relational place of communality, nurturing, and sanctuary. *Gurbet* translates as 'exile' (Said 2000 [1984]; see also Abusharaf 2002; Elliot 2021; Saloul 2012; Sayad 2000) or the state of being 'out of place' (Said 2000 [1999]), and signifies anywhere that is not *sıla* – as easily a single step outside the natal village as the other side of the world. It is associated with danger, and its emotive qualities have been communicated for centuries in poetic traditions that – superimposed onto the contemporary migration context – feed the so-called 'myth of return' (see also Soysal 2008). *Gurbet*, like *sıla*, is both a place – one actually goes *to* it (*gurbete gitmek*) – and an experiential assignation, described by Carol Delaney as 'an unenviable condition' (1991, 271) characterised by a melancholic nostalgia for the past as a faraway place. In the collective socio-spatial imaginary, then, no one 'in their right mind' (I expand on this phrasing below) would depart the embrace of *sıla* voluntarily, and 'the journey towards *gurbet* [is] never thought of as being one way' (Zırh 2012, 1760; see also Mandel 2008).

The classic Turkish term for 'migrant' is *gurbetçi*, where the professionalising suffix *-çi* conveys that one goes to *gurbet* as a duty. Kemal Karpat described *gurbetçiler* (plural) as men who 'left the village every year seeking jobs as chefs, drivers, porters, menial workers, and so on' before returning to their *sıla* 'to rest and to reproduce and … receive there special respect and care as breadwinners and hardship sufferers' (1976, 54, 55). Men who spend extended periods in *gurbet* are thought of as kites without strings; ideally, then, they will be joined by wives and children before too long. Across the Aegean, Roxanne Caftanzoglou described a shifting of familiar networks of convergence to a new location – her informants, who worked as labourers in Athens, would send for sisters from the home village in the Cyclades – as the transplantation of 'homeland memories' into 'new and unchartered living space … thus symbolically appropriating it and bridging the distance between the homeland and the new settlement' (2001, 30). This analogous example supports the idea that *sıla* place-making is considered achievable only with the inclusion of female kin (Sıla is also used as a given name for women in Turkey). Within this normative socio-spatial framework, then, migrants comprehend their absence from home in the same way as those they left behind, and so remain intelligible to their home communities even across vast distances.

As for the issue of mobility as a counterpoint to migration, the distinction between the two can be understood through Deleuze and Guattari, whose nomad–sedentary model would position mobility and migration as fundamentally different categories in that migrants are also 'the sedentary', only dis-*placed* (1987 [1980], 380–87; see also Braidotti 1994; Clifford 1997; Cresswell 1996; Malkki 1992). *Voluntary* long-term absence from *sıla* and/or affective distance from *gurbet* are thereby associated with the state of *not* being in one's right mind. The most common term that incorporates this imagery is *delikanlı* (adj. crazy-blooded, n. one with crazy blood), which is used to both demarcate a period and suggest a style of youth characterised by social experimentation and spatial movement. As Leyla Neyzi explained,

> Turkish society [acknowledges] a stage of potentially unruly behavior, particularly among young men, who are referred to as delikanlı. ... Historically it was single young men who became involved in acts of collective rebellion [so] it was preferable for reasons of social control to keep the period between puberty and marriage ... as short as possible. 'Wild blood' was to be channeled along tracks acceptable to adult society. (2001, 415; see also Kandiyoti 1994)

Those *not* successfully channelled back into the fold, on the other hand, would become defined by this externality – and by spatial movement – the most successful being storied for their capacity to thrive in far-off lands or inhospitable geographies. Two categories of Eric Hobsbawm's (1981 [1969]) peasant-to-bandit typology run parallel to this: Potential bandits may be 'the age group of male youth between puberty and marriage' (31) – which corresponds to *delikanlı* – but may also

> [consist] of the men who are unwilling to accept the meek and passive role of the subject peasant; the stiffnecked and the recalcitrant, the individual rebels. They are, in the classic familiar peasant phrase, the 'men who make themselves respected'. ... Theirs is an individual rebellion, which is socially and politically undetermined, and which under normal – i.e. non-revolutionary – conditions is not a vanguard of mass revolt, but rather the product and counterpart of the general passivity of the poor. They are the *exception* which proves the rule. (35–36, my emphasis)[6]

Terms linking spatial movement to lack of sanity proliferated in the Ottoman era. Many of these, like *delibaş* (crazy head), *başıbozuk* (damaged head; see Image 8.2), and *garip yiğit* (defined below), originated as designations for irregular and/or mercenary forces under the umbrella category of *gönüllü* (volunteer, lit. 'with heart') before passing into colloquial usage. Upon being decommissioned, these militia tended

Image 8.2: Ottoman-era postcard featuring *başıbozuk* irregulars.
Source: https://commons.wikimedia.org/wiki/File:Bashi-bazouk_Ottoman_Postcard.jpg.
Accessed 13 January 2018. Image is in the public domain.

not to return to the peasantry, instead cutting ties to land to comprise the storied bandit cohorts found around the empire (Blok 1972; Gallant 1988; Hobsbawm 1981 [1969]; Sant Cassia 1993; Todorova 2009 [1997]). The cycles of war and peace could see a 'deterritorialised' (Deleuze and Guattari 1987 [1980]; Malkki 1992) ex-peasant swapping allegiances for and against the state multiple times in a career, so it was in the best interest of the powers that be to approach relations pragmatically. A few bandits even 'ended their days at the Sublime Porte and as guests of the Sultan were treated on par with his closest advisers' (Barkey 1994, 192). In short, spatial and social mobility were formally linked and could be exploited to transgress the boundary between centre and periphery.

Garip yiğit, among such terms, speaks directly to *sıla* and *gurbet*. *Garip* means 'strange' in both the sense of being 'odd' and of being a 'stranger in a strange land'. Like *gurbet*, it is negatively connoted – the lyrics of classic Turkish songs like 'Bir Garip Yolcu' (A Strange Trav-

eller) feature protagonists complaining self-pityingly of the hopeless-
ness, emptiness, and disorientation of lives spent on the road. *Gurbet*
and *garip* actually share an etymological root, the former emphasising expulsion from the community of origin and the latter entry into
the new milieu.[7] When *garip* is paired with *yiğit* (adj. valiant, n. hero),
on the other hand, the compound term connotes facing the perceived
ills of 'strangerhood' with a certain swagger. Its history as a term follows the aforementioned military-to-vernacular arc, dating in Ottoman records to 16th-century calls for 'fit for fighting, effective fellows
able (to acquire) a horse and garment' (Fodor 2000, 251). By the 17th
century the term had spread beyond military usage, as when Ottoman
traveller Evliya Çelebi reported on an incident in which '*bir garîb yiğit*'
(translated as 'a young stranger' in Sariyannis 2006, 168) slew several
people in the capital city's Tophane marketplace. As of the 19th century
it was still in use as a descriptor for single young men roaming the
empire, but has all but disappeared since, seemingly (albeit specula-
tively) lost in the structural upheavals of the transition from empire to
bounded, modern nation-state.

While both *garip* and *yiğit* remain in the lexicon individually, in
the era of national borders and the institutional mediation of movement, the sort of swashbuckling approach to *gurbet* that epitomised
the *garip yiğit* no longer has an intelligible corollary. Self-generated
impulses toward spatial mobility for personal enrichment or pleasure
are now conceived of as the domain of privileged classes, while others
are migrants, glossed as the culturally insular masses moving only in
reluctant response to economic or political imperatives, and existing
at the societal margins in a form of exile. Indeed, the settlement patterns of migrants to Istanbul described at the top of this section seem
to support this, suggesting a preoccupation with reproducing *sıla* in
gurbet through various place-making efforts (see also Mandel 1996 for
the case of Turkish migrants to Germany). But I contend that the phenomenological descendants of the *garip yiğit* did not go extinct with
the vocabulary used to describe them:

> We can say I'm in *gurbet* because I left the village but I don't feel so. Usu-
> ally in *gurbet* people are missing their homes and always dream of going
> back. (Informant from rural southeastern Turkey; living in Istanbul at
> the time of interview, currently living in Australia)

> Do I feel in *gurbet*? … For me *gurbet* is missing your city and … foods
> and blah blah. I was never a fan of my own traditional things. I don't
> mean I never liked these things, I just don't feel that way. (Informant
> from urban northwestern Turkey; living in France at the time of inter-
> view and currently)

With *gurbet* maintaining the socio-spatial perimeter around the category of 'migrant', here two informants from divergent parts of Turkey –
but who have in common self-described poor backgrounds and unfinished secondary educations – also share a disassociation from *gurbet*
that reinforces my contention that, while the young men in question
may be 'elsewhere in geographical space' relative to *sıla*, they are nevertheless not 'displaced' in the exilic sense associated with migrants.
Notably, the second quoted informant actually articulated this disposition during a conversation largely dedicated to complaints about his
difficulty finding a satisfying job and making lasting friendships after
nearly three years in France, yet this had done nothing to coax his personal trajectory back in the direction of 'home'.

By way of comparison, later in the chapter we will meet a group
of informants whose lives in Istanbul vividly portray the influence of
gurbet. Primarily, though, this study focuses on Turkey's 'contemporary *garip yiğitler*', single young men from modest backgrounds who
roam the landscape outside their *sıla* 'with heart' (*gönüllü*) in an effort
to parlay their 'performative excellence' – along with a dose of luck
(Su 2022) – into lifestyles that socially and spatially exceed the usual
limits associated with their peripheral origins. I label this 'mobility'
and define an ethnographic community through it even though, with
current paradigms of movement accommodating no middle ground
or third way between exile and expat (see Schielke 2015, 2020 for an
emerging take), contemporary *garip yiğitler* (plural) find themselves
lumped in with the deluge of migrants absorbed by Istanbul in recent
decades (see also Kaplan 1996), and they chafe at both the socially
stifling demands of those back in *sıla* and the perpetually dim view
Istanbulites take of them. The slippage between their aspirational subjectivities and the weight of public judgement feeds a desire to create
distance between themselves and Turkish sociability in general. In turn,
this becomes part of the attraction of the Sultanahmet district, whose
peculiar history and connection to international tourism beget its own
unintelligibility. This also shapes the belief that in order to enact the

lives they envision for themselves – as opposed to those determined by normative sociability – they should leave Turkey altogether.

Manhood-via-Mobility

It is tempting to evaluate claims of indifference toward *gurbet* like those quoted above as youthful bluster rather than evidence of a 'lost' or unintelligible social archetype, especially since my informants are demographically indistinguishable (e.g. by ethnolinguistic or educational background) from Istanbul's majority migrant population. Distinguishing between *delikanlı* and *garip yiğit*, then, requires tracking both word and action over time: are their gendered selfhoods eventually 'channelled' by normative sociability or do they become expressed as 'masculine trajectories', a term Farha Ghannam employed to '[depart] from the "life cycle" concept, which assumes a fixed and repetitive socialization of individuals into clearly defined roles that support existing social structures' (2013, 6–7)? In other words, separating mobility from migration requires a diachronic approach.

And so, for the same reasons that 'migration' fails to capture my informants' subjectivities, the existing literature on 'migration-as-rite-of-passage' (e.g. Mondain and Diagne 2013; Monsutti 2007; Osella and Osella 2000) fails to capture their trajectories. That is, without minimising the challenges facing migrants, such challenges are nevertheless institutionalised within 'cultures of migration' (e.g. Ali 2007; Cohen and Sirkeci 2011; Horváth 2008; Kandel and Massey 2002), and are viewed by the 'home community' – both diasporic and in *sıla* – as temporary and for the purpose of shaping the next generation of community pillars. A different diachronic model becomes necessary to describe trajectories linked to mobility, which expose contemporary *garip yiğitler* unmitigated to the uncertainties of *gurbet*. Indeed, if it were as simple as 'young men having an adventure before marriage', then Lemi – one among relatively few educated, middle-class urbanites whose profession grants him substantial direct exposure to such young men – might have seen little in Kaan that he found 'exceptional'. I employ instead 'manhood-via-mobility', wherein self-actualisation as a man is considered achievable through spatial movement outside the normative gaze. In the short term, liminal Sultanahmet fulfils this requirement, but many of my informants also feel this means a move abroad in the longer term. And, since their primary social interactions are with tourists, they most commonly come to imagine this through marriage to a foreign woman and emigration to her country of residence.

Three factors make manhood-via-mobility qualitatively different from migration-as-rite-of-passage: first is the sense of social rather than economic or political constraint that draws my informants away from *sıla*. Second is the high risk of failure in the absence of mitigating 'cultures of migration' support structures abroad, including aid from diasporic community members and 'hometown associations'.[8] And third is the lack of *re*incorporation among those who eventually leave Turkey into communities that grant them full social and political rights of membership (see also Su 2022). In fact, the first of these may overlap with or also resemble *delikanlı*, as this represents a starting point. The second and third, however, demonstrate divergence from the life cycle. This divergence is already seen in the choice to avoid settling in one of the aforementioned satellite communities of migrants, instead choosing to base themselves in Sultanahmet *because* it is outside the gaze of normative sociability and its associated baggage. The eventual move abroad that some of these young men make follows this logic as well, since when they choose to leave Turkey through marriage to a foreign woman they do not choose their place of settlement.

To synthesise, my informants' subjectivities are unintelligible to the normative gaze because that gaze has lost the capacity in the modern era to recognise non-normative 'affective bonds with place', at least among those from less privileged classes who may not have the option to enact mobile subjectivities by institutionalised means (e.g. a study abroad programme). And this renders their trajectories resistant to being channelled back toward the life cycle by family and friends in *sıla*, or by the diasporic community in a migrant setting.

On Being a Migrant: Introducing the Bitlis Boys

In the continuing effort to make Sultanahmet boys' projects of manhood-via-mobility intelligible, in this section I ethnographically portray the normative gaze through the eyes of those who embrace it – those who are *not* exceptions, we might say. From the Bitlis boys, as I call them, we get a sense of the material and affective presence of *gurbet* in daily life among migrants.

One of the hostels I spent time in during my fieldwork was owned by three brothers who had been raised in the Aegean province of Manisa before coming to Istanbul to pursue professional opportunities, but who self-identified as being from their ancestral homeland of Bitlis, and as Kurdish. The affective constellation positioning Istanbul as the location of *gurbet* is the norm in Turkey; in addition, it is notable that *sıla* here is not Manisa but Bitlis; that is, the ancestral homeland takes precedence over the place of birth and/or upbringing where these are not the same.[9] Two of the brothers were actually high school teachers who gave their evenings, weekends, and summers to the family business, while the middle brother managed it full time. The family were relative newcomers to Sultanahmet, part of a late wave of entrepreneurs attracted to the district strictly as an investment opportunity after the profitability of tourism-driven enterprises had been proven, but who had no special interest in hosting foreign visitors. Not only that, they also expressed suspicion of others in the district. All staffers but one were family members, and the non-family member told me he believed the reason he'd been chosen for the job was because he was also Kurdish (albeit from a different province). In addition to the three brothers and the non-familial staffer were two male cousins – neither of whom had any skills or experience that made them particularly suitable to work in tourism (one indeed had studied to be an imam!) – brought directly from Bitlis to work as housekeepers and general support staff. The cousins also lived at the hostel, typically only venturing outside its immediate environs to run errands. Upon leaving the job, both returned directly to *sıla*.

It didn't take long for the Bitlis boys' mode of interaction with Sultanahmet tourism to distinguish them from many others I knew in the district. The differences were evident even in the material environs of the hostel's interior. For example, the Ministry of Culture and Tourism distributes promotional posters representing major locations of interest around the country to tourism-related enterprises. The managers of most such businesses request posters depicting the most popular sites with foreign visitors – especially those associated with classical antiquity, or with the beach towns dotting the Mediterranean shore – in hopes of whetting their appetites for onward travel within Turkey. This is because, if tourists book accommodation or activities for those destinations while still in Istanbul, commissions can be earned not just by the travel agents who make the bookings but also by the third parties (often hotel or hostel staffers) who initiate conversations about these places of interest with potential customers and then refer them to a 'friend' at a nearby agency. But at Outback Hostel, as I call it, only posters of sites associated with Bitlis were on display: Lake Van in the lobby, Nemrut Volcano in the common room, and so on. Other material cues included the customisable picture-frame keychain that held the master keys, into which had been inserted a photo of musician Ahmet Kaya on one side of the clear plastic casing, and of film-maker Yılmaz Güney on the other. Both were renowned Kurdish artists revered almost as much for the nature of their deaths 'in exile' in Paris – Kaya is said to have died of a broken heart from missing his homeland – as they are for their bodies of work.[10]

Most evenings I would find the staff huddled together around a table in the hostel's semi-enclosed rooftop terrace café, with the TV trained on Kurdish-language news programmes or folk music performances. This is usefully contrasted against what would be found on the televisions at other hostels, namely FIFA, UEFA, and Turkish Superlig football matches; or international and Turkish-language series and music videos. Note that at Outback Hostel the programming was always set according to the tastes of the staff, and the remote control rested permanently at their table, as opposed to being mounted under the television so guests could go looking for whatever they liked, as is more conventional in Sultanahmet hospitality. Indeed, although they were never unfriendly, the Bitlis boys infrequently socialised with the guests who ventured up to the café; the guests, in turn, tended to stay there only long enough to finish a glass of tea or write in their journals before heading back down to their rooms or dorms, returning the space to its proprietors. Meanwhile, the norm in Sultanahmet's hostels is for guests to congregate in these spaces, spending evenings there befriending other travellers or asking staffers cultural questions about Turkey, sometimes extending these interactions late into the evening by going together to bars or nightclubs in the more exciting Beyoğlu district (the contemporary city centre).

The case of the Bitlis boys is recognisable as that of migrants rather than of the affectively mobile, not only according to the understanding of *gurbet* in the Turkish collective consciousness but also according to the common frameworks of migration literature: the family members had been motivated by economic factors to move to Istanbul, and entered the tourism industry while nevertheless avoiding interaction with those they deemed 'outsiders' – customers and colleagues alike – a category they defined in overlapping place-based, kinship, and sociopolitical terms. Unlike the case of today's unintelligible *garip yiğit* youth, the boundaries of *gurbet* were not imposed on the Bitlis boys any more severely than they also imposed them on themselves and others, as they barricaded themselves counterintuitively inside their guesthouse.

Conclusion

The connection between a subject and *gurbet* not only continues to exist in contemporary Turkey and elsewhere around the former Ottoman Mediterranean, it even retains some of its sense of legend despite its unintelligibility. For example, Penelope Papailias (2003) detailed the case of Flamur Pisli, a 24-year-old Albanian labourer in Greece, who became storied as a 'hero of *kurbet*' (p. 1084) after hijacking a public bus at Kalashnikov-point in May 1999.[11] The event, which ended by sniper-fire in the deaths of both the perpetrator and a Greek hostage, became immortalised in poems, songs, and 'a privately-recorded memorial *rapsodi*, a genre of folk epic, [which] became a pirate cassette hit that travelled beyond the borders of Albania and Kosovo, Greece and the Albanian areas of [Macedonia]' (pp. 1062–63). According to Papailias, 'What ultimately turned his typical migration experience into a heroic event … is that Pisli spoke back to the Greek people. … He thus succeeded in turning the humdrum, often miserable experience of migration into the stuff of history' (pp. 1065–66).

In the absence of *gurbet*'s signature melancholic nostalgia, my informants demonstrated non-normative 'affective bonds with place' that obliterate the socio-spatial 'striations' in the otherwise 'smooth' space of mobility (Deleuze and Guattari 1987 [1980]). Through a socio-historical analysis of constellations of relative location and understandings of spatial movement, I have in this chapter isolated 'mobility' as a discrete phenomenon alongside 'migration' for the Turkish context. I have also fleshed out this framework ethnographically, sharing Sultanahmet boys' articulations of their positionality relative to *gurbet* and discussing how the dissonance between their affective mobility and the 'sedentarist' (Malkki 1992) normative gaze compel them to try to actualise their subjectivities outside Turkey.

Despite the phenomenological residue of *garip yiğitler*, bandits, and other swashbuckling youth of old in contemporary social life, the substance of my informants' distinctiveness is unintelligible today. This was demonstrated in Lemi's attempt to explain away as aberrant Kaan's 'performative excellence', especially around visiting foreign women. Lemi is in fact is also a migrant; he grew up in another province and moved to Istanbul only after graduating university. However, such factors as his sought-after neighbourhood of residence and skilled profession granted him the social and modern institutional capital to obviate many of the ills of *gurbet*, and protecting that privilege had everything to do with his ire toward Kaan. It is also important to recognise that the gaze of Lemi and the gaze of the Bitlis boys on the location of *gurbet* and its subject are one and the same, only the former is cast from the centre and the latter from the periphery. Kaan, meanwhile, preferred to evade their gaze altogether. In another time, he might have been able to exploit societal mechanisms through which to manoeuvre himself up the socio-spatial hierarchy, but in the here and now he simply wanted to leave.

Notes

1 This chapter builds partly on Su 2022.
2 All parties are referred to by pseudonyms.
3 Lemi's comment about closing in on prey was meant in self-deprecating jest at the perceived absurdity of the outcome, which I note in case it is interpreted as disparagement of the women in question.
4 According to the United Nations World Tourism Organization's annual reports, Turkey has consistently ranked in the top ten for tourism, measured in international arrivals, since 2007 (UNWTO 2021).
5 For reference, the city's mid-century population was around one million; at the time of writing it stands well above 15 million.
6 There are four parts to Hobsbawm's typology; the other two are those who are forced to the margins of the home society due to antisocial behaviour, or to economic exclusion. These two types we could think of as 'involuntary bandits'. A key point about my informants, then – whom I liken to Hobsbawm's 'individual rebels' – is that no interpersonal or systemic obstacles stand between them and living their lives wholly within normative sociability; the issue lies only in their desire not to do so.
7 Both descend from *garb*, which means 'west' in Arabic. The original reference was to the setting of the sun and the sense of disorientation, isolation, and fear associated with trying to find one's way in the dark (Sayad 2000, 166–67). That said, this imagery does not directly inform contemporary Turkish usage, as the word for 'west' is *batı*.

8 See Zırh (2017) on the ubiquity of 'hometown associations' serving the Turkish diaspora in Europe – in this case among the Alevi religious minority.

9 The distinction between place of birth and/or upbringing and ancestral homeland is not just an affective orientation, it is also administratively codified. The national ID cards of all Turkish citizens contain two location-related fields: *ikametgah* and *kütük*. The former is one's current location of residence according to the civil registry, from which things like voter registration are determined. The latter is one's patrilocal ancestry originating in Ottoman census records. One's *kütük* and one's *sıla* tend to be the same, although one category is not derived from the other as such. In the context of the Bitlis boys' understanding of 'home', despite being raised in Manisa, its official significance was erased when they moved to Istanbul and changed their *ikametgah* at the registrar's office, while Bitlis remained the *kütük* of all three brothers even though the youngest had never even lived there, having been born after the family's move to Manisa.

10 The official cause of death for Ahmet Kaya was a heart attack.

11 *Kurbet* is the Albanian variant of *gurbet*. It is also *gurbet* in Bulgaria and the former Yugoslav republics. Elsewhere around the former empire it is *kourbeti* in Greece and *ghurba* (transliteration varies) around the Arabic-speaking world. In addition, the ethnonym used by Romani populations in the former Yugoslavia, Albania, and Cyprus is Gurbeti.

References

Abusharaf, Rogala Mustafa. 2002. *Wanderings: Sudanese Migrants and Exiles in North America*. Ithaca, NY: Cornell University Press.

Ali, Syed. 2007. '"Go West Young Man": The Culture of Migration among Muslims in Hyderabad, India'. *Journal of Ethnic and Migration Studies* 33 (1): 37–58. https://doi.org/10.1080/13691830601043489.

Augé, Marc. 1995 [1992]. *Non-Places: Introduction to an Anthropology of Supermodernity*. Translated by John Howe. London: Verso.

Barkey, Karen. 1994. *Bandits and Bureaucrats: The Ottoman Route to State Centralization*. Ithaca, NY: Cornell University Press.

Blok, Anton. 1972. 'The Peasant and the Brigand: Social Banditry Reconsidered'. *Comparative Studies in Society and History* 14 (4): 494–503. https://doi.org/10.1017/S0010417500006824.

Braidotti, Rosi. 1994. *Nomadic Subjects: Embodiment and Sexual Difference in Contemporary Feminist Theory*. New York, NY: Columbia University Press.

Butler, Judith. 2009. 'Performativity, Precarity and Sexual Politics'. *AIBR, Revista de Antropología Iberoamericana* 4 (3): 1–13. https://doi.org/10.11156/aibr.040305.

Caftanzoglou, Roxane. 2001. 'In the Shadow of the Sacred Rock: Contrasting Discourses of Place under the Acropolis'. In *Contested Landscapes: Movement, Exile and Place*, edited by Barbara Bender and Margot Winer, 21–35. Oxford: Berg.

Clifford, James. 1997. *Routes: Travel and Translation in the Late Twentieth Century*. Cambridge, MA: Harvard University Press.

Cohen, Jeffrey H., and Ibrahim Sirkeci. 2011. *Cultures of Migration: The Global Nature of Contemporary Mobility*. Austin, TX: University of Texas Press.

Cresswell, Tim. 1996. *In Place/out of Place: Geography, Ideology, and Transgression*. Minneapolis, MN: University of Minnesota Press.

Delaney, Carol. 1991. *The Seed and the Soil: Gender and Cosmology in Turkish Village Society*. Berkeley, CA: University of California Press.

Deleuze, Gilles, and Félix Guattari. 1987 [1980]. *A Thousand Plateaus: Capitalism and Schizophrenia*. Translated by Brian Massumi. Minneapolis, MN: University of Minneapolis Press.

Demirtaş, Neslihan, and Seher Şen. 2007. 'Varoş Identity: The Redefinition of Low Income Settlements in Turkey'. *Middle Eastern Studies* 43 (1): 87–106. https://doi.org/10.1080/00263200601079732.

Elliot, Alice. 2021. *The Outside: Migration as Life in Morocco*. Bloomington, IN: Indiana University Press.

Erder, Sema. 1999. 'Where Do You Hail from? Localism and Networks in Istanbul'. Translated by Çağlar Keyder. In *Istanbul: Between the Global and the Local*, edited by Çağlar Keyder, 161–71. Lanham, MD: Rowman & Littlefield.

Fodor, Pál. 2000. 'Making a Living on the Frontiers: Volunteers in the Sixteenth-Century Ottoman Army'. In *Ottomans, Hungarians, and Habsburgs in Central Europe: The Military Confines in the Era of Ottoman Conquest*, edited by Pál Fodor and Géza Dávid, 229–64. Leiden: Brill.

Gallant, Thomas W. 1988. 'Greek Bandits: Lone Wolves or a Family Affair?' *Journal of Modern Greek Studies* 6 (2): 269–90. https://doi.org/10.1353/mgs.2010.0264.

Ghannam, Farha. 2013. *Live and Die Like a Man: Gender Dynamics in Urban Egypt*. Stanford, CA: Stanford University Press.

Gustafson, Per. 2001. 'Roots and Routes: Exploring the Relationship between Place Attachment and Mobility'. *Environment and Behavior* 33 (5): 667–86. https://doi.org/10.1177/00139160121973188.

Herzfeld, Michael. 1985. 'The Poetics of Manhood: Contest and Identity in a Cretan Mountain Village'. Princeton, NJ: Princeton University Press.

Hobsbawm, Eric. 1981 [1969]. *Bandits*. Revised edition. New York, NY: Pantheon.

Horváth, Istvan. 2008. 'The Culture of Migration of Rural Romanian Youth'. *Journal of Ethnic and Migration Studies* 34 (5): 771–86. https://doi.org/10.1080/13691830802106036.

Kandel, William, and Douglas S. Massey. 2002. 'The Culture of Mexican Migration: A Theoretical and Empirical Analysis'. *Social Forces* 80 (3): 981–1004. https://doi.org/10.1353/sof.2002.0009.

Kandiyoti, Deniz. 1994. 'The Paradoxes of Masculinity: Some Thoughts on Segregated Societies'. In *Dislocating Masculinity: Comparative Ethnographies*, edited by Andrea Cornwall and Nancy Lindisfarne, 196–212. London: Routledge.

Kaplan, Caren. 1996. *Questions of Travel: Postmodern Discourses of Displacement*. Durham, NC: Duke University Press.

Karpat, Kemal H. 1976. *The Gecekondu: Rural Migration and Urbanization*. Cambridge: Cambridge University Press.

Keyder, Çağlar. 2005. 'Globalization and Social Exclusion in Istanbul'. *International Journal of Urban and Regional Research* 29 (1): 124–34. https://doi.org/10.1111/j.1468-2427.2005.00574.x.

Malkki, Liisa. 1992. 'National Geographic: The Rooting of Peoples and the Territorialization of National Identity Among Scholars and Refugees'. *Cultural Anthropology* 7 (1): 24–44. https://doi.org/10.1525/can.1992.7.1.02a00030.

Mandel, Ruth. 1996. 'A Place of Their Own: Contesting Spaces and Defining Places in Berlin's Migrant Community'. In *Making Muslim Space in North America and Europe*, edited by Barbara Daly Metcalf, 147–64. Berkeley, CA: University of California Press.

Mandel, Ruth. 2008. *Cosmopolitan Anxieties: Turkish Challenges to Citizenship and Belonging in Germany*. London: Duke University Press.

Mills, Amy. 2008. 'The Place of Locality for Identity in the Nation: Minority Narratives of Cosmopolitan Istanbul'. *International Journal of Middle East Studies* 40: 383–401. https://doi.org/10.1017/S0020743808080987.

Mondain, Nathalie, and Alioune Diagne. 2013. 'Discerning the Reality of "Those Left Behind" in Contemporary Migration Processes in Sub-Saharan Africa: Some Theoretical Reflections in the Light of Data from Senegal'. *Journal of Intercultural Studies* 34 (5): 503–16. https://doi.org/10.1080/07256868.2013.82 7831.

Monsutti, Alessandro. 2007. 'Migration as a Rite of Passage: Young Afghans Building Masculinity and Adulthood in Iran'. *Iranian Studies* 40 (2): 167–85. https://doi.org/10.1080/00210860701276183.

Neyzi, Leyla. 2001. 'Object or Subject? The Paradox of "Youth" in Turkey'. *International Journal of Middle East Studies* 33 (3): 411–32. https://doi.org/10.1017/S002074380100304X.

Osella, Filippo, and Caroline Osella. 2000. 'Migration, Money and Masculinity in Kerala'. *Journal of the Royal Anthropological Institute* 6: 117–33.

Papailias, Penelope. 2003. '"Money of *Kurbet* is Money of Blood": The Making of a "Hero" of Migration at the Greek-Albanian Border'. *Journal of Ethnic and Migration Studies* 29 (6): 1059–78. https://doi.org/10.1080/1369183032000171 366.

Said, Edward W. 2000 [1984]. *Reflections on Exile and Other Essays*. Cambridge, MA: Harvard University Press.

Said, Edward W. 2000 [1999]. *Out of Place: A Memoir*. New York, NY: Vintage Books.

Saloul, Ihab. 2012. *Catastrophe and Exile in the Modern Palestinian Imagination: Telling Memories*. Basingstoke: Palgrave Macmillan.

Sant Cassia, Paul. 1993. 'Banditry, Myth, and Terror in Cyprus and Other Mediterranean Societies'. *Comparative Studies in Society and History* 35 (4): 773–95.

Sariyannis, Marinos. 2006. '"Neglected Trades": Glimpses into the 17th Century Istanbul Underworld'. *Turcica* 38: 155–79.

Sayad, Abdelmalek. 2000. 'El Ghorba: From Original Sin to Collective Lie'. *Ethnography* 1 (2): 147–71. https://doi.org/10.1177/14661380022230714.

Schielke, Samuli. 2015. *Egypt in the Future Tense: Hope, Frustration, and Ambivalence before and after 2011*. Bloomington, IN: Indiana University Press.

Schielke, Samuli. 2020. *Migrant Dreams: Egyptian Workers in the Gulf States*. Cairo: The American University in Cairo Press.

Soysal, Levent. 2008. 'The Migration Story of Turks in Germany: From the Beginning to the End'. In *The Cambridge History of Turkey*, vol. 4, edited by Resat Kasaba, 199–225. Cambridge: Cambridge University Press.

Su, Janine. 2022. "'Asılmak Tehlikeli Ve Yasaktır": Unintelligible Mobility and Uncertain Manhood in Istanbul's Old City'. In *Extraordinary Risks, Ordinary Lives: Logics of Precariousness in Everyday Contexts*, edited by Beata Świtek, Allen Abramson and Hannah Swee, 223–48. Cham: Palgrave Macmillan. https://doi.org/10.1007/978-3-030-83962-8_9

Todorova, Mariia. 2009 [1997]. *Imagining the Balkans*. Oxford: Oxford University Press.

UNWTO (UN World Tourism Organization). 2021. *International Tourism Highlights*. 2020 edition. Madrid: UNWTO. https://doi.org/10.18111/9789284422456.

White, Jenny B. 2010. 'Tin Town to Fanatics: Turkey's Rural to Urban Migration from 1923 to the Present'. In *Turkey's Engagement with Modernity: Conflict and Change in the Twentieth Century*, edited by Celia Kerslake, Kerem Öktem and Philip Robins, 425–42. Basingstoke: Palgrave Macmillan.

Zırh, Besim Can. 2012. 'Following the Dead beyond the "Nation": A Map for Transnational Alevi Funerary Routes from Europe to Turkey'. *Ethnic and Racial Studies* 35 (10): 1758–74. https://doi.org/10.1080/01419870.2012.659274.

Zırh, Besim Can. 2017. "'Kırmančiya belekê": Understanding Alevi Geography in between Spaces of Longing and Belonging'. In *Alevis in Europe: Voices of Migration, Culture and Identity*, edited by Tözün Issa, 158–72. London: Routledge.

CHAPTER 9

The Hedgehog from Jordan
Or, How to Locate the Movement of Wild
Animals in a Partially Mediterranean Context[1]

Sarah Green

University of Helsinki

Abstract

This chapter considers Mediterranean crosslocations in terms of non-human animals. It begins with a hedgehog crossing the border between Jordan and Israel, and describes some of the ways it has been spatially located. One involves formal scientific classification systems: Latin naming conventions, concepts of habitat and ideas about indigeneity. The hedgehog's designated habitat overlaps with another locating system in the region, the state border territorial structure, which is not at all relevant to hedgehogs. A third layer is to consider how the hedgehog might fit into the idea of Mediterranean, to which the short answer is: awkwardly. The chapter then moves away from hedgehogs to briefly describe how people in different parts of the geographical Mediterranean have accounted for the dramatic rise in populations of wild boar in their area in recent years. Wild boar are among a number of animals that have suddenly appeared, or rapidly increased in number, in many

How to cite this book chapter:
Green, Sarah. 2022. 'The Hedgehog from Jordan: Or, How to Locate the Movement of Wild Animals in a Partially Mediterranean Context'. In *Locating the Mediterranean: Connections and Separations across Space and Time*, edited by Carl Rommel and Joseph John Viscomi, 199–221. Helsinki: Helsinki University Press. DOI: https://doi.org/10.33134/HUP-18-9.

areas in the geographical Mediterranean region. Looking at how people have accounted for this provides one way to briefly explore how the logic of locating regimes might be deployed to explain changes in the spatial presence of non-human animals.

Animal Locations

Non-human animals within the geographical Mediterranean region are located in a variety of ways, only one of which involves explicitly referring to them as Mediterranean animals. They could be referred to as invasive species (in which case they do not belong in the Mediterranean) or desert animals (which only partially overlaps with the Mediterranean). These are different ways of locating where animals belong that coexist, and spatially overlap with, the way that other kinds of things are located. For example, the habitat of an animal can stretch across several state borders, creating a 'crosslocation' of animal habitat and political borders. This chapter briefly unpacks the means by which animals are located within Euro-American scientific standards – i.e. the Linnaean classification system first developed in the 18th century in Northern Europe – and then looks at how that system coexists with other locating regimes, most particularly state border regimes, and the use of the idea of Mediterranean as a locating mechanism. I begin with an entirely insignificant event – a hedgehog crossing the Jordan–Israel border on a sunny day in 2019 – in order to explore the different logics used to spatially locate places (e.g. states) and things (e.g. hedgehogs), logics that often overlap and crosscut one another. This is followed by an exploration of what kind of locating practice is involved in the idea of Mediterranean and considers how the hedgehog might fit into that kind of locating regime. Finally, I briefly describe how people in different parts of the geographical Mediterranean have accounted for the dramatic rise in populations of wild boar in their area in recent years, in order to explore how they draw on diverse locating logics in order to make sense of the new way in which the wild boar have made their presence felt. I suggest that the key element many people draw upon in this process is to locate the newly arrived animals into one or more power structures that create certain kinds of connections, separations, and hierarchies in their region: in crosslocations terms, the wild boar are located through drawing upon one or more locating regimes and fitting their new use of location into it. I will begin with the hedgehog.

Taxonomies

On a warm day in June 2019, a hedgehog crossed the border from Jordan into Israel, made its way to a spare flowerpot that was lying outside a house in a kibbutz about 30 kilometres north of Eilat, and then promptly snuggled into it (see Image 9.1). Nobody was concerned. Nor have hedgehogs attracted a great deal of attention in anthropology; when they are mentioned, it is usually a metaphorical reference to a comparison between foxes and hedgehogs first made by Archilochos and then made famous by Isaiah Berlin: 'a fox knows many things, but a hedgehog one important thing' (Berlin 1954; Carrithers 2005, 582; Jung 1987, 322). Viveiros de Castro mentioned the fact that hedgehogs were used as footballs in *Alice in Wonderland* (Viveiros de Castro 2015, 14–15); Mike Michael mentioned them in some research on roadkill (Michael 2004).

Image 9.1: Hedgehog from Jordan, June 2019.
Photo: Joan Neiberg.

Although these references only mention hedgehogs in generic terms, it is almost certain that the animal they had in mind is the European hedgehog, named *Erinaceus europaeus* within the Linnaean taxonomic system. There are currently 17 types (species) of hedgehog listed within that classification system, subdivided into five genera (*Atelerix*, *Erinaceus*, *Hemiechinus*, *Mesechinus*, and *Paraechinus*). Yet almost all references to hedgehogs in Euro-American literature, including Beatrix Potter's Mrs Tiggy-winkle, actually mean *Erinaceus europaeus* (or *Ee* for short), rather than any of the other 16 species.[2] This is not surprising, as *Ee* was the original model for the generic idea of hedgehog-ness, as it were: Linnaeus himself named *Ee* in 1758, in the tenth edition of *Systema Naturae* – the same edition that introduced the binomial (genus and species) nomenclature system for animals (Linné 1758). Thereafter, all animals found around the world that were deemed to be sufficiently similar to *Ee*, according to the criteria set out by the Linnaean taxonomic system, were classified as belonging to the same group: the family Erinaceidae, which also includes moonrats (they look like hedgehogs, but have no spines), and the subfamily Erinaceinae (named by Gotthelf Fischer von Waldheim in 1814), which contains only hedgehogs. These 17 variations of the 'same' creature are not to be confused with porcupines, which belong to the order of rodents, taxonomically speaking; nor should they be confused with the lesser hedgehog tenrec (*Echinops telfairi*) or greater hedgehog tenrec (*Setifer setosus*), which are endemic to Madagascar and are not hedgehogs at all, according to the taxonomic system, even though they are called hedgehogs in English, since they look quite a lot like *Ee*. The taxonomic system is all about establishing similarities and differences that make a difference within the logic of Linnaean taxonomy. That logic also draws strongly on certain understandings of location in its classification practices, particularly through concepts of indigeneity, habitat, and niche – in what one critical animal geographer has referred to as 'a gigantic act of enclosure'.[3]

The hedgehog that crossed the border from Jordan to Israel and nestled into a flowerpot in a kibbutz on that day in June 2019 was not an *Ee* hedgehog but an example of one given the taxonomic name *Paraechinus aethiopicus* (or *Pa* for short). In contemporary terms, the name is a little misleading, as *Pa*'s listed habitat covers most of North Africa and all of the Arab world but is not listed as existing in today's Ethiopia (Amori et al. 2012). The locational reference for *Pa*'s name, 'aethiopicus', is a reference to Aethiopia, which was a rather vaguely located place that occasionally appeared in classical history. The historian Herodotus discussed Aethiopia several times and, to him, the area was located directly south of Egypt, which would place it in contemporary Sudan (Godley 1975 [1920], 299). Earlier classical references placed Aethiopia to the east of the Nile and up to the Red Sea. My point is that the German naturalist who classified and named *Pa* in 1832, a man called Christian Gottfried Ehrenberg, who made a scientific expedition to North Africa and the East Mediterranean in the early 1820s, took the locational name from his reading of classical history, and not from whatever names such animals might have been given by people living in the regions that he visited.[4] The main point was to create a non-local, universal, standardised nomenclature that could be used anywhere, with the implication that this system would describe an objective and timeless reality. Yet the use of classical history to name a location also reveals that all standards have histories and come from somewhere in particular – in this case, from late-19th-century Northern Europe (Lampland and Star 2009, 14).

In any case, whether or not these hedgehogs live in today's Ethiopia, they certainly live in Jordan,[5] and on that day in June one of these little creatures walked across the Jordanian border to an Israeli kibbutz, which is, by all accounts, quite a common occurrence.[6]

The point of that lengthy and technical description of a non-event was to demonstrate the historically and epistemologically contingent process of describing locations – in this case, of a hedgehog that was on the move. I described two ways to locate *Pa*'s place in the world: the Linnaean taxonomic system, which embeds within it the concepts of habitat, niche, and indigeneity; and the fact that *Pa* crossed a state border, drawing on modern state territorial border logic. These two locating systems coexist in parallel rather than in conflict: it does not matter that *Pa*'s habitat crosscuts a range of political borders: the borders are not built for hedgehogs. Of course, there are other occasions when the crossing of animal habitats and political borders do cause problems – for example, in the Pyrenees, where policies involving national parks and the protection of wildlife come into direct conflict with the interests of livestock farmers living in the same areas (Vaccaro and Beltran 2009). The same can be said of trouble involving wild boar, as I describe further below. The key issue here is that coexisting classification systems that locate things differently (state borders, animal habitats) do not necessarily cause conflicts, even when they overlap in the same geographical spaces. The particular political border *Pa* crossed on that day had been through a number of transitions during the 20th century: British, French, Palestinian, Egyptian, Jordanian, and Israeli interests jostled for space around there at various different moments and with varying degrees of violence (Robins 2004). Yet *Pa*'s designated habitat remained the same throughout, and neither she nor any other hedgehogs were prevented from crossing whatever new political borders were being created there at any given moment.

Nevertheless, all that political jostling was significant for *Pa*'s naming and the classification of her location, including that location being given a name that came from classical history, which was something of an obsession in European scientific circles at the time. North European involvement in, and agreements concerning, this region made it not only possible for people such as Ehrenberg to travel to the region in the 1820s so he could collect specimens of *Pa*; in addition, the whole idea of going off on expeditions to discover and classify things according to this logic also provided the motivation and resources for Ehrenberg to do so. Along with many other European explorers, Ehrenberg collected all kinds of samples, both of plants and animals, and then returned to Europe to analyse, sort, and order them, and then give them Linnaean taxonomic names. The naming marked a scientific discovery.

In other words, my description of *Pa*'s name, movements, and location have their roots in historically and geographically specific understandings of location, both for the animal's habitat and for the territory (Elden 2013). And it is important to note that the Linnean taxonomic system has been regularly challenged, despite having been globally adopted. Rousseau went out of his way to challenge it, and, perhaps most famously, Goethe questioned the whole underlying premise of Linnaean taxonomy: rather than rely on a static system of fixed similarities and differences, as Linnaeus did, Goethe began from the premise that all living entities are constantly in a process of transformation and change, so that a static classification system was actually wrongheaded (Larson 1967). Thus the historical and epistemological contingency of these descriptions means it could have been otherwise: there have been other ways to classify and organise political and legal territoriality, and there have been other ways to understand hedgehogs and their habitats.[7] Still, *Paraechinus aethiopicus* (*Pa*) is in practice the contemporary formal taxonomic name of that hedgehog and the same

Latin name is used throughout the world in all languages, irrespective of whatever she is called locally, and irrespective of how people in the area might classify her, how they might understand her association with the local area, or how they might understand her character (her hedgehog-ness, as it were).[8] And the border between Jordan and Israel that *Pa* crossed is a political border that belongs to an historically specific way to classify territory and establish political and legal powers over particular patches of the earth, and one that is currently the internationally agreed standard for doing so. It could have been otherwise, but it ended up this way.

Mediterranean Partial Locations

So, how does the Mediterranean fit into this story? As Chapter 1 in this volume outlines, the classification of the Mediterranean has undergone a variety of transformations, giving the word shifting meaning and significance. As Rommel and Viscomi note, a key part of this has been movement from Braudel's understanding of Mediterranean as a process to drawing more on Horden and Purcell's approach of regarding Mediterranean as being characterised by its connections as well as being a process. These shifts have specific histories associated with perspectives that could loosely be described as Euro-American modern and, more recently, postmodern, perspectives. Anthropologists have of course engaged in those debates as much as classicists, historians and political scientists.[9] Critiques often suggest that there is something partial about earlier understandings of Mediterranean – that such accounts are both incomplete and describe things from a particular vantage point or perspective.[10] All-encompassing accounts are often replaced by ones that are multiple, generating a sense of ongoing change and transformation, or ones that reject the idea that there is some-*thing* to discuss at all: the Mediterranean as an intellectual invention, or as no longer having relevance, whether or not it is a process of shifting connections.

The approach within this volume comes closer to one that suggests ongoing change and transformation, but with an additional twist: that the changes stop and start, and that they are not random; that disconnections, separations, and fragmentations are often as relevant as connections in understanding how the process of ongoing change works. That focus on disconnection as well as connection places emphasis on the hierarchical and power-inflected way that differences between people and places are effected, which is anything but random.

There are three implications here that are worth making explicit. The first is that it is probably not helpful to search for a final answer to the Mediterranean, as the question appears to be scale- and context-dependent, both across time and space. The second is that different understandings of Mediterranean have held purchase within different disciplines, which means that diverse meanings coexist within scholarship as well as across the geographical Mediterranean region. For example, ecosystems researchers have linked together parts of the world that have 'Mediterranean-type' environmental conditions, which includes parts of Chile, California, and Australia (Esler, Jacobsen, and Pratt 2018). In that account, Mediterranean could be geographically located anywhere in the world: so long as certain ecological conditions are present, it is a Mediterranean location. The historically contingent issue there is to note that such ecosystems are called Mediterranean-type rather than, for example, California-type ecosystems: just as the first hedgehog to be taxonomically classified was a European one, the Mediterranean ecosystem provides the model for the rest of the world. The third implication is that, despite all that diversity and complexity, there are non-random and deliberate ways in which 'the' Mediterranean has been made to appear, and that these can have both trivial and serious material effects for people.

Collectively, all of this makes it tempting to understand Mediterranean in the same way that Janet Carsten understands kinship: by considering how the concept is meaningful for particular people and at particular moments, fully abandoning the 19th-century view from nowhere (Carsten 1995, 236). That approach, which is highly familiar in anthropology (looking for ethnographic meaning, which is by definition relative and context-dependent), is certainly worthwhile, and has resulted in excellent contributions to understanding the Mediterranean within the discipline (e.g. Herzfeld 2005; Ben-Yehoyada 2017). At the same time, even ethnographic meaning focuses on questions of what things are – or, at least, a sense of their value. While keeping the idea of focusing on the relative (and often hierarchical) value involved, I am instead, and drawing on the crosslocations approach, shifting my attention to location rather than identity: looking at how Mediterranean is deployed as a way to relatively locate things, which coexists with other ways to locate things. This approach emphasises relative locations (where something is located relative to its connections to and disconnections from other locations) rather than identities (what something is, as such), and it focuses on the coexistence of a range of different ways to locate things rather than only one. And that allows a focus on the dynamics of connections and separations, both within and across different logics. This does not replace research on identities; instead, by shifting attention to location, something can be added to the debate, something that concerns the dynamics of connections and separations between different ways of ascribing things a place in the world.[11]

The example I have been using is the coexistence of a logic informing the creation of political state borders (in this case, Israel and Jordan), and a North European 18th-century taxonomic system that names and spatially locates living entities, including hedgehogs (in this case, *Paraechinus aethiopicus*). So, the next question to be addressed is: how does Mediterranean as a way of locating things come into the story of animals moving across a landscape that is criss-crossed with several different locating regimes?

In the case of *Pa*, the short answer is: indirectly. *Pa's* Mediterranean location is a rather small and not very explicit part of her story; although she is found in many areas that are described as being part of the geographical Mediterranean, including a portion of southern Israel, a thin strip along the coasts of Egypt and Libya, and then in wider strips along northern Algeria, Tunisia, and Morocco, the bulk of her designated habitat covers almost the entirety of the Arabian Peninsula, all of Jordan, some of Syria and Iraq, and the Western Sahara, plus a small population further south in Sudan, none of which are included in the geographical Mediterranean. And, in practice, *Pa* is not classified as a Mediterranean animal; her most common non-Latin name is 'desert hedgehog'. The desert is an environment that also straddles the border between Mediterranean and that which is not Mediterranean; desert points towards the 'tug-of-war' Herzfeld has referred to between imagining Mediterranean as the birthplace of Western civilisation while simultaneously being Middle Eastern (Herzfeld 2014). *Pa* is somewhere in between there, and, perhaps significantly, her habitat does not include anywhere in the north Mediterranean, the part of the region most often referred to as Southern Europe.

Here, it is worth briefly noting the well-known hierarchies involved in evoking the word Mediterranean, ones that assert and ascribe a sliding scale of relative values to different parts of the Mediterranean, and which clearly distinguish between the locations that surround the Mediterranean Sea: North Africa, Southern Europe, and the eastern shores, which are variously called Mediterranean, eastern Mediterranean, Near East and Middle East. The explicit assertion of being Mediterranean – what Herzfeld refers to as 'Mediterraneanism' (Herzfeld 2005, 2014) – is often an intentional political project, one that aims to generate certain distinct associations with some places (e.g. Europe) and separations from others (e.g. the Middle East and North Africa).

This dynamic has been noted in many places, but perhaps most particularly in Israel (Ohana 2011). Monterescu and Handel, in a recent study of the use of the concept of 'terroir' for Israeli viticulture, argue that, '[s]eeking to "undo Palestine," [Israeli terroir] steps over the Arab Middle East by conjuring up the Mediterranean as a gateway to the global market and to cultural normalcy' (Monterescu and Handel 2020, 255). Herzfeld, in a commentary on architectural styles deployed in Israel, suggests that evoking Mediterranean helped to resolve 'a conflict between romantic Orientalism on the one hand and the Eurocentric fear of cultural absorption into something "Middle Eastern" on the other. In that tension, appealing to a Mediterranean identity ... offered a relatively cosmopolitan compromise' (Herzfeld 2014, 125).

Clearly, there are stakes involved in locating a place as Mediterranean, which requires some deliberate performative effort in Israel to balance the desert against the vineyards. As noted by Hirsch in her study of the development of a hummus 'cult' in Israel, this does not necessarily mean entirely rejecting the Arab world (Hirsch 2011) but it does require generating a clear separation, a difference that makes a difference (Bateson 1972, 453). *Pa*, located as a desert animal, exists only on one side of that difference; yet, as a hedgehog, she is classified as belonging to a family of animals that also belong entirely to the other side: the other species of hedgehogs, who are in the family Erinaceidae and the subfamily Erinaceinae, and, particularly, Mrs Tiggy-winkle, *Erinaceus europaeus*, the European hedgehog that Linnaeus himself named. In that sense, *Pa* can be located as being at the heart of Mediterranean: by being labelled a desert hedgehog, she is distinguished from the European hedgehog but she belongs to the same family (literally). It depends on the locating regime and how you read it.

Locating Wild Boar

Speaking of deserts, issues relating to the environment regularly come up in discussions of Mediterranean things, and are often even given a determining status. It is as if the topography, climate, and soils explain everything (a particularly good example is McNeill 1992). Braudel devoted over 270 pages to discussing the Mediterranean's environment, climate, topography and the like, and Horden and Purcell embedded the idea of 'micro-ecologies' into their entire framework for understanding Mediterranean: a place that combined 'easy seaborne communications with a quite unusually fragmented topography of microregions' (Horden and Purcell 2000, 5). In both of these studies, the physical characteristics of the Mediterranean are key aspects of the dynamics of the place. Interestingly, these descriptions rarely describe wild animals. Both Braudel (1995) and Horden and Purcell (2000) passed over wildlife with almost no comment, except occasional mentions of hunting.

Among the animals hunted in the 16th century were wild boar, which can live in a wide variety of environments and are known to be exceptionally adaptable. That makes them potentially troublesome animals, as they are highly capable of interfering with human activity: a crossing of paths that disturbs. And indeed, in recent years, wild boar in all parts of the geographical Mediterranean and also in many other parts of the world, including North America (both the US and Canada), have been causing trouble.[12] There has been a very significant increase in their numbers in recent years, along with their appearance in towns and cities, and they regularly dig up land searching for roots, often destroying lawn and other plants, and they are capable of eating, or at least destroying, entire fields of crops in one night. The animals in question, which again Linnaeus himself named in 1758 as *Sus scrofa*, is taxonomically the same as the domesticated pig, which is named as a subspecies: *Sus scrofa domesticus* (named by Johann Christian Polycarp Erxleben in 1777).

This capacity for animals to be adaptable, especially their capacity to move out of what is classified as their indigenous habitats and into some other place, can lead to a particularly negative classification: 'invasive species'. That concept combines the classificatory logic of habitat with the political border logic of territories, generating an idea of territorial transgression that has long been associated with colonial, nationalist, and racist approaches towards questions of location.[13] Whether or not the wild boar appearing in ever greater numbers across the geographical Mediterranean region count as 'invasive' depends on who you ask: some argue that the animals are the same species that always existed in the area anyway; others suggest they are a new species that came in from somewhere else; some extend the idea of 'invasive' to mean transgressive, by moving into somewhere they have no right to be (cities, cultivated fields, etc.). The media regularly carry stories about wild boar 'trashing' places, even in cities, around the entire region.[14]

In any case, while I was carrying out some preliminary ethnographic research in 2019 and early 2020 on the transportation of livestock across the Mediterranean region, as well as looking into efforts to track wild animals and manage the spread of zoonotic disease, just about every veterinarian, zoological researcher, agriculture ministry official, farmer, animal trader, and hunter that I met spontaneously mentioned a huge increase in the numbers of wild boar in their region in recent years. This has also been noticed by the officials in the European Union, which has funded a substantial project called ENETWILD, which in 2019 was specifically focusing on the wild boar issue.[15]

Here, it is worth noting that there is an increasing trend among animal geographers to remove the nature–culture border between cities and countryside and insist that cities are also, normally and as a matter of course, wild animal habitats. Indeed, Jennifer Wolch, in noting that cities have always contained a wide variety of non-human animals, has called for an *Anima Urbis* movement, which regards urban environments to be as much non-human animal environments as they are human ones (Wolch 2002). This is an idea that encompasses most of the critiques of zoos, gardens, nature–culture distinctions, and classificatory constraints that usually accompany this approach of blurring the lines between human and non-human. In particular, critiques question the way such places (zoos, gardens, etc.) generate clear spatial separations between wild, natural, and cultural, arguing that 18th-century thinking on such matters in fact imposed those separations, rather than reflecting them. In effect, the argument is that Linnaean classificatory logic generated these different locations (by creating distinctions using a particular logic), rather than recording them.

A similar argument is made by Irus Braverman in her study of three zoos separated by three different kinds of border regime in Israel–Palestine (Braverman 2013). In an account that is quite similar to the earlier studies I mentioned on Mediterraneanism, Braverman demonstrates a deep level of intertwining of political, religious, and classificatory logic that plays out in the connections and separations between these zoos. The work of researchers such as Wolch and Braverman argues that 18th- and 19th-century scholars were strongly influenced by the idea of the human–animal distinction, a distinction that some argue has been crucial to Euro-American ideas of both civility and sovereignty.[16] In that sense, the classification of animals and attempts to contain them in zoos, which after the 1750s became repositories for keeping all the specimens being collected from around the world, as well as showcasing the colonial and modern mastery of the natural world (Urbanik 2012, 78), was never entirely successful. Apart from the fact that animals would quite often get out of their zoos, there were also always animals that were out anyway. These borders were never intended for the animals, as such.[17]

So perhaps the wild boar were always there. In any case, looked at from the perspective of location, many comments I received from people in my travels around the geographical Mediterranean were not quite in line with the idea of the need to maintain a distinction between places that animals belong and human places. Instead, people most often discussed how the wild boar arrived: stories about how something or someone, somewhere, had either accidentally or deliberately arranged things so that the boar would move into certain spaces.

Penny Johnson provides a similar report from the West Bank (Johnson 2019). Johnson devotes an entire chapter of her book to 'A conspiracy of wild boars' (Chapter 6). She received repeated reports from Palestinian farmers whose crops were being regularly destroyed by the animals that the Israeli settlers were dumping the boar onto Palestinian lands. Johnson herself argued that, whether or not that occurred, Israelis' habit of building walls and boundaries, and dumping raw sewage into the rivers and onto the landscape, probably contributed considerably to attracting the animals and changing where they travelled. Johnson points out that Palestinians' knowledge of powerful human forces causing bad effects in the area could easily be turned into a convincing theory that the boar had also been deliberately placed so as to cause maximum damage to Palestinians.

During my own brief visit to Israel–Palestine in March 2019, the wild boar issue was raised as well. One of the Israeli government's representatives of the World Organization for Animal Health (OIE), a veterinarian, suggested that a considerable number of wild boar were coming across to Israel from Jordan; he also suggested that these animals were the source of the spread of various diseases to domestic livestock (sheep and goats, mostly) on the Israeli side. This was one of several occasions during my travels that the crossing of state borders was brought into the discussion. The Israeli veterinarian believed that the surveillance and management of infectious animal diseases were not nearly as good on the Jordanian side of the border, which had bad consequences for Israel, as the animals wandered across the border and spread their diseases there. The stark difference between that and the accounts given by Palestinians speaking to Johnson give a fairly good impression of what kinds of locational threats each was concerned about.

A different account was provided by an Israeli activist working on behalf of the Bedouin. She had spent decades campaigning to try to reverse the illegal building of Israeli settlements on Bedouin grazing lands in the West Bank. She also campaigned to try to prevent the 'boxing in' of the Bedouin, which stopped them from travelling the routes that they once did with their camels, goats, and sheep. She believed, as did those who spoke to Penny Johnson, that the wild boar had been deliberately released by settlers into the Bedouin grazing lands in order to drive the Bedouin away. The several Bedouin whom I met during that short trip, both in the West Bank and in the Negev Desert, did not spontaneously mention any trouble with wild boar. Instead, they focused squarely on the difficulties they confronted in their efforts to move across the landscape with their animals (goats, sheep, and camels), which nowadays involves the crossing of multiple highly securitised borders, and the fact that, when their animals wandered out of their designated areas, they were frequently confiscated or even shot by the authorities (a point that Johnson also mentions). This is an obvious example of how two different locating logics contradict one another: the one involving animal herding and the routes developed by Bedouin to move their animals across the landscape with the seasons; and the second involving state borders and other kinds of political territorial barriers that crosscut them in a way that prevented or deterred movement of any animals.

Beyond the Israel–Palestine region, in Lebanon in July 2019, a researcher who specialised in studying small mammals (fruit bats and mice, mostly) suggested that the wild boar had been introduced to Lebanon for recreational hunting, and that it had got out of hand because of the lack of goats and sheep on the hills. He added that the dramatic drop in the number of wolves in Lebanon in recent years had also meant that the wild boar could breed unhindered. He further believed there were several 'non-indigenous' species of wild boar in the area as a result of them being introduced by humans. And, as an afterthought, he suggested that the number of wolves and jackals were now increasing again in Lebanon, perhaps because of the rise in numbers of wild boar.

A different suggestion was made by a veterinarian who ran a veterinary surgery and supplies shop in Beirut, and who was a specialist in artificial insemination for cattle. While he himself agreed with the small mammal researcher's explanation for the rise in wild boar numbers, he also recounted a conspiracy theory he had heard from some of his customers. This was a variation on the theme reported by Palestinian farmers: the theory was that Israelis were gathering up wild boar on their side of the border, sedating them with alpha-chloralose, and then dumping the sleeping boar on the Lebanese side of the border. The veterinarian grinned, and added that, of course, he did not believe that story, despite providing highly specific information on the drug used to allegedly sedate the animals.

In all these reports, a sense of the tensions created by overlapping locations that are crosscut by power-inflected hierarchies is palpable: people locate the wild boar within a dense interspersing of different ways of managing, controlling, and subdividing the landscape, and unsurprisingly conclude that those with the greatest power are the ones who are probably controlling the new appearance of any animals in the area.

Although the story was somewhat different, a similar dynamic appeared in a remote part of Calabria in July of 2019, where wild boar were not only pottering around local towns and villages, particularly at night and when piglets had recently been born, but they were also causing 'havoc' in the rural areas, according to a local vet who also bred domestic pigs. The vet said they dug up fields, damaged trees and walls, and generally created a mess. He commented that he had to give up growing maize because the boar ate it all. A local landowner in the same small town, along with a number of others, suggested that the wild boar had been deliberately introduced to the area by wealthy investors in order to cause so much destruction that the value of the land would drop, so the investors could buy it all up at a bargain price and make a huge profit out of developing the land. One of them commented that these new wild boar were not the same species as the local wild boar, suggesting that they were bigger and bred much faster than their 'local' boar. This assertion might have been related to the widespread belief that part of the town had been deliberately permitted to fall into disrepair so that it could be cleared and developed for profit. Someone else in the town suggested that the wild boar had been introduced in order to develop hunting tourism in the area (as was also suggested in Lebanon), but the plan had gone wrong and the boar were now running amok.

A similar story about hunting development was recounted in Epirus in north-western Greece, which I visited in March 2020 (just before the Covid-19 lockdown in most of Europe). A national parks officer there reported that wild boar had been introduced to encourage recreational hunting, but little hunting had occurred, and so the boar population had got out of hand. I was aware that, indeed, there had been such a plan to develop wild boar hunting in Epirus, as I happened to have been researching in the area in the early 2000s when a wild boar sanctuary was being built there with EU funding (Green 2005, 240–42). However, the story at that time was that the wild boar were indigenous to the area, rather than being introduced, and the sanctuary was to encourage an increase in their numbers.

A sheep and goat pastoralist from the Pogoni area of Epirus, a Sarakatsani man who had been practising pastoralism in the area for decades, had a somewhat different story. He suggested that the wild boar had increased because of the decline of sheep and goat pastoralism in the area, which had given the wild boar much more space in which to breed and thrive. He also suggested that the wild boar were not the same animals as they had been years ago – not because new species had been introduced but because the local wild boar had crossbred with domestic pigs. It was only in recent decades that pig farming had become big business in the region and, inevitably, some of these farm animals had escaped from the farm and bred with wild boar. This, he said, had resulted in a considerable improvement in the reproductive capacity of the wild boar: the domestic pigs had been specially bred to produce as many piglets as possible, and to be able to have more than one litter per year. As a result, the wild boar's reproductive capacities were also much improved.

Combining all these explanations together – along with many similar ones I heard during my visits to various parts of the geographical Mediterranean – it is possible to generate a clear sense of what people cared about, and how they understood the location dynamics of these wild boar. While many people suggested the boar might be 'invasive' or at least not local, that idea was not connected to the agency of the animals themselves but to the actions of some powerful group of people. Either by accident or design, some humans had unleashed these highly annoying and destructive creatures into the landscape. People attempted to fit the boar into the variety of locating processes that they felt were responsible for how things ended up where they did around their area. Nobody believed that the wild boar had appeared randomly or entirely by their own agency; all accounts assumed that there was some kind of change in the engagement between people and the landscape that led to the wild boar either to move in, or to increase in numbers. Some suggested that powerful people, or wealthy people, or familiar enemies from across the border, were behind it; others suggested that a series of transformations – such as the growth of pig farming in Epirus – had the unintended effect of increasing the birth rate of the wild boar. People did not focus on nature–culture divisions or urban–rural divisions; rather, the discussions focused mostly on the experience that these animals were creating a mess that local residents found difficult, costly, and annoying. And, in attempting to account for their presence, people drew on the dynamics of different locating regimes – the operations of various types of economic power; or the logic of ecology, in which an imbalance caused in one part of the ecosystem (e.g. the removal of sheep and goat pastoralism from the mountains) will result in a compensation in another part (the increase in wild boar); or the operations of political border regimes (wild boar coming from Jordan, or being spread by Israeli settlers, or being dumped in Lebanon by Israelis). In that sense, these accounts could all be described as people's experiences and understanding of the workings of coexisting locating regimes: a means to try to understand where the boar came from by locating them within those power dynamics.

Conclusion

Wild boar, like desert hedgehogs, are to be found in the geographical Mediterranean region, though they have not been marked out as being stereotypically Mediterranean animals: they have not been drawn into Mediterraneanist efforts to create particular hierarchies, relative values between locations, or particular connections and separations between them. Instead, they have been located by people according to a variety of coexisting logics of where things are in the world, and how they got there. *Pa* passes mostly unnoticed, and only appears to be firmly located through her names – as *Paraechinus aethiopicus*, which locates her within a taxonomic system invented by North Europeans; as a desert hedgehog, which places her on one side of a particular internal division within Mediterraneanist discourse; and as a hedgehog, which means, in taxonomic family terms, she belongs on all sides of the Mediterranean and beyond. Nobody suspects that *Pa* has crossed the Jordan–Israel border because of some kind of deliberate or accidental action; her location coexists in parallel with other locating regimes in the area. In contrast, the wild boar, whose numbers have been dramatically increasing over the last few years to the consternation of just about everybody, has been identified as being considerably more transgressive. And, rather than place the blame on the boar for this trouble, people have looked to human intervention, and identified a variety of dynamics that have either reflected or created hierarchies, connections, and separations across the landscape that the wild boar have either exploited or been pushed into deliberately. Their location is not accidental in the way that *Pa*'s appears to be; instead, the wild boar are caught up in conflicting locating regimes, and their transgression of other people's places, as well as the mess that they cause, are placed firmly in the hands of those who control locating dynamics in the area. Through exploring how these two creatures have been drawn into these dynamics, and the way that people make sense of their locations in the world, I have tried to provide a brief glimpse of crosslocations at work.

Notes

1 The research for this chapter has received funding from the European Research Council (ERC) under the European Union's Horizon 2020 research and innovation programme (grant agreement no 694482, Crosslocations, https://www2.helsinki.fi/en/researchgroups/crosslocations, last accessed 4.4.2022). I am grateful to the anonymous reviewers of this volume for their helpful comments, which have improved this chapters considerably – most particularly Reviewer 1, who identified a slippage in language in the previous version of this chapter regarding the concept of relations and separations.

2 *E. europaeus* is the more common way of abbreviating taxonomic names, but that is still overly long in my view.

3 Michael J. Watts in Philo and Wilbert (2000, 292).

4 Souguir-Omrani et al. (2018); Beck (2018, 100).

5 Archaeological research confirms that hedgehogs have been around the area of Jordan for a very long time (Byrd 1989).

6 I am very grateful to Ruth Mandel, who sent me a photograph of *Pa*, taken by her sister. Permission received to reproduce it here.

7 Bolton and Degnen (2010); Fairchild (2003); Foucault (1974); Gilfoyle, Brown, and Beinart (2009); Goldman (1991); Haraway (1988); Law and Mol (2003); Poovey (1998).

8 Bolton and Degnen's edited volume *Animals and Science* provides a range of excellent examples of the way that scientific classification of animals both contradict other ways that people understand them and have often been used for political and economic ends (Bolton and Degnen 2010).

9 Bechev and Nicolaidis (2010); Ben-Yehoyada (2017); Braudel (1995); Herzfeld (1984); Mitchell (2002); Petri (2016); Pina-Cabral (1989); Bromberger (2006).

10 Examples of such critiques include Herzfeld (1980, 1984); Pina-Cabral (1989); Giaccaria and Minca (2011); Bechev and Nicolaidis (2010); Mitchell (2002).

11 I am avoiding the term 'relations' so as not to cause confusion between 'connection' and 'relation' in this context. While often used interchangeably in English, in this chapter the difference is important. My focus is on classification systems and how their logics generate separate and distinct locations – ones that often overlap and coexist. I am not concerning myself with the subtler question of whether these classification systems imply autonomous entities in which relations are created between them; or, alternatively, whether such classification systems imply that entities come into being through their relations (see Strathern 2020 for a richly described analysis of this distinction). That is a different question from the one I am addressing here. I am grateful to an anonymous reviewer who pointed out the slippage in my language in a previous version of this chapter.

12 See, for example, Weeks and Packard (2009); Gren et al. (2020); Sordi (2020); Toger et al. (2018). See also regular media reports on the wild boar issue – for example, https://undark.org/2020/09/14/feral-pig-swine-bomb-ontario-montana (accessed 30 December 2021) and https://www.nationalgeographic.com/animals/article/huge-feral-hogs-swine-spreading-through-north-canada?fbclid=IwAR05CxFtKkN7UwRAjpaHzfVycJaBKhuNx67FsWM-BXkJuBsqT-5P9oGUJ8ZI (accessed 30 December 2021).

13 See, for example Comaroff (2017); Comaroff and Comaroff (2001); Franklin (2006); Vaccaro and Beltran (2009); Wolch (2002).
14 https://www.theguardian.com/world/2019/jul/30/boar-wars-how-wild-hogs-are-trashing-european-cities (accessed 1 June 2020).
15 https://enetwild.com/the-project (accessed 1 June 2020).
16 Vaughan-Williams (2015, 87–93); Derrida (2009).
17 In recent years, there has been an increased use of GIS technologies to track where animals actually go when left to their own devices (Cheshire and Uberti 2017). That is leading to considerable revision of concepts of habitat: the findings not only suggest that many earlier assumptions were inaccurate; they also suggest a high level of variation across space and time, and a tendency for animals to take a number of issues into account in deciding how, when, and where to move – not all of which are related to food, shelter, or safety.

References

Amori, Giovanni, Sabrina Masciola, Jenni Saarto, Spartaco Gippoliti, Carlo Rondinini, Federica Chiozza, and Luca Luiselli. 2012. 'Spatial Turnover and Knowledge Gap of African Small Mammals: Using Country Checklists as a Conservation Tool'. *Biodiversity and Conservation* 21 (7): 1755–93. https://doi.org/10.1007/s10531-012-0275-5

Bateson, Gregory. 1972. *Steps to an Ecology of Mind*. Chicago, IL, and London: University of Chicago Press.

Bechev, Dimitar, and Kalypso Nicolaidis, eds. 2010. *Mediterranean Frontiers: Borders, Conflict and Memory in a Transnational World*. London: Tauris Academic Studies.

Beck, Lothar A., ed. 2018. *Zoological Collections of Germany: the Animal Kingdom in Its Amazing Plenty at Museums and Universities*. Cham: Springer International.

Ben-Yehoyada, Naor. 2017. *The Mediterranean Incarnate: Region Formation Between Sicily and Tunisia since World War II*. Chicago, IL, and London: University of Chicago Press.

Berlin, Isaiah. 1954. *The Hedgehog and the Fox: An Essay on Tolstoy's View of History*. London: Weidenfeld & Nicolson.

Bolton, Maggie, and Cathrine Degnen, eds. 2010. *Animals and Science: From Colonial Encounters to the Biotech Industry*. Newcastle: Cambridge Scholars.

Braudel, Fernand. 1995. *The Mediterranean and the Mediterranean World in the Age of Philip II*. vols I and II. Translated by Siân Reynolds. Berkeley and Los Angeles, CA: University of California Press.

Braverman, Irus. 2013. 'Animal Frontiers: A Tale of Three Zoos in Israel/Palestine'. *Cultural Critique* 85: 122–62. https://doi.org/10.5749/culturalcritique.85.2013.0122

Bromberger, Christian. 2006. 'Towards an Anthropology of the Mediterranean'. *History and Anthropology* 17 (2): 91–107. Byrd, Brian F. 1989. 'The Natufian: Settlement Variability and Economic Adaptations in the Levant at the End of the Pleistocene'. *Journal of World Prehistory* 3 (2): 159–97. https://doi.org/10.1080/02757200600624339

Carrithers, Michael. 2005. 'Why Anthropologists Should Study Rhetoric'. *Journal of the Royal Anthropological Institute* 11 (3): 577–83.

Carsten, Janet. 1995. 'The Substance of Kinship and the Heat of the Hearth: Feeding, Personhood, and Relatedness among Malays in Pulau Langkawi'. *American Ethnologist* 22 (2): 223–41.

Cheshire, James, and Oliver Uberti. 2017. *Where the Animals Go: Tracking Wildlife with Technology in 50 Maps and Graphics*. New York, NY: W.W. Norton & Company.

Comaroff, Jean. 2017. 'Invasive Aliens: The Late-Modern Politics of Species Being'. *Social Research* 84 (1): 29–52. https://doi.org/10.1353/sor.2017.0004

Comaroff, Jean, and John L. Comaroff. 2001. 'Naturing the Nation: Aliens, Apocalypse and the Postcolonial State'. *Journal of Southern African Studies* 27 (3): 627–51.

Derrida, Jacques. 2009. *The Beast and the Sovereign*. vol. I. Translated by Geoffrey Bennington. Chicago, IL: University of Chicago Press.

Elden, Stuart. 2013. *The Birth of Territory*. Chicago, IL: University of Chicago Press.

Esler, Karen J., Anna L. Jacobsen, and R. Brandon Pratt. 2018. *The Biology of Mediterranean-Type Ecosystems*. New York, NY: Oxford University Press.

Fairchild, Amy L. 2003. *Science at the Borders: Immigrant Medical Inspection and the Shaping of the Modern Industrial Labor Force*. Baltimore, MD: Johns Hopkins University Press.

Foucault, Michel. 1974 [1966]. *The Order of Things. An Archaeology of the Human Sciences*. Translated from the French. London: Tavistock.

Franklin, Adrian. 2006. *Animal Nation: The True Story of Animals and Australia*. Sydney: UNSW Press.

Giaccaria, Paolo, Claudio Minca. 2011. 'The Mediterranean Alternative'. *Progress in Human Geography* 35 (3): 345–65. https://doi.org/10.1177/0309132510376850

Gilfoyle, Daniel, Karen Brown, and William Beinart. 2009. 'Experts and Expertise in Colonial Africa Reconsidered: Science and the Interpenetration of Knowledge'. *African Affairs* 108 (432): 413–33. https://doi.org/10.1093/afraf/adp037

Godley, Alfred Denis, ed. 1975 [1920]. *Herodotus: Histories*. Books I–II. Cambridge, MA: Harvard University Press.

Goldman, Lawrence. 1991. 'Statistics and the Science of Society in Early Victorian Britain: An Intellectual Context for the General Register Office'. *Social History of Medicine* 4 (3): 415–34. https://doi.org/10.1093/shm/4.3.415

Green, Sarah. 2005. *Notes from the Balkans: Locating Marginality and Ambiguity on the Greek-Albanian Border*. Princeton, NJ and Oxford: Princeton University Press.

Gren, Ing-Marie, Henrik Andersson, Justice Tei Mensah, and Thérèse Pettersson. 2020. 'Cost of Wild Boar to Farmers in Sweden'. *European Review of Agricultural Economics* 47 (1): 226–46. https://doi.org/10.1093/erae/jbz016

Haraway, Donna. 1988. 'Situated Knowledges: The Science Question in Feminism and the Privilege of Partial Perspective'. *Feminist Studies* 14 (3): 575–99. https://doi.org/10.2307/3178066

Herzfeld, Michael. 1980. 'Honour and Shame: Problems in the Comparative Analysis of Moral Systems'. *Man (n.s.)* 15 (2): 339–51. https://doi.org/10.2307/2801675

Herzfeld, Michael. 1984. 'The Horns of the Mediterraneanist Dilemma'. *American Ethnologist* 11 (3), 439–54.

Herzfeld, Michael. 2005. 'Practical Mediterraneanism: Excuses for Everything, from Epistemology to Eating'. In *Rethinking the Mediterranean*, edited by William V. Harris, 45–63. Oxford: Oxford University Press.

Herzfeld, Michael. 2014. 'Po-Mo Med'. In *A Companion to Mediterranean History*, edited by Peregrine Horden and Sharon Kinoshita. Chichester: John Wiley & Sons, 122–35.

Hirsch, Dafna. 2011. '"Hummus Is Best When It Is Fresh and Made by Arabs": The Gourmetization of Hummus in Israel and the Return of the Repressed Arab'. *American Ethnologist* 38 (4): 617–30. https://doi.org/10.1111/j.1548-1425.2011.01326.x

Horden, Peregrine, and Nicholas Purcell. 2000. *The Corrupting Sea: A Study of Mediterranean History*. Oxford and Malden, MA: Blackwell Publishers.

Johnson, Penny. 2019. *Companions in Conflict: Animals in Occupied Palestine*. New York, NY: Melville House Publishing.

Jung, Hwa Yol. 1987. 'Being, Praxis, and Truth: Toward a Dialogue between Phenomenology and Marxism'. *Dialectical Anthropology* 12 (3): 307–28.

Lampland, Martha, and Susan Leigh Star, eds. 2009. *Standards and Their Stories: How Quantifying, Classifying, and Formalizing Practices Shape Everyday Life*. Ithaca, NY and London: Cornell University Press.

Larson, James L. 1967. 'Goethe and Linnaeus'. *Journal of the History of Ideas* 28 (4): 590–96. https://doi.org/10.2307/2708532

Law, John, and Annemarie Mol. 2003. *Situating Technoscience: An Inquiry into Spatialities*. Lancaster: Centre for Science Studies, Lancaster University.

Linné, Carl von. 1758. *Caroli Linnæi … Systema naturæ per regna tria naturæ, secundum classes, ordines, genera, species, cum characteribus, differentiis, synonymis, locis* Holmiæ: impensis L. Salvii.

McNeill, John Robert. 1992. *The Mountains of the Mediterranean World: An Environmental History*. Cambridge and New York, NY: Cambridge University Press.

Michael, Mike. 2004. 'Roadkill: Between Humans, Nonhuman Animals, and Technologies'. *Society & Animals* 12 (4): 277–98.

Mitchell, Jon P. 2002. 'Modernity and the Mediterranean'. *Journal of Mediterranean Studies (Special Issue)* 12 (1): 1–22.

Monterescu, Daniel, and Ariel Handel. 2020. 'Terroir and Territory on the Colonial Frontier: Making New-Old World Wine in the Holy Land'. *Comparative Studies in Society and History* 62 (2): 222–61. https://doi.org/10.1017/S0010417520000043

Ohana, David. 2011. *Israel and Its Mediterranean identity*. New York, NY: Palgrave Macmillan.

Petri, Rolf. 2016. 'The Mediterranean Metaphor in Early Geopolitical Writings'. *History* 101 (348): 671–91. https://doi.org/10.1111/1468-229X.12326

Philo, Chris, and Chris Wilbert, eds. 2000. *Animal Spaces, Beastly Places: New Geographies of Human-Animal Relations*. London and New York, NY: Routledge.

Pina-Cabral, João de. 1989. 'The Mediterranean as a Category of Regional Comparison: A Critical View'. *Current Anthropology* 30 (3): 399–406.

Poovey, Mary. 1998. *A History of the Modern Fact: Problems of Knowledge in the Sciences of Wealth and Society*. Chicago, IL, and London: University of Chicago Press.

Robins, Philip. 2004. *A History of Jordan*. Cambridge and New York, NY: Cambridge University Press.

Sordi, Caetano. 2020. 'Bicho Bandido: Wild Boars, Biological Invasions and Landscape Transformations on the Brazilian-Uruguayan Border (Pampas Region)'. *Social Anthropology* 28 (3): 614–28. https://doi.org/10.1111/1469-8676.12785

Souguir-Omrani, Hejer, Jomaa Chemkhi, Akila Fathallah-Mili, Yusr Saadi-BenAoun, Insaf BelHadjAli, Ikram Guizani, and Souheila Guerbouj. 2018. 'Paraechinus aethiopicus (Ehrenberg 1832) and Atelerix algirus (Lereboullet 1842) Hedgehogs: Possible Reservoirs of Endemic Leishmaniases in Tunisia'. *Infection Genetics and Evolution* 63: 219–30. https://doi.org/10.1016/j.meegid.2018.05.029

Strathern, Marilyn. 2020. *Relations: An Anthropological Account*. Durham, NC: Duke University Press.

Toger, Marina, Itzhak Benenson, Yuqi Wang, Daniel Czamanski, and Dan Malkinson. 2018. 'Pigs in Space: An Agent-Based Model of Wild Boar (Sus scrofa) Movement into Cities'. *Landscape and Urban Planning* 173: 70–80. https://doi.org/10.1016/j.landurbplan.2018.01.006

Urbanik, Julie. 2012. *Placing Animals: An Introduction to the Geography of Human-Animal Relations*. Lanham, MD: Rowman & Littlefield.

Vaccaro, Ismael, and Oriol Beltran. 2009. 'Livestock Versus "Wild Beasts": Contradictions in the Natural Patrimonialization of the Pyrenees'. *Geographical Review* 99 (4): 499–516. https://doi.org/10.1111/j.1931-0846.2009.tb00444.x

Vaughan-Williams, Nick. 2015. *Europe's Border Crisis: Biopolitical Security and beyond*. New York, NY: Oxford University.

Viveiros de Castro, Eduardo. 2015. 'Who Is Afraid of the Ontological Wolf? Some Comments on an Ongoing Anthropological Debate'. *The Cambridge Journal of Anthropology* 33 (1): 2–17.

Weeks, Priscilla, and Jane Packard. 2009. 'Feral Hogs: Invasive Species or Nature's Bounty?' *Human Organization* 68 (3): 280–92. https://doi.org/10.17730/humo.68.3.663wn82g164321u1

Wolch, Jennifer. 2002. 'Anima urbis'. *Progress in Human Geography* 26 (6): 721–42. https://doi.org/10.1191/0309132502ph400oa

On the Topic of Location

Matei Candea

University of Cambridge

Abstract

What does it mean to 'locate' the study of location in the Mediterranean? Would studying location somewhere other than the Mediterranean make location itself look different? Conversely – this is the same question, inside out – is there something distinctively Mediterranean about the topic of location? This afterword considers the way in which the volume contributes to rethinking not just Mediterranean anthropology but also the broader assumption that anthropology is about studying general topics in particular places.

Commonplaces

Anthropologists, as Eriksen (2018) notes, typically study some-*thing*, some-*where*. This recurrent anthropological form is evidenced in the distinctive and recognisable aesthetic of titles and abstracts (dance in rural Greece, neo-liberalism in Puerto Rican street markets, infrastructural politics in Kinshasa, etc.). But this 'topic–location'[1] pairing is more than a verbal tic, a writerly trope. It is a profound structuring device of anthropological knowledge production. Pairing a topic with

How to cite this book chapter:
Candea, Matei. 2022. 'Epilogue: On the Topic of Location'. In *Locating the Mediterranean: Connections and Separations across Space and Time*, edited by Carl Rommel and Joseph John Viscomi, 223–31. Helsinki: Helsinki University Press. DOI: https://doi.org/10.33134/HUP-18-10.

a location forces each to cut across the other in ways anthropologists typically value. Locations[2] specify theme and concepts, tie them to empirical experiential realities. Conversely, making particular locations speak to themes, topics, and concepts that are shared beyond a 'regionalist' audience opens up conversations with anthropologists working elsewhere (cf. Howe and Boyer 2015). This is why, despite the recurrent ways in which anthropologists rail against the topic–location binary, try to challenge it, destroy it, or radically reimagine it,[3] they keep coming back to it in the immanent practice of the discipline. Supervisors continue to instruct students, and reviewers to invite authors, to find that 'topic–location' sweet spot. In this enduring anthropological aesthetic, a something without a somewhere feels 'ungrounded', a somewhere without a something feels 'uninteresting', a 'mere case study'.

Having got the topic–location device in clear view, we can see in what ways this volume's call to study location in the Mediterranean is both classic and new. The form is familiar: these chapters consider an enduring anthropological topic ('location'), in a recognisable albeit problematic location ('the Mediterranean'). Yet the fact that the topic here is precisely location brings an exciting recursivity and also a hint of paradox to the exercise. What does it mean to 'locate' the study of location? Would studying location somewhere other than the Mediterranean make location look different? Conversely – this is the same question, inside out – is there something distinctively Mediterranean about the topic of location?

Returns

As the Introduction (Chapter 1) to this volume reminds us, the topic of Mediterranean distinctiveness (or, conversely, the coherence of the Mediterranean as a location) has had a problematic life in anthropology. Andrew Shryock has noted in a perceptive recent comment that anthropologists seem to be forever 'returning' to the Mediterranean (2020). Collections such as the present one are critically aware that they are returning to a location that was once the scene of a thriving regionalist anthropology, dissolved by critical fiat in the 1980s. Such returns frame their efforts as much against as within that older history. Yet, as Shryock notes, Julian Pitt-Rivers himself in one of the foundational texts of the 'old' Mediterraneanist anthropology, already saw his discipline as returning, after a hiatus, to 'the Mediterranean that figured so large in the writings of the founders of anthropology' (Pitt-Rivers 1963, 10; quoted in Shryock 2020, 151). Shryock's explanation of this phenomenon turns on the distinctive and problematic way in which topics cling to locations.

On the one hand, with each return, the problematics of Mediterranean anthropology seem to change drastically. The present collection clearly bears out Shryock's observation that 'The old problem of Mediterranean anthropology was comparison. As a way of articulating the region and defining its distinctive qualities, it failed. The new problems of Mediterranean anthropology are connection, movement, protection, and border-crossing' (Shryock 2020, 153). Indeed, the chapters in this volume do not, in the main, gravitate to the classic topics – honour and propriety, tradition and modernity, patronage and egalitarianism – through which an older Mediterranean anthropology tried to frame the region as a comparative unit.[4] The themes most in evidence in these pages are along the 'new' lines to which Shryock points: migration, materiality, and postcolonial legacies loom large here. As if to drive the point home, the present volume's Introduction persistently casts itself as being against 'comparison'. If there is one thing this volume is setting out *not* to do, it is identifying (stereo)typical features of Mediterranean distinctiveness.

On the other hand, there is a deep continuity beneath these changes. The old problem of comparison and the new problems of connection (and disconnection) are both refractions of an anthropological ambivalence about the Mediterranean as a location. What has remained constant throughout the troubled history of the anthropological Mediterranean is the challenging yet productive way in which holding the Mediterranean together as a focus of analysis disturbs anthropological practice. In particular, the Mediterranean recurrently disturbs the operation of that key anthropological device, frontal comparison – comparison between 'us and them' (Candea 2019b).

For the old Mediterraneanist anthropology, a key challenge and promise of the area lay in its sitting astride two figures of contemporary anthropological imagination: 'traditional Africa', classic stomping ground of anthropology, and 'modern Europe', anthropological *terra incognita*.[5] Critics of this first wave of Mediterranean studies returned to the troubling in-betweenness of the Mediterranean, re-reading it as a figure of anthropological imagination, not as a feature of the world itself (Herzfeld 1987). Even as Mediterraneanist anthropology was being dissolved, the Mediterranean – now an imaginary location – was being put to work to reveal the internal workings of anthropological epistemology and European power/knowledge. Now, studies of Mediterranean region formation (e.g. Ben-Yehoyada 2017; Ben-Yehoyada, Cabot, and Silverstein 2020; Ben-Yehoyada and Silverstein 2020) are returning to that frontal contrast once again, worrying away at it in two distinct registers. One register is epistemological: the study of 'practical Mediterraneanism' (Herzfeld 2005) poses the question of what 'we', anthropologists, are to do with the fact that 'they', people living around the Mediterranean, are still after all characterising themselves in the very terms 'we' have abandoned (cousinage, gendered performance, honour and propriety, North/South, Christian/Muslim, tradition and modernity, patronage and egalitarianism). The other register is political: as almost every chapter in this collection attests, locating one's study in the Mediterranean forces an attention to the sheer complexity of the afterlives of European colonialism and imperialism in non-European locations – the Mediterranean seems to relentlessly call up that dualism in order to complicate it.

In picking the Mediterranean as a location in which to experiment with location, this volume is therefore building on a long tradition. True, the current resistance to identifying Mediterranean distinctiveness through comparison is the diametrical opposite of the pointedly comparative aspirations of an earlier anthropology that sought to draw it together. Yet both attitudes point to the same distinctive ways in which the Mediterranean keeps interrogating anthropological uses of location. One might be tempted to ask whether this tells us more about the Mediterranean itself (its geographic, ecological, sociological, or cultural realities), or about the intellectual history and conceptual devices of anthropology (its changing uses of geography, its enduring concern with frontal comparison), but I will not. I will follow the Introduction's lead, in which we are enjoined to stop trying to split the real Mediterranean from its imagined counterpart. Trying to disentangle anthropological knowledge practices from the locations in relation to which they have been crafted is a similarly hopeless endeavour. Such hopeless endeavours can sometimes be productive, but that is for another day. Suffice it to say for now that the persistent way in which the Mediterranean interrogates anthropology's techniques of location speaks to a relationship that pre-exists its terms.

Dislocations

The present volume moves this relationship along in a number of ways, key among which is the sustained attention these chapters give to issues of disconnection, immobility, and arbitrariness. If, as Shryock writes, the old problem was comparison, and the new problems are connection and border-crossing, the editors rightly show that both of these problems share an additive aesthetic: they are about bringing the Mediterranean together. By contrast, this volume makes a point of reminding us that such achieved unities in the Mediterranean are only ever partial, and showcase 'practices that intentionally work to dissolve region, to foster separation, and to generate remoteness' (Rommel and Viscomi). These practices include the borders and walls that make their presence felt in Melilla (Soto Bermant) or Lampedusa (Elbek), and the multiple historical repartitionings of 'public' space in Beirut (Lähteenaho). More subtly, they include the menus and pricing of the various 'Mediterranean' restaurants along one road in Marseille (Bullen), which shape as much as they reflect classed and racialised divides, or the distinctive ways in which touristic over-exposure leeches out meaning and identity from Istanbul's Old City (Su). The partitionings and divisions of an old imperial order run like a backbeat through these chapters, as does the theme of selective memorialising and historical forgetfulness – from the fraught re-enactments of religious conflict around the Nafpaktos 'bridge to nowhere' (Douzina-Bakalaki), via the historic replay of siege mentalities in Melilla, all the way to the well-meaning but somewhat arbitrary reboot of the Virgin Mary of Trapani as a patron saint of migrants (Russo), which one cannot help feeling is also an unintentional act of historical erasure of the figure's rich and layered earlier lives. Nowhere is the value of paying attention to disconnection more clearly visible than in Green's exploration of the ways ecosystemic and national political visions of the Mediterranean cut across each other. At times these collude to make certain animal border-crossings into a 'problem'. At other times each vision's own determinisms works to render the other's utterly irrelevant. And of course, one might add that these practices of disconnection are as much those of anthropologists as they are those of the people whose lives are described in these pages: the dogged resistance against 'comparison of cultural traits and separate cases' is an intentional device for ensuring, as much as acknowledging, the incomplete unity of the Mediterranean.

And yet this focus on disconnection and arbitrariness, on processes that 'although always beginning somewhere, often finish nowhere in particular' (Chapter 1) raises its own paradox. For, as soon as it is identified explicitly and brought to mind, every disconnection is also perforce a connection. Or, to put it otherwise, an arbitrary location (Candea 2007) turns into a relative location (Green 2005), as soon as you make explicit what it was arbitrary *in relation to*. Thus, the remoteness of Melilla speaks to the marginality of Lampedusa; in both cases, 'locals' relate to outsiders (powerful people in the metropolitan centre, struggling migrants breaching the border) precisely as they mark their separation from them. Historical re-enactments at Lepanto call up reflections on contemporary inter-faith encounters. It is because the eateries along one street in Marseille are so neatly lined up as instances of the same thing (Mediterranean food outlets) that one can pick out how they differ and how they differentiate their *clientèle*.

More broadly, despite the self-conscious rejection of comparison in the Introduction, the chapters in this book cannot help but line up – like those eateries – as 'separate cases' of the same problematic: location in the Mediterranean. The stubbornly comparative form of 'the edited volume' trumps the self-conscious rejection of comparison. For, after all, we have here a set of texts, each set in or around the Mediterranean Sea, each exploring the question of location, and these texts are collected under a common title and framed by an introduction that elucidates how they hang together and where they diverge. Comparison is like a boomerang: the harder you throw it away, the harder it comes back.[6]

Remappings

The problem brings to mind Umberto Eco's meditations on mnemotechnics and the impossibility of an 'art of forgetting' (1988). The classical arts of memory, Eco reminds us, operated by associating ideas to locations: an orator would visualise a familiar location (a house, street, or townscape) and 'place' the topics of their speech around that location in the form of vivid images. They could then mentally travel that space in order to remember the sequence of their speech. If this connecting of places to topics is the art of remembering, Eco asks, how then might we imagine an art of forgetting? The difficulty is that you cannot unmake a connection any more than you can unring a bell. Connections may fade on their own in time, but to intentionally 'disconnect' a topic from a location is to connect them once more – rather like in the famous injunction 'don't think of a pink elephant'. If there is a way of intentionally forgetting, Eco argues, it is not through the removal of connections but on the contrary through their accumulation. The more cross-cutting connections anything has to anything else, the more faintly each of these connections registers. The art of forgetting is the art of overwriting, the art of the palimpsest.

Eco's meditation helps us get the novelty of the present collection into sharper focus. Yes, focusing explicitly on disconnection means, inescapably, making more connections. But the question each time is what is being remembered and what is being forgotten, what is being written anew and what is being overwritten. The 'new Mediterraneanist' focus on cross-cutting connections, border-crossings and region formation is calculated to overwrite the recurrent binaries (north/south, modern/traditional, real/imagined) that had haunted both the old Mediterraneanism and its 1980s critique. The present volume partakes of that sensibility, and in that respect belongs squarely to this new wave of Mediterraneanist studies. But its abiding concern with remoteness, arbitrariness, and the trailing edges of processes that finish nowhere in particular writes over this emergent picture of Mediterranean region formation in a distinctive way. This is not an erasure but rather a delicate shading in, adding darker touches of absence and interruption that allow unexpected patterns to come into view. This makes a subtle yet important difference to that topical location – the Mediterranean. The topic of location, too, emerges refreshed.

Notes

1 Elsewhere I called this the 'place–concept binary' (Candea 2019a). On reflection, though, this is too specific and too general at the same time. 'Topic–location' fits the bill better, if only because of the pleasing etymological reminder that these two terms are ultimately interchangeable. There is an arbitrariness and reversibility to the way anthropological themes operate upon anthropological locations. Both are also, literally and metaphorically, 'commonplaces'.

2 Not necessarily geographic, of course. The classic 'among the' is another recurrent way of 'locating' a topic.

3 See Candea (2019a) for a roll call of some of these attempts and concerns.

4 These topics do loom large, however, in the collection that Shryock is commenting on (Ben-Yehoyada, Cabot, and Silverstein 2020), and that is precisely his point. Despite the critical exorcisms of the 1980s, the topics of the 'old' Mediterranean anthropology are returning to haunt contemporary ethnographers, if only because they are the topics that, for better or worse, still matter to people living around that sea. The new anthropology of Mediterranean 'region formation' represents a creative and sophisticated engagement with this dilemma. But it still very much bears out Shryock's point about shifts in perspective. What is at stake in revisiting these topics is not the task of building up a 'culture area' but rather an attentiveness to how concepts, stereotypes, and expectations move around the Mediterranean, connecting people across borders.

5 Evans-Pritchard's rather defensive foreword to Pitt-Rivers's *People of the Sierra* (1954) gives a measure of the discomfort this in-betweenness caused. Inside the book itself, Pitt-Rivers's model of the way the nation state articulates to the local community through bonds of patronage and models of honour was one of the more sophisticated early products of this perceived in-betweenness.

6 For sure, this is not comparison as a mere 'sifting out' of similarities that unite a region. But then, arguably, neither was the comparatism of the old Mediterranean anthropology, although it is beyond the scope of this epilogue to make good on that assertion.

References

Ben-Yehoyada, Naor. 2017. *The Mediterranean Incarnate: Region Formation between Sicily and Tunisia Since World War II*. Chicago, IL, and London: University of Chicago Press.

Ben-Yehoyada, Naor, Heath Cabot, and Paul A. Silverstein. 2020. 'Introduction: Remapping Mediterranean Anthropology'. *History and Anthropology* 31 (1): 1–21. https://doi.org/10.1080/02757206.2019.1684274

Ben-Yehoyada, Naor, and Paul A. Silverstein. 2020. *The Mediterranean Redux: Ethnography, Theory, Politics*. London: Routledge.

Candea, Matei. 2007. 'Arbitrary Locations: In Defence of the Bounded Field-Site'. *Journal of the Royal Anthropological Institute* 13: 167–84.

Candea, Matei. 2019a. 'Comparison, Re-placed'. In *Going to Pentecost: An Experimental Approach to Studies in Pentecostalism*, edited by Annelin Eriksen, Ruy Llera Barnes and Michell MacCarthy. Berghahn Books. Accessed 1 March 2019. http://www.jstor.org/stable/10.2307/j.ctv9hj8pw.

Candea, Matei. 2019b. *Comparison in Anthropology: The Impossible Method*. Cambridge: Cambridge University Press.

Eco, Umberto. 1988. 'An Ars Oblivionaris? Forget It'. *PMLA* 103: 254–61.

Eriksen, Annelin. 2018. 'Going to "Pentecost": How to Study Pentecostalism – in Melanesia, for Example'. *Journal of the Royal Anthropological Institute* 24: 164–80. https://doi.org/10.1111/1467-9655.12757

Green, Sarah. 2005. *Notes from the Balkans*. Princeton, NJ: Princeton University Press.

Herzfeld, Michael. 1987. *Anthropology through the Looking-Glass: Critical Ethnography in the Margins of Europe*. Cambridge: Cambridge University Press.

Herzfeld, Michael. 2005. 'Practical Mediterraneanism: Excuses for Everything, from Epistemology to Eating'. In *Rethinking the Mediterranean*, edited by William V. Harris, 45–63. Oxford: Oxford University Press.

Howe, Cymene, and Dominic Boyer. 2015. 'Portable Analytics and Lateral Theory'. In *Theory Can Be More than It Used to Be: Learning Anthropology's Method in a Time of Transition*, edited by Dominic Boyer, James D. Faubion, and George E. Marcus. Ithaca, NY: Cornell University Press.

Pitt-Rivers, Julian Alfred. 1954. *The People of the Sierra*. London: Weidenfeld and Nicholson.

Pitt-Rivers, Julian Alfred, ed. 1963. *Mediterranean Countrymen. Essays in the Social Anthropology of the Mediterranean*. Paris, la Haye: Mouton & Co.

Shryock, Andrew. 2020. 'Rites of Return: Back to the Mediterranean, Again'. *History and Anthropology* 31: 147–56. https://doi.org/10.1080/02757206.2019.1684273

Index

Page numbers in *italic* refer to illustrations; page numbers in **bold** indicate a table.